READINGS IN WORLD HISTORY

HBJ Harcourt Brace Jovanovich
Holt, Rinehart and Winston

Printed in the United States of America
ISBN 0-15-373498-1

Cover: Germans atop the Berlin Wall, November 10, 1989. Eric Bouvet/Gamma-liaison

ACKNOWLEDGMENTS

For permission to reprint copyrighted material, grateful acknowledgment is made to the following sources:

Angus & Robertson Publishers/Collins: "Before Action," "A Night Attack," and "The Attack at Dawn" by Leon Gellert from *Songs of a Campaign*. Copyright 1918 by Mrs. C. Gellert.

Edward Arnold (Publishers) Ltd.: From "An Official Report on 'Bloody Sunday' in St. Petersburg" from *Octobrists to Bolsheviks Imperial Russia, 1905–1917* by Martin McCauley, assisted by Peter Waldron. Copyright © 1984 by Martin McCauley.

Mrs. R. Bronowski: From *The Ascent of Man* by J. Bronowski. Copyright © 1973 by J. Bronowski. Published by BBC Books, a division of BBC Enterprises Ltd., 1973.

Cambridge University Press: From "Zik on Africa" (Retitled: "The New Africa") from *ZIK: A Selection From the Speeches of Nnamdi Azikiwe*. Copyright © 1961 by Cambridge University Press. From Chapters XIV-XVIII (Retitled: "Advice to Princes") from *The Prince* by Niccolo Machiavelli, edited by Quentin Skinner and Russell Price. Copyright © 1988 by Cambridge University Press.

Jonathan Cape Ltd.: "A Letter from Aragon" (Retitled: "Two Poems of the Spanish Civil War") by John Cornford.

Jonathan Cape Ltd. on behalf of the Estate of C.V. Wedgwood: From "A King for Bohemia" (Retitled: "Revolt in Bohemia") from *The Thirty Years War* by C.V. Wedgwood. First published in 1938.

Frank Cass & Co. Ltd.: From "A Working Day" (Retitled: "A Working Day in a Manchester Cotton Mill") from *Labour and the Poor in England and Wales, 1849–1851,* Vol. 1, edited by J. Ginswick. From "Conclusion: Value of British Rule" (Retitled: "A Justification of British Colonialism in Africa") from *The Dual Mandate in Tropical Africa* by Lord Lugard. First published in 1922.

John Chadwick and Blackwell Scientific Publications Ltd.: From "Aphorisms" by Hippocrates from *The Medical Works of Hippocrates,* translated by John Chadwick and W.N. Mann. Published by Blackwell Scientific Publications Ltd., 1950.

Columbia Broadcasting System, Inc.: From "10:56:20 PM (edt) 7/20/69" from *The historic conquest of the moon as reported to the American people by CBS News over the CBS Television Network* (Retitled: "A Message From the Apollo 11 Astronauts"). Copyright © 1970 by Columbia Broadcasting System, Inc.

Columbia University Press: From "Asoka's Edicts," from "Aurobindo Ghose" (Retitled: "The Doctrine of Passive Resistance"), and from "The Four-Class Division of Society" (Retitled: "Social Classes in Muslim India") from *Sources of Indian Tradition,* compiled by Wm. Theodore de Bary, et al. Copyright © 1958 by Columbia University Press. From "Majjhima Nikaya," and from "Manu Smrti" from *Sources of Indian Tradition,* Volume 1, Wm. Theodore de Bary, General Editor. Copyright © 1970 by Columbia University Press. From pp. 244–246 (Retitled: "Drinking Tea for Long Life"), from "Hashimoto Kingorō" (Retitled: "A Justification of Japanese Expansionism"), and from "Yoshida Shōin" (Retitled: "Yoshida Shōin: Philosopher of the Meiji Restoration") from *Sources of the Japanese Tradition,* Wm. Theodore de Bary, Editor. Copyright © 1958 by Columbia University Press. From *The Chronicle of Jean de Venette,* edited and translated by Richard A. Newhall from *Records of Civilization,* Vol. L. Copyright 1953 by Columbia University Press. From "Criminal Clerks at Paris, 1269" (Retitled: "Rowdy Paris Students") from *University Records and Life in the Middle Ages* by Lynn Thorndike. Copyright 1944 by Columbia University Press. From "The Russian Law" (Retitled: "The Pravda Russkaia") from *Medieval Russian Laws,* translated by George Vernadsky. Copyright 1947 by Columbia University Press. From "Universal Love, Part III" (Retitled: "Mo Tzu on Universal Love") by Mo Tzu from *Basic Writings of Mo Tzu, Hsün Tzu, and Han Fei Tzu,* translated by Burton Watson. Copyright © 1963, 1964 by Columbia University Press.

Constable & Co. Ltd.: From *The Home Fronts: Britain, France and Germany, 1914–1918* by John Williams (Retitled: "The Home Front in Germany"). Copyright © 1972 by John Williams.

(Acknowledgments continued on p. 301)

TABLE OF CONTENTS

THE BEGINNINGS OF CIVILIZATION

CIVILIZATIONS OF THE MEDITERRANEAN WORLD

THE WORLD IN TRANSITION

THE EMERGENCE OF MODERN NATIONS

THE DEVELOPMENT OF INDUSTRIAL SOCIETY

WORLD WAR IN THE TWENTIETH CENTURY

THE WORLD SINCE 1945

The Beginnings of Civilization

1 THE TASK OF THE ARCHAEOLOGIST

Since no written records of prehistory exist, historians depend on the work of archaeologists for evidence of what life was like during those far-off times. In the excerpt below from Digging Up the Past *by Sir Leonard Woolley, the excavator of Ur and other Sumerian cities, the author explains how the ideal archaeologist works. As you read the excerpt, ask yourself how archaeology and history are related.*

The prime duty of the field archaeologist is to collect and set in order material with not all of which he can himself deal at first hand. In no case will the last word be with him; and just because that is so his publication of the material must be minutely detailed, so that from it others may draw not only corroboration of his views but fresh conclusions and more light. Should he not then stop at this? It might be urged that the man who is admirably equipped to observe and record does not necessarily possess the powers of synthesis and interpretation, the creative spirit and the literary gift which will make of him a historian. But no record can ever be exhaustive. As his work in the field goes on, the excavator is constantly subject to impressions too subjective and too intangible to be communicated, and out of these, by no exact logical process, there arise theories which he can state, can perhaps support, but cannot prove: . . . in any case, they have their value as summing up experiences which no student of his objects and his notes can ever share. . . . The conclusions which the archaeologist draws from his own work ought to carry weight, and he is bound to put them forward; if they are palpably wrong then his observations also may justly be held suspect. Between archaeology and history there is no fenced frontier, and the digger who will best observe and record his discoveries is precisely he who sees them as historical material and rightly appraises them. . . . It is true that he may not possess any literary gifts, and that, therefore, the formal presentation of results to the public may be better made by others; but it is the field archaeologist who, directly or indirectly, has opened up for the general reader new chapters in the history of [civilization]; and by recovering from the earth such documented relics of the past as strike the imagination through the eye, he makes real and modern what otherwise might seem a far-off tale.

An archaeologist at work

READING REVIEW

1. According to Sir Leonard Woolley, what is the prime duty of the field archaeologist?
2. Why should archaeologists go beyond simply observing and recording their finds?
3. "The archaeologist finds the evidence, the historian breathes life into it." Do you agree or disagree with this statement? Why or why not?

---

2 THE NOMADIC LIFE

Before the Neolithic Revolution, people lived as nomads, wandering from place to place in search of food. But what was nomadic life like? In the excerpt below from The Ascent of Man, *scientist and broadcaster Jacob Bronowski provides an answer by describing the life of the Bakhtiari, a group of modern-day nomads who herd sheep and goats in the Zagros Mountains of Iran. As you read the excerpt, ask yourself why civilization could not develop while people lived as nomads.*

Everything in nomad life is immemorial. The Bakhtiari have always travelled alone, quite unseen. Like other nomads, they think of themselves as a family, the sons of a single founding-father. . . . The

Bakhtiari take their name from a legendary herdsman . . . Bakhtyar. The legend of their own origin that they tell of him begins,

> And the father of our people, the hill-man, Bakhtyar, came out of the fastness of the southern mountains in ancient times. His seed were as numerous as the rocks on the mountains, and his people prospered.

. . . Before 10,000 B.C. nomad peoples used to follow the natural migration of wild herds. But sheep and goats have no natural migrations. They were domesticated about ten thousand years ago. . . . And when man domesticated them, he took on the responsibility of nature; the nomad must lead the helpless herd.

The role of women in nomad tribes is narrowly defined. Above all, the function of women is to produce men-children. . . . Apart from that, their duties lie in preparing food and clothes. For example, the women among the Bakhtiari bake bread—in the biblical manner, in unleavened cakes on hot stones. But the girls and the women wait to eat until the men have eaten. Like the men, the lives of the women centre on the flock. They milk the herd, and they make a clotted yoghourt from the milk by churning it in a goatskin bag on a primitive wooden frame. They have only the simple technology that can be carried on daily journeys from place to place. The simplicity is not romantic; it is a matter of survival. Everything must be light enough to be carried, to be set up every evening and to be packed away again every morning. When the women spin wool with their simple, ancient devices, it is for immediate use, to make the repairs that are essential on the journey—no more.

It is not possible in the nomad life to make things that will not be needed for several weeks. They could not be carried. And in fact the Bakhtiari do not know how to make them. If they need metal pots, they barter them from settled peoples. . . . A nail, a stirrup, a toy, or a child's bell is something that is traded from outside the tribe. The Bakhtiari life is too narrow to have time or skill for specialisation. There is no room for innovation, because there is not time, on the move, between evening and morning, coming and going all their lives, to develop a new device or a new thought—not even a new tune. The only habits that survive are the old habits. The only ambition of the son is to be like the father.

It is a life without features. Every night is the end of a day like the last, and every morning will be the beginning of a journey like the day before. When the day breaks, there is one question in everyone's mind: Can the flock be got over the next high pass? . . . For the tribe must move on, the herdsman must find new pastures every day. . . .

Every year the Bakhtiari cross six ranges of mountains on the outward journey (and cross them again to come back). They march through snow and the spring flood water. And in only one respect has their life advanced beyond that of ten thousand years ago. The nomads of that time had to travel on foot and carry their own packs. The Bakhtiari have pack-animals—horses, donkeys, mules—which have only been domesticated since that time. Nothing else in their lives is new. And nothing is memorable. Nomads have no memorials, even to the dead. (Where is Bakhtyar . . . buried?) The only mounds that they build are to mark the way.

READING REVIEW

1. What is the role of women in nomadic tribes?
2. What is the one change that has taken place in the nomadic life of the Bakhtiari in the last 10,000 years?
3. In the introduction to his discussion of the Bakhtiari, Bronowski contends that "civilization can never grow up on the move." How does information in the excerpt support this contention?

---

3 THE FIRST PAINTERS

The cave paintings by the Cro-Magnon people provide us with a fascinating picture of the way they lived—most notably, the animals they hunted and the weapons they used. The excerpt below from Life on Earth: A Natural History *by David Attenborough describes how the Cro-Magnons created these paintings and offers some explanations of why they produced these artworks. As you read the excerpt, ask yourself why these paintings are important to our understanding of prehistoric times.*

The first flowering [of painting] can be seen in . . . ancient European caves. The men who lived there ventured deep into the black holes that lead from the back of many of them, finding their way by the feeble flickering light of stone lamps filled with animal fat. There, in some of the most remote parts of the caverns, sometimes in passages and chambers that could only be reached after hours of crawling, they painted designs on the walls. For pigments they used the red, brown and yellow ochres of iron, and black from charcoal and manganese ore. For brushes, they used sticks burred at the end, their fingers, and sometimes blew paint on to the rock, probably from the mouth. Sometimes the designs are engraved with a flint tool and there are a few examples of carving in the round, and modelling in clay. Their subjects were almost always the animals they hunted—mammoth, deer, horse, wild cattle, bison and rhinoceros. Often they are superimposed, one on top of the other. There are no landscapes and only very rarely human figures. In one or two caves, the people left a particularly evocative symbol of their visit, the image of their hands made by blowing paint over them so that the outline is left stencilled on the rock. Scattered among the animals, there are abstract designs—parallel lines, squares, grids and rows of dots, curves . . . [and] chevrons that might be arrows. . . .

Even now, we do not know why these people painted. Perhaps the designs were part of a religious ritual—if the chevrons surrounding a great bull represent arrows, then maybe they were drawn to bring success in hunting; if the cattle shown with swollen sides are intended to

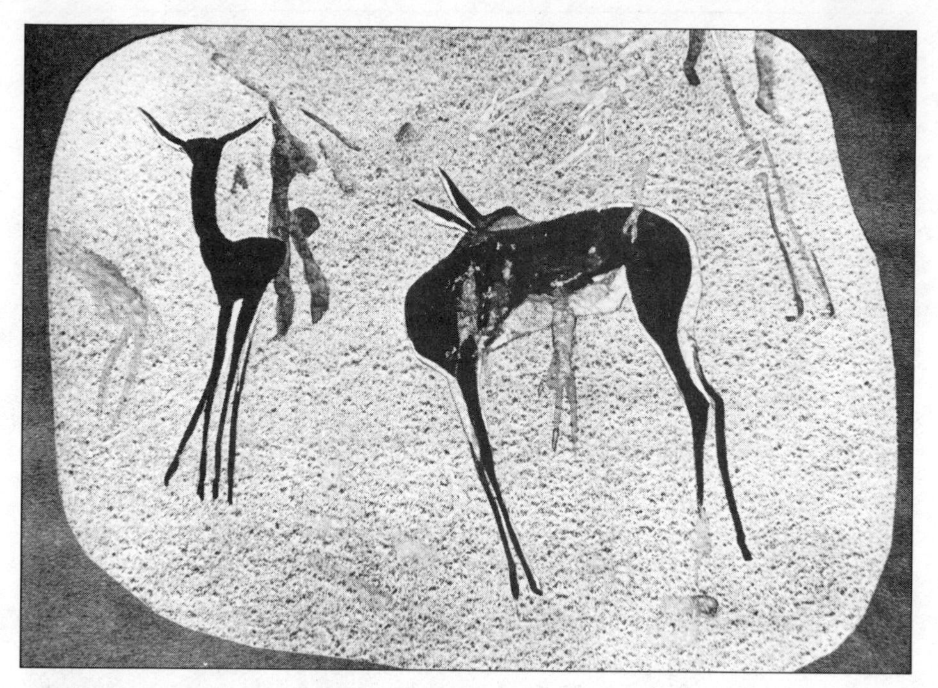

Cave paintings by an unknown prehistoric artist

appear pregnant, then maybe they were made during increase rituals to ensure the fertility of the herds. Maybe their function was less complicated and the people painted simply because they enjoyed doing so, taking pleasure in art for art's sake. Perhaps it is a mistake to seek a single universal explanation. The most ancient of the paintings is thought to be about 30,000 years old, the youngest maybe 10,000. The interval between these two dates is about six times the length of the entire history of western civilisation, so there is no more reason to suppose that the same motives lay behind all these paintings than there is to believe that background music saturating a modern hotel serves the same function as a [religious] chant. But whether they were directed at the gods, at young initiates or appreciative members of the community, they were certainly communications. And they still retain their power to communicate today. Even if we are baffled by their precise meaning, we cannot fail to respond to the perceptiveness and . . . sensitivity with which these artists captured the significant outlines of a mammoth, the cocked heads of a herd of antlered deer or the looming bulk of a bison.

READING REVIEW

1. What were the usual subjects of the cave paintings?
2. Why does the author think that it is a mistake to seek a single universal explanation of the cave paintings?
3. What explanations does the author give for why the Cro-Magnon people painted? Why do you think early people created the cave paintings? Explain your answer.

4 AN EARLY AGRICULTURAL VILLAGE

The agricultural revolution allowed people of Neolithic times to build homes and settle permanently in one area. In time small agricultural villages grew up around these settlement sites. One of the earliest of these villages, dating from about 6750 B.C., was Jarmo, located in what today is northern Iraq. In the excerpt below from Prehistoric Men, *Robert Braidwood, the archaeologist who unearthed Jarmo, describes what he found there. As you read the excerpt, ask yourself what artifacts discovered at Jarmo suggest that the village had connections with the outside world.*

The site of Jarmo has a depth of deposit of about twenty-seven feet, and approximately a dozen layers of architectural renovation and change. Nevertheless it is a "one period" site; its assemblage remains essentially the same throughout, although there are developments in some categories of artifacts and one or two new items are added in later levels. The site covers about four acres of the top of a bluff, below which runs a small stream. It lies in the hill country east of the modern oil town of Kirkuk. . . .

The people of Jarmo grew the barley plant and two different kinds of wheat. They made flint sickles with which to reap their grain, mortars . . . on which to crack it, ovens in which it may have been parched, and stone bowls out of which they might eat their porridge. We know that they had domesticated goats, sheep, dogs, and, in the latest levels, pigs. . . . As well as their grain and the meat from their animals, the people of Jarmo consumed great quantities of land snails. . . .

The houses of Jarmo were only the size of a small cottage by our standards, but each was provided with several rectangular rooms. The walls of the houses were made of puddled mud, often set on crude foundations of stone. . . . The village probably looked much like the simple Kurdish farming village of today, with its mud-walled houses and low mud-on-brush roofs. I doubt that the Jarmo village had more than twenty houses at any one moment of its existence. Today, an average of about seven people live in a comparable Kurdish house; possibly the population of Jarmo was about 150 people.

It is interesting that portable pottery does not appear until the . . . last third of the life of the Jarmo deposit, and even then not over the whole site. Throughout the duration of the village, however, its people had experimented with the plastic qualities of clay. As well as building puddled-mud houses, they modeled little figurines of animals and human beings in clay. One type of human figurine they favored was that of a markedly pregnant woman, probably the expression of some sort of fertility spirit. They provided their house floors with baked-in-place depressions, either as basins or as hearths, and later with domed ovens of clay. . . . The houses themselves were of clay or mud; one could almost say they were built up like a house-sized pot. Then, finally, the idea of making portable pottery itself appeared....

On the other hand, the old tradition of making flint blades and microlithic tools was still very strong at Jarmo. The sickle blade was made in quantities, but so also were many of the much older tool types. Strangely enough, it is within this age-old category of chipped stone tools that we see one of the clearest pointers to a newer age. Many of the Jarmo chipped stone tools... were made of obsidian, a black volcanic natural glass. The obsidian beds nearest to Jarmo are over three hundred miles to the north. Already a bulk carrying trade had been established, the forerunner of commerce, and the routes were set by which, in later times, the metal trade was to move.

READING REVIEW

1. What was the diet of the people of Jarmo?
2. Why does Braidwood find it interesting that portable pottery did not appear until late in the life of Jarmo?
3. (**a**) Why does the existence of obsidian tools indicate that the people of Jarmo were involved in trade? (**b**) Why did these obsidian tools "point to a newer age"?

---

5 ADVICE FOR EGYPTIAN STUDENTS

Ancient Egyptians had the highest regard for education. Their word for school, for example, meant "house of life." Knowledge of reading, writing, and math was considered an utmost necessity for boys of all social classes. Students learned such skills through the constant copying of classical texts and moral guidelines. The excerpt below from Wings of the Falcon: Life and Thought of Ancient Egypt, *translated by Joseph Kaster, includes a number of the latter, written in the form of instructions from father to son, advising the son to diligently follow the life of a scribe. As you read the excerpt, note the problems of ancient Egyptian education that affect our educational system today.*

I

I place you at school along with the children of the notables, to educate you and to have you trained for [the scribe's] calling.

Behold, I relate to you how it fares with the scribe when he is told: "Wake up and at your place! The books lie already before your comrades! Place your hand on your clothes and look to your sandals!"

When you get your daily task, be not idle and read diligently from the book. When you reckon in silence, let no word be heard.

Write with your hand and read with your mouth. Ask counsel of them who are clever. Be not slack, and spend not a day in idleness, or woe betide your limbs! Enter into the methods of your teacher and hear his instruction. Behold I am with you every day!

II

O scribe, be not idle, be not idle, or you will be soundly chastised! Set not your heart on pleasures, or you will be ruined. Write with your hand, read with your mouth, and ask counsel of them that have more knowledge than you.

. . . Persevere every day; thus shall you obtain mastery over the knowledge of writing. Spend no day in idleness or you will be beaten. The ear of the boy is on his back, and he hearkens when he is beaten!

. . . Persevere in asking counsel, neglect it not; and in writing, sicken not of it.

Set your heart upon hearing my words; you will find them profitable.

III

Be not a foolish man, that has no instruction.

By night you are taught, and by day you are instructed, but you do not listen to instruction, and you do after your own devices!

. . . Lions are taught, horses are broken in, but you—the like of you is not known in the whole land! Know that, if you please!

IV

My heart is sick of giving you further teaching! I may give you a hundred blows, and yet you cast them all off! You are as a beaten ass unto me, that is stubborn. You are as a jabbering [slave] unto me, that is brought with the tribute! . . .

Giant statues of Pharaoh Ramses II at Abu Simbel in the Nile Valley

V

I am told that you forsake writing, that you give yourself up to pleasures. You go from street to street, where it smells of beer, to destruction. Beer . . . will send your soul to perdition. . . .

You are encountered climbing a wall and breaking in; men run away from before you, for you inflict wounds upon them.

Would that you knew that wine is an abomination, that you would take an oath in respect to wine, that you would not set your heart on the bottle, and would forget [drink]! . . .

VII

I am told that you forsake writing, that you have gone and run away. You forsake writing as fast as your feet can manage it, like a pair of horses. . . .

You are like a skipper's mate who does not look out for adverse winds, and searches not for the wave. If the outer rope is let go, it pulls him by the neck. . . .

X

Ah, what mean you by saying: "It is thought that the soldier is better off than the scribe?"

Come, let me tell you how the soldier fares, the often-belabored, when he is brought while yet young, to be shut up in the barracks. He receives a burning blow on his body, a ruinous blow on his eye, a blow on his eyebrow that lays him out, and his pate is cleft with a wound. . . . He is battered and bruised with flogging.

Comc, let me tell you how he goes to Syria, and how he marches over the mountains. His bread and water are borne upon his shoulder like the load of an ass; they make his neck as bent as that of an ass, and the joints of his back are bowed. His drink is stinking water. He falls out only to keep watch. When he reaches the enemy, he is like a trapped bird, and he has no strength in his limbs. . . .

O scribe, turn you away from the thought that the soldier is better off than the scribe! . . .

XIII

Be a scribe who is freed forth from forced labor, and protected from all work. He is released from hoeing with the hoe, and he need not carry a basket.

It separates you from plying with the oar, and it is free from vexation. You have not many masters, nor a host of superiors.

No sooner has a man come forth from his mother's womb, than he is stretched out before his superiors. The boy becomes a soldier's henchman, the stripling a recruit, the grown man is made into a husbandman, and the townsman into a groom. The lame [one] is made into a doorkeeper, and the nearsighted into one who feeds cattle; the fowler goes among the marshes, and the fisherman stands in the wet. . . .

When the baker stands and bakes and lays bread on the fire, his head is inside the oven, and his son holds fast his feet. Comes it to pass that he slips from his son's hand, he falls into the blaze!

But the scribe, he directs every work that is in the land!

READING REVIEW

1. What could students expect if they did not study diligently?
2. How does the father persuade the son that the calling of scribe is the best one to follow?
3. What problems mentioned in the excerpt are found in the American educational system today?

---

6 AN EARLY CITY IN THE TIGRIS-EUPHRATES VALLEY

By about 300 B.C., the Tigris-Euphrates Valley was divided into a number of city-states, each one consisting of a city and the surrounding country it controlled. In the excerpt below from The Rise and Fall of the Ancient World, *historian Chester G. Starr describes an imaginary tour around a typical city-state of this period. As you read the excerpt, ask yourself how a Mesopotamian city was similar to and different from modern cities.*

We should find ourselves first walking down a high road, with fields stretching out on either side. . . . The roads are relatively straight, the fields are carefully marked out by the use of geometry, and here and there drainage and irrigation canals cut their regular courses. Farming with stone hoes and wooden plows is still hard work, despite the use of oxen; but the rewards of barley, wheat, and vegetables are relatively sure. Shepherds in the pastures watch the sheep and cattle, which are carefully registered in the temple accounts; groves of date palms and fruit trees stud the landscape.

But one cannot stay in the fields, though they are the backbone of [the] economy. Some of the farmers still live in minor villages, but many trudge out to their small plots every day from the city proper. Framed by a moat and a high brick wall, the city has heavily fortified gates which are guarded by the soldiers of the state; the wall of [Erech] was five-and-a-half miles long and had over nine hundred towers. When one passes within the gates, the difference from a purely agricultural village is extraordinary. The mud-brick, flat-roofed houses of the ordinary inhabitants are still primitive, but they press closely on one another and are divided by twisting, narrow, blank-walled streets. One [city-state] king . . . boasts himself master of thirty-six thousand souls. This may be a purely conventional figure, but many of the cities must have had populations of about this size.

In one part of the city are lanes of artisans, smiths, potters, and the like, who live by making and exchanging their wares for barley, fish, and so on. In another is the palace of the king. Looming over all are the temples, very literally conceived as the "houses of the gods." What we would call the temple proper was frequently built on an artificial mound, beside which might loom up in later days a stepped tower. . . . Within the palace of the deity are also the abodes of the priests, wool-workers, brewers, and countless other servants of the temple complex. . . .

In theory the [city-]state was an earthly estate of the gods, and its early economic activities were focused on the temple. The land, which was owned by the gods, was partly farmed directly for the temple; the rest was allotted to individual farmers, who paid between one-third and one-sixth of their produce to the temple granaries. The temple owned great quantities of livestock, date orchards, even its own boats and plows; about the temple lived and worked . . . slaves and free people who brewed and baked, carded and wove wool, or made jewelry and statues. Fishers and traders as well carried on their work for the temples.

READING REVIEW

1. According to the excerpt, what was the most marked difference between a purely agricultural village and a city-state?
2. What were the most prominent buildings in the city-state? Why?
3. (**a**) How were the cities of ancient Mesopotamia different from modern cities? (**b**) How were they the same?

---

7 SARGON II'S CONQUESTS

The Assyrians had the best equipped and most ferocious army of ancient times. They were the first to employ effectively the cavalry charge, and their formidable array of modern weaponry included iron-tipped lances and arrows and the battering ram. The Assyrian army's most powerful weapons, however, were fear and terror. In the excerpt below from Ancient Near Eastern Texts, *edited by James B. Pritchard, Sargon II, who ruled the Assyrians from 722 B.C. to 705 B.C., discusses his conquests. As you read the excerpt, note the tactics that Sargon II used to strike fear into his opponents.*

Hanno, king of Gaza and also Sib'e, the [top general] of Egypt, set out . . . against me to deliver a decisive battle. I defeated them; Sib'e ran away, afraid when he [only] heard the noise of my [approaching] army, and has not been seen again. Hanno, I captured personally. . . .

Iamani from Ashdod, afraid of my armed force, left his wife and children and fled to the frontier . . . and hid there like a thief. I installed an officer of mine as governor over his entire large country and its prosperous inhabitants, [thus] aggrandizing [again] the territory belonging to Ashur, the king of the gods. The terror[-inspiring] glamor of Ashur, my lord, overpowered . . . the king of [Ethiopia] and he threw [Iamani] . . . in fetters on hands and feet and sent him to me, to Assyria. I conquered and sacked the towns Shinuhtu and Samaria, and all Israel. I caught, like a fish, the Greek [Ionians] who live [on islands] amidst the Western Sea. . . .

Ia'ubidi from Hamath, a commoner without claim to the throne, a cursed Hittite, schemed to become king of Hamath, induced the cities Arvad, Simirra, Damascus, and Samaria to desert me, made them collaborate and fitted out an army. I called up the masses of the soldiers of Ashur and besieged him and his warriors in Qarqar, his favorite city. I conquered [it] and burnt [it]. Himself I flayed; the rebels I killed in their cities and established [again] peace and harmony. A contingent of 200 chariots and 600 men on horseback I formed from among the inhabitants of Hamath and added them to my royal corps.

Azuri, king of Ashdod, had schemed not to deliver tribute any more and sent messages [full] of hostilities against Assyria, to the kings [living] in his neighborhood. On account of the[se] act[s] which he committed, I abolished his rule over the people of his country and made Ahimiti, his younger brother, king over them. But the[se] Hittites, always planning evil deeds, hated his reign and elevated to rule over them a Greek who, without claim to the throne, had no respect for authority—just as they themselves. In a sudden rage, I did not [wait to] assemble the full might

An Assyrian winged bull from the palace of King Ashurnasirpal II

of my army . . . but started out towards Ashdod [only] with those of my warriors who, even in friendly areas, never leave my side. But this Greek heard about the advance of my expedition, from afar, and he fled into the territory of Musru—which belongs [now] to Ethiopia—and his [hiding] place could not be detected. I besieged [and] conquered the cities . . .; I declared his images, his wife, his children, all the possessions and treasures of his palace as well as the inhabitants of his country as booty. I reorganized [the administration of] these cities [and] settled therein people from the [regions] of the East which I had conquered personally. I installed an officer of mine over them and declared them Assyrian citizens and they pulled [as such] the straps [of my yoke]. The king of Ethiopia, who [lives] in [a distant country], in an inapproachable region, . . . whose fathers never—from remote days until now—had sent messengers to inquire after the health of my royal forefathers, he did hear, even [that] far away, of the might of Ashur, Nebo, [and] Marduk. The awe-inspiring glamor of my kingship blinded him and terror overcame him. He threw [the Greek] in fetters, shackles and iron bands, and they brought him to Assyria, a long journey.

READING REVIEW

1. What in the excerpt suggests that Sargon II felt himself in constant danger of assassination?
2. Why did the king of Ethiopia return the Greek pretender to the throne of Ashdod to Assyria?
3. Give two examples of Sargon II's use of terror.

8 A DEBATE ON GOVERNMENT

After the death of the Persian king Cambyses—the son of Cyrus—in 522 B.C., a palace official of the Magian tribe seized the throne. However, seven Persian nobles—Darius the Great among them—formed a conspiracy and removed the usurper from power. According to the Greek historian Herodotus, the seven nobles then discussed what kind of government Persia should have in the future. As you read the excerpt, note the arguments the nobles gave for and against the various types of government.

When the confusion had settled, five days later, the conspirators against the Magians held a debate about the entire condition of affairs. Here speeches were made that some of the Greeks refuse to credit, but the speeches *were* made, for all that. Otanes proposed that power should be entrusted to the main body of the Persians: "It is my conviction that we should no longer have a monarch over us. It is neither pleasant nor good, the monarchy. You yourselves know how far Cambyses' outrages went, and you have had a taste of the outrageousness of the Magian. How can a monarchy be a suitable thing? The monarch may do what he pleases, with none to check him afterwards. Take the best man on earth and put him into a monarchy and you put him outside of the thoughts that have been wont to guide him. Outrageousness is bred in him by reason of the good things he has, and envy is basic in the nature of man. He has these two qualities, then, and in them he has all evil. Out of his satiety his outrageousness grows, and he does appalling things out of that; but he does many, too, out of envy. You would think that a man who was an absolute sovereign would be free of jealousy, for he has all good things at his disposal, but the contrary is true of him with respect to his fellow citizens. He is jealous that the best of them should continue alive; he is pleased that the worst of them should continue alive. He is a master at receiving slanders. He is the most difficult of all men to deal with: if your admiration of him is moderate, he is offended because the flattery is not abject; if the flattery is abject, he is offended with you as a toady. I have still my biggest charge to make against him: he turns upside down all ancestral observances . . . and kills men without trial. When the people is ruler, in the first place its title is the fairest of all—namely, equality before the law; secondly, it does none of those things I have objected against the monarch. The government holds office by decision of lot, and the power it holds is subject to . . . check . . . and all its propositions it must put before the commonalty for judgment. I vote therefore that we abolish the monarchy and increase the power of the people; for in the Many lies All."

. . . Megabyzus would have them turn things over to an oligarchy, and his speech was as follows: "What Otanes has said about the abolition of the monarchy you may regard as being my opinion also. But when he proposes to turn over power to the Many, he has fallen short of the nicest judgment. There is nothing stupider, nothing more given to outrage, than a useless mob. Yet surely for men who are fleeing the outrage of the despot to fall into the clutches of the outrageous Many, on whom, too, there is no restraint, is in no way bearable. The despot, if he does something, does it of knowledge; but knowledge is what does not inhere in the Many. How can men know anything when they have never been taught what is fine, nor have they any innate sense of it? They rush into things and push them this way and that without intelligent purposes, like a river in a winter spate. Let those who have ill will to the Persians press for a democracy; but let us choose a society of the Best Men and entrust the power to them. Among this number we shall be ourselves, and we may reasonably assume that, when the men are the Best, their counsels will be so too."

. . . Darius gave his judgment as third among them: "What Megabyzus has said about the Many seems to me truly said; not so his comments on oligarchy. Suppose, for the argument, that all three constitutions are of the very best—the best democracy, the best oligarchy, the best monarchy. I declare to you that, of these three at their best, monarchy is far superior. Nothing is manifestly better than the one best man. He will have judgment to match his excellence and will govern the Many blamelessly, and what measures he must devise against ill-doers will be wrapped in a similar well-judging silence. In an oligarchy, many try to practice virtue for the public good, but in doing so they engender bitter private enmities. Each of the oligarchs wants to be chief man and to win with his opinions, and so they come to great hatreds of one another, and from this comes faction, and from faction comes murder. From murder there is a relapse into despotism—and *there* is an indication again how much despotism is the best! When the Many are rulers, it cannot but be that, again, knavery is bred in the state; but now the knaves do not grow to hate one another—they become fast friends. For they combine together to maladminister the public concerns. This goes on until one man takes charge of affairs for the Many and puts a stop to the knaves. As a result of this, he wins the admiration of the Many, and, being so admired, lo! you have your despot again; in this case, too, it is clear that monarchy is the best of the systems. In one word: from what source did we gain our freedom, and who gave it us? The people, the oligarchy, or the despot? I give my vote that, as we were freed by one man [Cyrus], so we should keep this freedom *through* one man; apart from this, we should not abolish any of our ancestral laws that are sound. It would be better so."

These were the three opinions that were put forward. Four of the Seven gave their support to the last—that of Darius.

READING REVIEW

1. Some of Herodotus' readers doubted that the Persians had the political sophistication to hold such a debate. What sentence in the excerpt alludes to these doubts?
2. How is the argument put forward by Otanes in support of democracy similar to those of the writers of the Declaration of Independence?
3. What convincing argument did Darius give in support of monarchy?

---

9 EVERYDAY LIFE IN MOHENJO-DARO AND HARAPPA

A highly developed civilization flourished in the Indus Valley about 1,000 years, first appearing around 2500 B.C. This early civilization developed at the site of the ancient cities of Mohenjo-Daro and Harappa. The excerpt below from The World of the Past, *edited by Jacquetta Hopkins Hawkes, draws on archaeological findings in the twin cities to build a picture of everyday life in the Indus civilization. As you read the excerpt, compare life in the Indus civilization from life in other civilizations of the same time period.*

Statue from the city of Mohenjo-Daro

The following picture of the life that was led by the Indus peoples . . . is drawn by Sir John Marshall . . . "Like the rest of Western Asia, the Indus Country is still in . . . that age in which arms and utensils of stone continue to be used side by side with those of copper or bronze. Their society is organized in cities; their wealth derived mainly from agriculture and trade, which appears to have extended far and wide in all directions. They cultivate wheat and barley as well as the date-palm. They have domesticated the humped zebu [ox], buffalo, and short horned bull, besides the sheep, pig, dog, elephant, and camel; but the cat and probably the horse are unknown to them. For transport they have wheeled vehicles, to which oxen doubtless were yoked. They are skilful metal workers, with a plentiful supply of gold, silver, and copper. Lead, too, and tin are in use, but the latter only as an alloy in the making of bronze. With spinning and weaving they are thoroughly conversant. Their weapons of war and of the chase are the bow and arrow, spear, axe, dagger, and mace. The sword they had not yet evolved; nor is there any evidence of defensive body armour. Among their other implements, hatchets, sickles, saws, chisels, and razors are made of both copper and bronze; knives . . . sometimes of these metals, sometimes of chert or other hard stones. For the crushing of grain they have the [hand mill] but not the circular grindstone. Their domestic vessels are commonly of earthenware turned on the wheel and not infrequently painted with . . . designs. . . . The ornaments of the rich are made of the precious metals or of copper, sometimes overlaid with gold, of faience [opaque colored glazes], ivory, carnelian, and other stones; for the poor, they are usually of shell or terracotta. Figurines and toys, for which there is a wide vogue, are of terracotta, and shell and faience are freely used, as they are in Sumer and the West generally. . . . With the invention of writing the Indus peoples are also familiar, and employ for this purpose a form of script which, though peculiar to India, is evidently analogous to other contemporary scripts of Western Asia and the Nearer East."

Besides the cultivation of wheat, barley, and date-palm, . . . the inhabitants of Harappa cultivated peas and sesanum too. Nevertheless, for their food they were not dependent entirely on agriculture, for . . . there is hardly a place at Harappa where bones are not upturned by the spade. Moreover, the sling balls of clay, the copper fish hooks, the arrow-heads, the flaying knives, constitute sufficient proof . . . of the extent to which the inhabitants of Harappa depended for their food on birds and beasts and fish.

READING REVIEW

1. Of what were the tools of the Indus peoples made?
2. What evidence suggests that the Indus peoples did not depend entirely on agriculture for their food?
3. How did daily life in Mohenjo-Daro and Harappa compare to daily life in Sumer?

10 BUDDHISM AND EQUALITY

Buddha believed that all people were born equal and refused to accept the Hindu caste system. This view upset many members of the highest caste, the Brahmans, for they could not accept that the lower castes were their equals. In the excerpt below from Volume 1 of Sources of Indian Tradition, *edited by William Theodore de Bary, a learned young Brahman named Assalayana attempts to refute Buddha's views on caste. As you read the excerpt, note the arguments that Buddha uses to answer Assalayana's challenges.*

Surrounded by a crowd of brahmans, [Assalayana] went to the Lord [Buddha], and, after greeting him, sat down and said:

"Brahmans maintain that only they are the highest class, and the others are below them. . . . Only they are pure, and not the others. Only they are the true sons of Brahma . . . born of Brahma, creations of Brahma, heirs of Brahma. Now what does the worthy Gautama say to that?"

"Do the brahmans really maintain this, Assalayana, when they're born of women just like anyone else, of brahman women who . . . conceive, give birth and nurse their children, just like any other women?"

"For all you say, this is what they think. . . ."

"Have you heard that in the lands of the Greeks and . . . other peoples on the borders there are only two classes, masters and slaves, and a master can become a slave and vice versa?"

"Yes, I've heard so."

"And what strength or support does that fact give to the brahmans' claim?"

"Nevertheless, that is what they think."

"Again if a man is a murderer, a thief, or an adulterer, or commits other grave sins, when his body breaks up on death does he pass on to purgatory if he's a kshatriya, vaishya, or shudra, but not if he's a brahman?"

"No, Gautama. In such a case the same fate is in store for all men, whatever their class."

"And if he avoids grave sin, will he go to heaven if he's a brahman, but not if he's a man of the lower classes?"

"No, Gautama. In such a case the same reward awaits all men, whatever their class."

"And is a brahman capable of developing a mind of love without hate or ill-will, but not a man of the other classes?"

"No, Gautama. All four classes are capable of doing so."

"Can only a brahman go down to the river and wash away dust and dirt, and not men of the other classes?"

"No, Gautama, all four classes can."

"Now suppose a king were to gather together a hundred men of different classes and to order the brahmans and kshatriyas to take kindling wood of sal, pine, lotus or sandal, and light fires, while the low class folk did the same with common wood. What do you think would happen? Would the fires of the high-born men blaze up brightly . . . and those of the humble fail?"

"No, Gautama. It would be alike with high and lowly. . . . Every fire would blaze with the same bright flame.". . .

"Suppose there are two young brahman brothers, one a scholar and the other uneducated. Which of them would be served first at memorial feasts, festivals, and sacrifices, or when entertained as guests?"

"The scholar, of course; for what great benefit would accrue from entertaining the uneducated one?"

"But suppose the scholar is ill-behaved and wicked, while the uneducated one is well-behaved and virtuous?"

"Then the uneducated one would be served first, for what great benefit would accrue from entertaining an ill-behaved and wicked man?"

"First, Assalayana, you based your claim on birth, then you gave up birth for learning, and finally you have come round to my way of thinking, that all four classes are equally pure!"

At this Assalayana sat silent . . . his shoulders hunched, his eyes cast down, thoughtful in mind, and with no answer at hand.

READING REVIEW

1. How did Buddha answer Assalayana's claim that only the Brahmans "are the true sons of Brahma"?
2. On what two factors did Assalayana base the Brahmans' claim to be the highest class?
3. Explain Buddha's views on how to judge people.

Hindu pilgrims bathing in the sacred waters of the Ganges River near Benares, India

11 ASOKA'S EDICTS

After Asoka's conversion to Buddhism, he attempted to rule the Maurya Empire in India according to Buddhist precepts. To this end, Asoka issued a number of edicts, or rules, that were engraved on rocks and pillars throughout the empire in places where people were likely to gather. The edicts were written in such a simple and sincere fashion that historians are convinced they are the work of Asoka himself. Several of Asoka's edicts appear in the selection below from Volume 1 of Sources in Indian Tradition, *edited by William Theodore de Bary. As you read ask yourself what were the edicts' major themes.*

Father and mother should be obeyed, teachers should be obeyed; pity . . . should be felt for all creatures. These virtues of Righteousness should be practiced. . . . This is an ancient rule, conducive to long life.

It is good to give, but there is no gift, no service, like the gift of Righteousness. So friends, relatives, and companions should preach it on all occasions. This is duty; this is right; by this heaven may be gained—and what is more important than to gain heaven?

This world and the other are hard to gain without great love of Righteousness, great self-examination, great obedience, great circumspection, great effort. Through my instruction respect and love of Righteousness daily increase and will increase. . . . For this is my rule—to govern by Righteousness, to administer by Righteousness, to please my subjects by Righteousness, and to protect them by Righteousness.

Here no animal is to be killed for sacrifice, and no festivals are to be held, for the king finds much evil in festivals, except for certain festivals which he considers good.

Formerly in the [king's] kitchen several hundred thousand animals were killed daily for food; but now . . . only three are killed—two peacocks and a deer. . . . Even these three animals will not be killed in the future.

I am not satisfied simply with hard work or carrying out the affairs of state, for I consider my work to be the welfare of the whole world. . . . There is no better deed than to work for the welfare of the whole world, and all my efforts are made that I may clear my debt to all beings. I make them happy here and now that they may attain heaven in the life to come. . . . But it is difficult without great effort.

. . . Whoever honors his own [religion] and disparages another man's, whether from blind loyalty or with the intention of showing his own [religion] in a favorable light, does his own [religion] the greatest possible harm. Concord is best, with each hearing and respecting the other's teachings. It is the wish of the [king] that members of all [religions] should be learned and should teach virtue.

The seated Buddha

All the good deeds that I have done have been accepted and followed by the people. And so obedience to mother and father, obedience to teachers, respect for the aged, kindliness . . . to the poor and weak, and to slaves and servants, have increased and will continue to increase. . . . And this progress of Righteousness . . . has taken place in two manners, by enforcing conformity to Righteousness, and by exhortation. I have enforced the law against killing certain animals and many others, but the greatest progress of Righteousness . . . comes from exhortation in favor of noninjury to life and abstention from killing living beings.

I have done this that it may endure . . . as long as the moon and sun, and that my sons and my great-grandsons may support it; for by supporting it they will gain both this world and the next.

READING REVIEW

1. What evidence in the edicts suggests that Asoka was a vegetarian?
2. According to Asoka, what is the result of religious intolerance?
3. In your opinion, what are the major themes of Asoka's edicts? Provide evidence to support your answer.

---

12 THE PLACE OF WOMEN IN HINDU SOCIETY

The Sacred Law, Manu Smrti, *described how Hindus should behave in their everyday lives. This law was so detailed that it provided instructions on everything from how to perform religious rights to who to serve first at a family dinner. The excerpt below is from one of the texts of the Sacred Law, dating from about the first century* B.C. *It describes how Hindu women should be treated. As you read the excerpt, note the contradiction in how Hindu women were viewed.*

Women must be honored and adorned by their fathers, brothers, husbands, and brothers-in-law who desire great good fortune.

Where women, verily, are honored, there the gods rejoice; where, however, they are not honored, there all sacred rights prove fruitless.

Where the female relations live in grief—that family soon perishes completely; where, however, they do not suffer from any grievance—that family always prospers. . . .

Her father protects her in childhood, her husband protects her in youth, her sons protect her in old age—a woman does not deserve independence.

The father who does not give away his daughter in marriage at the proper time is censurable; censurable is the husband who does not [treat his wife correctly]; and after the husband is dead, the son, verily, is censurable, who does not protect his mother.

Even against the slightest provocations should women be particularly guarded; for unguarded they would bring grief to both the families.

Regarding this as the highest dharma of all four classes, husbands, though weak, must strive to protect their wives.

His own offspring, character, family, self, and dharma does one protect when he protects his wife scrupulously. . . .

The husband should engage his wife in the collection and expenditure of his wealth, in cleanliness, in [religious rites], in cooking food for the family, and in looking after the necessities of the household. . . .

Women destined to bear children, enjoying great good fortune, deserving of worship, the resplendent lights of homes on the one hand and divinities of good luck who reside in the houses on the other—between these there is no difference whatsoever.

READING REVIEW

1. According to the Sacred Law, what was the highest dharma, or morality, of all four Hindu classes?
2. According to the Sacred Law, what were suitable tasks for a Hindu woman?
3. How is this excerpt contradictory in the way it views Hindu women?

---

13 THE WISDOM OF CONFUCIUS

The teachings of Confucius, who lived from 551 B.C. to 479 B.C., are so rooted in Chinese culture that an understanding of China is almost impossible without knowledge of them. The importance of the family and respect for one's elders are two themes that frequently recur in Confucian philosophy. In the following excerpt from China: Selected Readings, *edited by Hyman Kublin, Confucius explains the meaning and importance of filial piety—reverence for one's mother and father. As you read the excerpt, note how Confucius suggests filial piety may be put into practice.*

The Scholars

The connecting link between serving one's father and serving one's mother is love. The connecting link between serving one's father and serving one's prince is reverence. Thus, the mother [brings forth] love, while the prince calls forth reverence. But to the father belong both—love and reverence. Therefore, to serve the prince with filiality is to serve him with loyalty.

"The connecting link between serving one's father and serving one's mother is love."

Likewise, to serve one's elders reverently paves the way for civic obedience. Loyal and obedient without fail in the service of their superiors, they will preserve their rank and offices. For the rest, they will carry on their family sacrifices. This is the filiality of scholars. The Odes say:

Rise early and retire late,
Not to discredit those [from whom you are born].

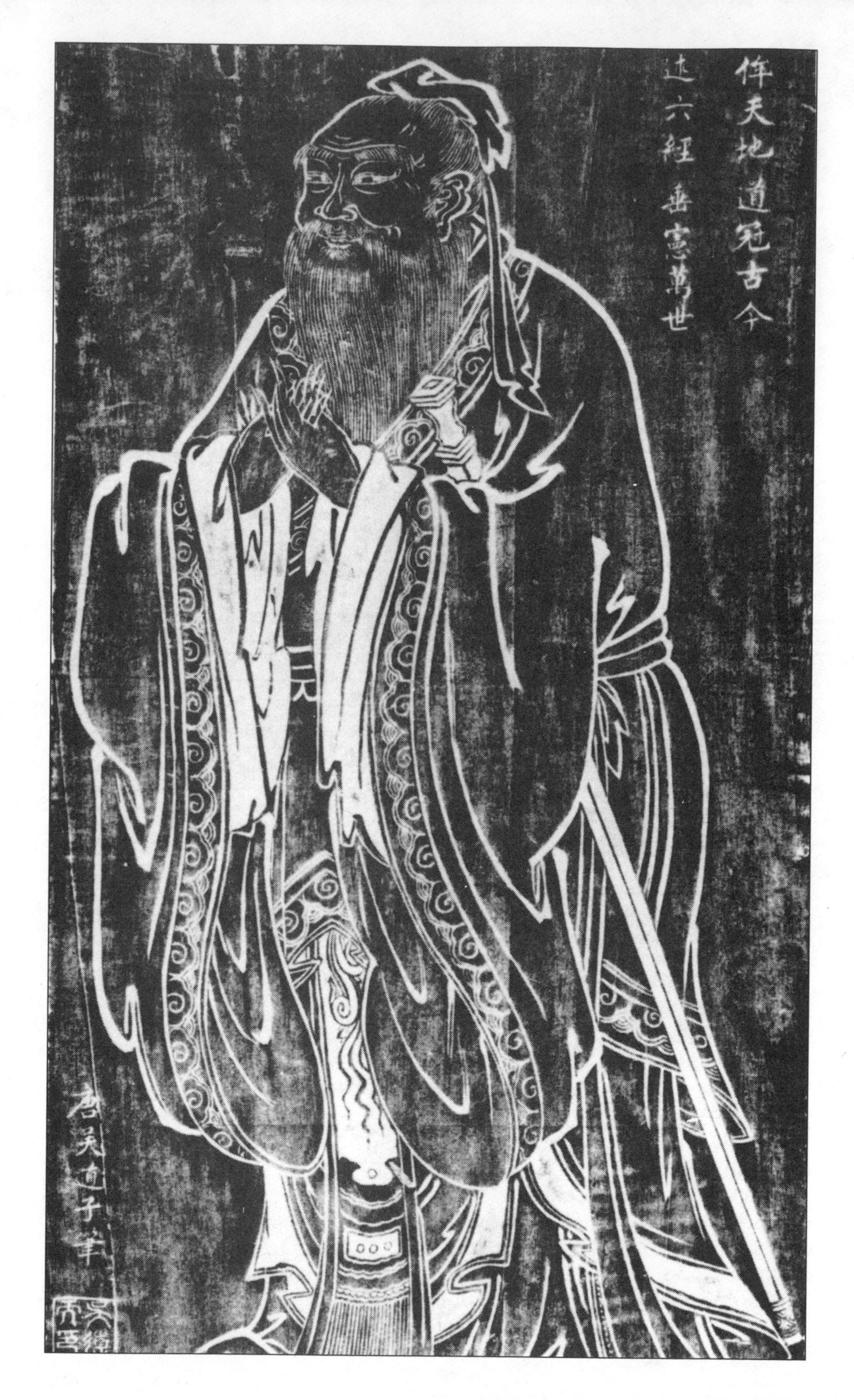

Confucius

The Common People

Following the laws of nature; utilizing the earth to the best advantage according to the various qualities of the soil; restricting one's personal desires and enjoyment in order to support one's parents—this is the filiality of the common people. So it is that, from the Son of Heaven [the Emperor] to the commoners, if filial piety is not pursued from beginning to end, disasters are sure to follow.

The Government of the Sage

The relation between father and son is rooted in nature and develops into the proper relation between prince and ministers. Parents give one life; no bond could be stronger. They watch over their child with utmost care; no love could be greater. Therefore, to love others without first loving one's parents is to act against virtue. To reverence other men without first reverencing one's parents is to act against propriety. If we model right upon such perversity, the people have no true [standard] to follow. In this there is no goodness; it is all evil. Although such a person may gain position, men of learning and virtue will not esteem him.

The practice of a virtuous man is different: his speech is praiseworthy; his actions are enjoyable; his righteousness is respected; his management of affairs is [worthy of imitation]; his deportment is pleasing; his gait is measured. He descends to his people; therefore, they look on him with awe and love; they imitate and seek to resemble him. Thus, he realizes his own virtuous teaching and puts into effect his own directives. The Odes say:

The virtuous man, the princely one,
Has nothing wrong in his deportment.

The Practice of Filiality

The master said: "In serving his parents a filial son renders utmost respect to them while at home; he supports them with joy; he gives them tender care in sickness; he grieves at their death; he sacrifices to them with solemnity. If he has measured up to these five, then he is truly capable of serving his parents.

"He who really loves his parents will not be proud in high station. He will not be insubordinate to an inferior position. Among his equals he will not be [quarrelsome]. To be proud in high station is to be ruined. To be insubordinate to an inferior position is to incur punishment. To be [quarrelsome] among one's equals leads to physical violence. As long as these three evils are not uprooted, a son cannot be called filial even though he feast his parents daily on the three kinds of choice meat. . . .

"When parents are alive, to serve them with love and reverence; when deceased, to cherish their memory with deep grief—this is the sum total of man's fundamental duty, the fulfillment of the mutual relations between the living and the dead, the accomplishment of the filial son's service of his parents."

READING REVIEW

1. According to Confucius what paves the way for civic obedience?
2. Why does Confucius call loving and reverencing others without first loving and reverencing one's parents a *perversity*?
3. Why do you think Confucius believes a son who is guilty of the three evils cannot be considered filial?

---

14 THE *DAO DE CHING* OF LAOZI

The ideas of Daoism are complementary to those of Confucianism. Whereas Confucianism is concerned with practical matters and is written in a straightforward manner, Daoism is concerned with spiritual life and is written in a mystical, otherworldly fashion. The most famous work of Daoism is the Dao De Ching, *or the "Classic of the Way and the Power," by the philosopher Laozi, from which the excerpt below is taken. As you read the excerpt, ask yourself why the* Dao De Ching *has been described as mystical and otherworldly.*

II

The whole world recognizes the beautiful as the beautiful, yet this is only the ugly; the whole world recognizes the good as the good, yet this is only the bad.

Thus Something and Nothing produce each other;
The difficult and the easy complement each other;
The long and the short off-set each other;
The high and the low incline towards each other;
Note and sound harmonize with each other;
Before and after follow each other.
Therefore the sage keeps to the deed that consists in taking no action and practices the teaching that uses no words. . . .

IV

The way is empty, yet use will not drain it.
Deep, it is like the ancestor of the [many] creatures.
Blunt the sharpness;
Untangle the knots;
Soften the glare;
Let your wheels move only along old ruts.
Darkly visible, it only seems as if it were there. . . .

Laozi holding the child Confucius

XI

Thirty spokes
Share one hub.

Adapt the nothing therein to the purpose in hand, and you will have the use of the cart. Knead clay in order to make a vessel. Adapt the nothing therein to the purpose at hand, and you will have the use of the vessel. Cut out doors and windows in order to make a room. Adapt the nothing therein to the purpose in hand, and you will have the use of the room. Thus what we gain is Something, yet it is by virtue of Nothing that this can be put to use.

READING REVIEW

1. Which verse in the excerpt is illustrated by the statement: "You can only know peace by having war"?
2. What do you think the "nothing" referred to in Verse XI is?
3. The *Dao De Ching* has been characterized as mystical. (**a**) What do you think this means? (**b**) Give two examples from the excerpt to support your statement.

---

15 MO TZU ON UNIVERSAL LOVE

The Chinese philosopher Mo Tzu was born about 470 B.C., a few years after the death of Confucius. Originally he was a follower of Confucianism, but he became disillusioned because of the emphasis on filial piety. Mo Tzu believed that people should make no distinctions between family and stranger or citizen and foreigner. Rather, they should love everyone equally. The excerpt below is taken from a collection of his teachings, the Mo Tzu. *As you read the excerpt, ask yourself what qualities constitute universal love.*

Mo Tzu said: It is the business of the benevolent man to try to promote what is beneficial to the world and to eliminate what is harmful. Now at the present time, what brings the greatest harm to the world? Great states attacking small ones, great families overthrowing small ones, the strong oppressing the weak, the many harrying the few, the cunning deceiving the stupid, the eminent lording it over the humble—these are harmful to the world. So too are rulers who are not generous, ministers who are not loyal, fathers who are without kindness, and sons who are unfilial, as well as those mean men who, with weapons, knives, poison, fire, and water, seek to injure and undo each other.

When we inquire into the cause of these various harms, what do we find has produced them? Do they come about from loving others and trying to benefit them? Surely not! They come rather from hating others and trying to injure them. And when we set out to classify and describe those men who hate and injure others, shall we say that their actions are motivated by universality or partiality? Surely we must answer, by partiality, and it is this partiality in their dealings with one another that gives rise to all the great harms in the world. Therefore we know that partiality is wrong.

Mo Tzu said: Whoever criticizes others must have some alternative to offer them. To criticize and yet offer no alternative is like trying to stop flood with flood or put out fire with fire. It will surely have no effect. Therefore Mo Tzu said: Partiality must be replaced by universality.

But how can partiality be replaced by universality? If men were to regard the states of others as they regard their own, then who would raise up his state to attack the state of another? It would be like attacking his own. If men were to regard the cities of others as they regard their own, then who would raise up his city to attack the city of another? It would be like attacking his own. If men were to regard the families of others as they regard their own, then who would raise up his family to overthrow that of another? Now when states and cities do not attack and make war on each other and families and individuals do not overthrow or injure one another, is this a harm or a benefit to the world? Surely it is a benefit.

When we inquire into the cause of such benefits, what do we find has produced them? Do they come about from hating others and trying to injure them? Surely not! They come rather from loving others and trying to benefit them. And when we set out to classify and describe those men who love and benefit others, shall we say that their actions are motivated by partiality or universality? Surely we must answer, by universality, and it is this universality in their dealings with one another that gives rise to all the great benefits in the world. Therefore Mo Tzu has said universality is right. . . .

Now if we seek to benefit the world by taking universality as our standard, those with sharp ears and clear eyes will see and hear for others, those with sturdy limbs will work for others, and those with a knowledge of the Way will endeavor to teach others. Those who are old and without wives or children will find means of support and be able to live out their days; the young and orphaned who have no parents will find someone to care for them and look after their needs.

READING REVIEW

1. According to Mo Tzu, what gives rise to all the great harms of the world?
2. How can universality replace partiality?
3. How did Mo Tzu view the nature of universal love, as spiritual or material? Provide evidence from the excerpt to support your answer.

---

16 THE *BOOK OF SONGS*

One of the Five Classics is the Book of Songs, *a collection of 305 poems about diverse subjects such as love, politics, and home life. Most of the poems are allegorical in nature. That is, they teach a lesson or make a moral point through a story. The excerpt below is taken from the* Greater Odes, *the last section of the* Book of Songs. *As you read the excerpt, ask yourself who is speaking in the poem and who that person is addressing.*

Grave and dignified manners
Are the helpmates of power.
Men indeed have a saying,
"There is none so wise but has his follies."
But ordinary people's follies
Are but sicknesses of their own.
It is the wise man's follies
That are a rampant pest.

"Nothing is so strong as goodness."

Nothing is so strong as goodness;
On all sides men will take their lesson from it.
Valid are the works of inward power;
In all lands men will conform to them.
He who takes counsel widely, is final in his commands,
Far-seeing in his plans, timely in the announcing of them,
  Scrupulously attentive to decorum,
Will become a pattern to his people.

But those that rule to-day
Have brought confusion and disorder into government;
Have upset their power
By wild orgies of drinking.
So engrossed are you in your dissipations
That you do not think of your heritage,
Do not faithfully imitate the former kings,
Or strive to carry out their holy ordinances.

Therefore mighty Heaven is displeased;
Beware lest headlong as spring waters
You should be swept to ruin.
Rise early, go to bed at night;
Sprinkle and sweep your courtyard
So that it may be a pattern to the people.
Put in good order your chariots and horses,
Bows, arrows, and weapons of offence,
That you may be ready, should war arise,
To keep at due distance barbaric tribes.

Ascertain the views of gentlemen and commoners,
Give due warning of your princely measures,
Take precautions against the unforseen,
Be cautious in your utterances.
Scrupulously observe all rules of decorum,
Be always mild and good-tempered.
A scratch on a sceptre of white jade
Can be polished away;
A slip of the tongue
Cannot ever be repaired.

Do not be rash in your words,
Do not say: "Let it pass.
Don't catch hold of my tongue!
What I am saying will go no further."
There can be nothing said that has not its answer,
No deed of Power that has not its reward.
Be gracious to friends and companions
And to the common people, my child.
So shall your sons and grandsons continue for ever,
By the [many] peoples each accepted.

READING REVIEW

1. Why do you think the person speaking in the poem feels that the follies of ordinary people are "but sicknesses of their own," but a wise man's follies are a "rampant pest"?
2. According to the speaker, why should the listener be "cautious in your utterances"?
3. Who do you think is speaking in the poem? Who is that person speaking to? Explain your answers.

Civilizations of the Mediterranean World

17 THESEUS AND THE SLAYING OF THE MINOTAUR

The Ancient Greeks developed myths about their gods, goddesses, and heroes to help explain the beginnings and early history of their country. Among the most famous of these myths is the story of how Theseus, the greatest hero of Athens, killed the bull-headed man, or Minotaur, that King Minos of Crete kept in a vast labyrinth. The excerpt below is a modern retelling of the story of Theseus and the Minotaur from Greek Myths *by Robert Graves. As you read the excerpt, note the role that the gods played in the story.*

In requital for the murder of Androgeus, [his son,] Minos had given orders that the Athenians should send seven youths and seven maidens every ninth year to the Cretan Labyrinth, where the Minotaur waited to devour them. This Minotaur, whose name was Asterius, was the bull-headed monster that [the wife of Minos] had born to the white bull. Soon after Theseus's arrival at Athens the tribute fell due for the third time, and he so deeply pitied those parents whose children were liable to be chosen by lot, that he offered himself as one of the victims, despite [his father] Aegeus's earnest attempts at dissuasion.

On the two previous occasions, the ship which conveyed the fourteen victims had carried black sails, but Theseus was confident that the gods were on his side, and Aegeus therefore gave him a white sail to hoist on return, in signal of success.

When the lots had been cast at the Law Courts, Theseus led his companions to the Dolphin Temple where, on their behalf, he offered Apollo a branch of consecrated olive, bound with white wool. The fourteen mothers brought provisions for the voyage, and told their children fables and heroic tales to hearten them. Theseus, however, replaced two of the maiden victims with a pair of effeminate youths, possessed of unusual courage and presence of mind. These he commanded to take warm baths, avoid the rays of the sun, perfume their hair and bodies . . .and practise how to talk, gesture and walk like women. He was thus able to deceive Minos by passing them off as maidens. . . .

Theseus sailed on the sixth day of . . . [April]. . . . When the ship reached Crete some days afterwards, . . . Minos's own daughter Ariadne fell in love with [Theseus] at first sight. "I will help you to kill my half-brother, the Minotaur," she secretly promised him, "if I may return to Athens with you as your wife." This offer Theseus gladly accepted, and swore to marry her. Now, before Daedalus left Crete, he had given Ariadne a magic ball of thread, and instructed her how to enter and leave the labyrinth. She must open the entrance door and tie the loose end of the thread to the lintel; the ball would then roll along, diminishing as it went and making, with devious turns and twists, for the innermost recess where the Minotaur was lodged. This ball Ariadne gave to Theseus, and instructed him to follow it until he reached the sleeping monster, whom he must seize by the hair and sacrifice to Poseidon. He could then find his way back by rolling up the thread into a ball again.

That same night Theseus did as he was told.... When Theseus emerged from the Labyrinth, spotted with blood, Ariadne embraced him passionately, and guided the whole of the Athenian party to the harbour. For, in the meantime, the two effeminate-looking youths had killed the guards of the women's quarters, and released the maiden victims. They all stole aboard their ship, and rowed hastily away....

Some days later, after disembarking on the island then named Dia, but later known as Naxos, Theseus left Ariadne asleep on the shore, and sailed away. Why he did so must remain a mystery. Some say that he

Theseus slaying the Minotaur

deserted her in favour of a new mistress . . . ; others that, while windbound on Dia, he reflected on the scandal which Ariadne's arrival in Athens would cause. Others again, that Dionysus, appearing to Theseus in a dream, threateningly demanded Ariadne for himself, and that, when Theseus awoke . . . he weighed anchor in sudden terror; Dionysus having cast a spell which made him forget his promise to Ariadne and even her very existence.

Whatever the truth of the matter may be, . . . when Ariadne found herself alone on the deserted shore, she broke into bitter laments, remembering how she had trembled while Theseus set out to kill her monstrous half-brother; how she had offered silent vows for his success; and how, through love of him, she had deserted her parents and motherland. She now invoked the whole universe for vengeance, and Father Zeus nodded assent. . . .

Ariadne was soon revenged on Theseus. Whether in grief for her loss, or in joy at the sight of the Attic coast, from which he had been kept by prolonged winds, he forgot his promise to hoist the white sail. Aegeus, who stood watching for him on the Acropolis, . . . sighted the black sail, swooned, and fell headlong to his death into the valley below. But some say that he deliberately cast himself into the sea, which was thenceforth named the Aegean.

READING REVIEW

1. What signal was Theseus supposed to give to indicate that his voyage to Crete had been successful?
2. How was Theseus able to slay the Minotaur and escape from the labyrinth?
3. In your opinion why did the gods play a major role in the story of Theseus and the Minotaur?

---

18 THE MAKING OF SPARTAN SOLDIERS

Spartan soldiers were renowned for their great courage, discipline, and fighting skill. But such qualities did not develop accidentally. Beginning at a very early age, Spartan boys underwent rigorous preparation and training for military life. The excerpt below from Lives from Plutarch *details some aspects of this preparation and training written by the Spartan lawmaker Lycurgus. As you read the excerpt, compare Spartan education with Athenian education.*

Children were actually considered to be the property of the Spartan state, the parents having little claim to them. . . .

. . . Custom demanded that [the father] bring the child before a jury of elders who would examine the infant. If the child were stout and healthy, they gave orders for his rearing and assigned him a share of land for his maintenance, but if he were unfit or lame, they ordered the infant exposed and destroyed.

The Spartans bathed their infants in wine rather than water, to test and toughen their bodies. Children were subject to strict discipline from the start, and were taught not to be afraid in the dark, not to be finicky about their food, and not to be peevish and tearful.

Lycurgus [a great Spartan leader] did not permit children to be taught by slaves, but he had them enrolled at the age of seven in companies or classes where they received uniform discipline and instruction. The major emphasis in their education was on perfect obedience. The old men witnessed the children's lessons and exercises and drills, and often started quarrels among the students to test which ones would be brave and which would be cowards when they later faced real dangers. The young studied only enough of reading and writing to be able to perform their civic duties. They were taught mainly to endure pain and to persevere in battle.

The children's heads were close-clipped; they usually went barefoot and frequently naked; and after they were twelve years old, they were no longer allowed to wear any underclothes. They bathed infrequently, and their bodies were tough, hard, and dry. They slept together in little bands and made their beds themselves from rushes they collected from the banks of the river . . . These they broke off with their hands, without using a knife. Scarcely was there a time or place when someone was not present to remind them of their duty and to punish them if they neglected it. In addition to all this, one of the best men in the city was appointed as governor over the boys. He arranged them in companies and set over each company a temperate and bold twenty-year-old captain.

This young man was their captain when they fought and their master at home, with the authority to use them as he saw fit. He would often assign them to steal, which they had to do cunningly and boldly, using their wits to deceive and acquire. If they were caught, they were punished by being whipped and deprived of food. They were so impressed by the seriousness of not being caught that one youth, having stolen a fox and hidden it under his coat, allowed it to tear out his very bowels with its claws and teeth and died rather than betray his theft.

After supper the captain would make the boys perform—singing, demonstrating, or answering questions and solving problems. He would ask, "Who is the best man in the city? Why? What do you think of a certain law?" Thus they were trained to judge men and issues.

READING REVIEW

1. How did the Spartans view children?
2. What was the major emphasis of Spartan education?
3. How did Spartan education compare to Athenian education?

19 A PLEA FOR EUNOMY

Before Solon became an archon of Athens, he was a poet of some distinction. In most of his poems, Solon discussed the problems that faced Athens and the ways in which these problems might be overcome. The poem below calls upon the people of Athens to embrace eunomy in order to end the greed and corruption that had gripped the city. Eunomy *and its opposite,* dysnomy, *are difficult words to define. Most people define* eunomy *as meaning equal laws or a well-ordered constitution. As you read the poem, ask yourself how Solon attempted to establish eunomy after becoming archon.*

Eunomy

Our city never shall be destroyed, by Zeus' decree
And by the will of the blessed immortal gods:
For, as a high-spirited guardian, Pallas Athena
Of the mighty father holds her hands over it.
But the citizens themselves are fain to ruin the great city
in their madness,
Lured by the insane pursuit of wealth,
Unjust is the mind of the people's leaders, who are bound
To suffer many troubles through their great hybris.
For they do not know how to restrain insolence
Nor decently to enjoy the present feast. . . .
Rich they are, giving in to deeds of injustice. . . .
With no respect for sacred goods or public
They steal and grasp everywhere
Nor leave they untouched the holy foundation of Right,
Who in silence witnesses their present actions and past
And in time shall come, for sure, to take revenge.
Inexorable this festering sore already spreads to the whole city,
And quickly she has fallen into wretched servitude,
Which wakes up civil strife and dormant war,
That destroys the lovely youth of many.
For, through the factions in which the unjust thrive,
Our beloved city is soon consumed by haters.
These are the evils loose upon the people:
Of the poor, many, sold, in shameful chains,
Take the road leading to a foreign land. . . .

Thus the public evil reaches each man at home;
Barred gates do not hold it;
It leaps over high fences, it never misses,
Even if one flees to the house's innermost corner.
This is what my heart bids me to teach the Athenians:
That dysnomy brings many evils to the city,

But eunomy makes all things orderly and fitting,
And often puts fetters [shackles] on the unjust ones;
She smooths the uneven, quiets insolence, destroys hybris, . . .
It rights crooked judgments, softens arrogance,
Quiets the zeal of opposing factions,
Stills the bile of vexing discord. Under its rule
All is even-fitting and full of wisdom everywhere.

READING REVIEW

1. According to Solon what will be the outcome of the corruption and greed that has gripped Athens?
2. According to Solon what impact would eunomy have on conditions in Athens?
3. How did Solon try to establish eunomy in Athens after he became archon?

---

20 THE GREATNESS OF ATHENS

Athens stood out among the Greek city-states because of its highly developed democratic system of government. In 431 B.C. Pericles outlined why Athens was so special in a funeral oration for Athenians killed in a war with Sparta. This oration was recorded by the historian Thucydides in his massive study of the struggle for supremacy among the Greek city-states, The Peloponnesian War. *As you read the excerpt, note Pericles' ideals of the Athenian way of life.*

Our constitution does not copy the laws of neighbouring states; we are rather a pattern to others than imitators ourselves. Its administration favours the many instead of the few; this is why it is called a democracy. If we look to the laws, they afford equal justice to all in their private differences; if to social standing, advancement in public life falls to reputation for capacity, class considerations not being allowed to interfere with merit; nor again does poverty bar the way, if a man is able to serve the state, he is not hindered by the obscurity of his condition. The freedom which we enjoy in our government extends also to our ordinary life. There, far from exercising a jealous surveillance over each other, we do not feel called upon to be angry with our neighbor for doing what he likes, or even to indulge in those injurious looks which cannot fail to be offensive, although they inflict no positive penalty. But all this ease in our private relations does not make us lawless as citizens. Against this fear is our chief safeguard, teaching us to obey the magistrates and the laws, particularly such as regard the protection of the injured, whether they are actually on the statute book, or belong to that code which, although unwritten, yet cannot be broken without acknowledged disgrace.

Further, we provide plenty of means for the mind to refresh itself from business. We celebrate games and sacrifices all the year round, and the elegance of our private establishments forms a daily source of pleasure and helps to banish the spleen; while the magnitude of our city draws the produce of the world into our harbour, so that to the Athenian the fruits of other countries are as familiar a luxury as those of his own.

If we turn to our military policy, there also we differ from our antagonists. We throw open our city to the world, and never by alien acts exclude foreigners from any opportunity of learning or observing, although the eyes of an enemy may occasionally profit by our liberality; trusting less in system and policy than to the native spirit of our citizens; while in education, where our rivals from their very cradles by a painful discipline seek after manliness, at Athens we live exactly as we please, and yet are just as ready to encounter every legitimate danger. . . . And yet if with habits not of labour but of ease, and courage not of art but of

The Erechtheum on the Acropolis in Athens

nature, we are still willing to encounter danger, we have the double advantage of escaping the experience of hardships in anticipation and of facing them in the hour of need as fearlessly as those who are never free of them.

Nor are these the only points in which our city is worthy of admiration. We cultivate refinement without extravagance and knowledge without effeminacy; wealth we employ more for use than for show, and place the real disgrace of poverty not in owning to the fact but in declining the struggle against it. Our public men have, besides politics, their private affairs to attend to, and our ordinary citizens, though occupied with the pursuits of industry, are still fair judges of public matters; for, unlike any other nation, regarding him who takes no part in these duties not as unambitious but as useless, we Athenians are able to judge at all events if we cannot originate, and instead of looking on discussion as a stumbling-block in the way of action, we think it an indispensable preliminary to any wise action at all. Again, in our enterprises we present the singular spectacle of daring and deliberation, each carried to the highest point, and both united in the same persons; although usually decision is the fruit of ignorance, hesitation of reflexion. But the palm of courage will surely be adjudged most justly to those, who best know the difference between hardship and pleasure and yet are never tempted to shrink from danger. In generosity we are equally singular, acquiring our friends by conferring not by receiving favours. . . . And it is only the Athenians who, fearless of consequences, confer their benefits not from calculations of expediency, but in the confidence of liberality.

In short, I say that as a city we are the school of Hellas; while I doubt if the world can produce a man, who where he has only himself to depend on, is equal to so many emergencies, and graced by so happy a versatility as the Athenian. And that this is no mere boast thrown out for the occasion, but plain matter of fact, the power of the state acquired by these habits proves. For Athens alone of her contemporaries is found when tested to be greater than her reputation, and alone gives no occasion to her assailants to blush at the antagonist by whom they have been worsted, or to her subjects to question her title by merit to rule. Rather, the admiration of the present and succeeding ages will be ours, since we have not left our power without witness, but have shown it by mighty proofs. . . . We have forced every sea and land to be the highway of our daring, and everywhere, whether for evil or for good, have left imperishable monuments behind us.

READING REVIEW

1. According to Pericles, why was the Athenian form of government called a democracy?
2. Why did Pericles say that the Athenian system of education provided Athenians with a "double advantage"?
3. Describe the major ideals of the Athenian way of life.

21 THE DEATH OF SOCRATES

In 399 B.C. the Athenian courts found Socrates guilty of "neglect of the gods" and "corruption of the young." He was sentenced to die by drinking poison. In the excerpt below from Phaedo, *Plato describes the last hours of Socrates' life. Although Plato was not present at his teacher's death, he was in close contact with those who were. As you read the excerpt, consider how Socrates' death resembles a Greek tragedy.*

Socrates got up and went into another room to bathe; and Crito went after him, but told us to wait. So we waited, discussing . . . the greatness of the calamity which had befallen us; for we felt just as though we were losing a father and should be orphans for the rest of our lives. Meanwhile, when Socrates had taken his bath, his children were brought to see him—he had two little sons and one big boy—and the women of his household . . . arrived. He talked to them in Crito's presence and gave them directions about carrying out his wishes; then he told the women and children to go away, and came back himself to join us.

It was now nearly sunset, because he had spent a long time inside. He came and sat down, fresh from the bath; and he had only been talking for a few minutes when the prison officer came in, and walked up to him. "Socrates," he said, "at any rate I shall not have to find fault with you, as I do with others, for getting angry with me and cursing when I tell them to drink the poison—carrying out Government orders. I have come to know during this time that you are the noblest and the gentlest and the bravest of all the men that have ever come here, and now especially I am sure that you are not angry with me, but with them; because you know who are responsible. So now—you know what I have come to say—goodbye, and try to bear what must be as easily as you can." As he spoke he burst into tears, and turning around, went away.

Socrates looked up at him and said, "Goodbye to you, too; we will do as you say." Then addressing us he went on "What a charming person! All the time I have been here he has visited me, and sometimes had discussions with me, and shown me the greatness kindness; and how generous of him now to shed tears for me at parting! But come, Crito, let us do as he says. Someone had better bring the poison. . . ."

"But surely, Socrates," said Crito, "the sun is still upon the mountains; it has not gone down yet. Besides, I know that in other cases people have dinner and enjoy their wine, and sometimes the company of those whom they love, long after they receive the warning; and only drink the poison quite late at night. No need to hurry; there is still plenty of time."

"It is natural that these people whom you speak of should act in that way, Crito," said Socrates, "because they think that they gain by it. And it is also natural that I should not; because I believe that I should gain nothing by drinking the poison a little later—I should only make myself ridiculous in my own eyes if I clung to life and hugged it when it has no more to offer. Come, do as I say and don't make difficulties."

At this Crito made a sign to his servant, who was standing near by. The servant went out and . . . returned with the man who was to administer the poison; he was carrying it ready prepared in a cup. When Socrates saw him he said, "Well, my good fellow, you understand these things; what ought I to do?"

"Just drink it," he said, "and then walk about until you feel a weight in your legs, and then lie down. Then it will act of its own accord."

As he spoke he handed the cup to Socrates, who received it quite cheerfully . . . without a tremor, without any change of colour or expression, and . . . quite calmly and with no sign of distaste, he drained the cup in one breath.

Up till this time most of us had been fairly successful in keeping back our tears; but when we saw that he was drinking, that he had actually drunk it, we could do so no longer; in spite of myself the tears came pouring out, so that I covered my face and wept broken-heartedly—not for him, but for my own calamity in losing such a friend. Crito had given up even before me, and had gone out when he could not restrain his

Socrates preparing to drink the poisonous hemlock

tears. But Apollodorus, who had never stopped crying even before, now broke into such a storm of passionate weeping that he made everyone in the room break down, except Socrates himself, who said:

"Really, my friends, what a way to behave! Why, that was my main reason for sending away the women, to prevent this sort of disturbance; because I am told that one should make one's end in a tranquil frame of mind. Calm yourselves and try to be brave."

This made us feel ashamed, and we controlled our tears. Socrates walked about, and presently, saying that his legs were heavy, lay down on his back. . . .

Such . . . was the end of our comrade, who was, may we fairly say, of all those whom we knew in our time, the bravest and also the wisest and most upright man.

READING REVIEW

1. Why did Plato and his friends consider the death of Socrates a great personal calamity?
2. Why did Socrates choose not to delay drinking the poison?
3. How was Socrates' death similar to a Greek tragedy?

---

22 ARISTOTLE'S VIEWS ON EDUCATION

Aristotle outlined the principles of government in a massive work titled The Politics. *In one section of the study, Aristotle discussed the relationship between good government and education. In the excerpt below, Aristotle offers his views on the kind of education government should provide for young people. As you read the excerpt, note how Aristotle's concerns are still debated issues today.*

It is clear then that there should be laws laid down about education, and that education itself must be made a public concern. But we must not forget the question of what that education is to be, and how one ought to be educated. For in modern times there are opposing views about the tasks to be set, for there are no generally accepted assumptions about what the young should learn, either for virtue or for the best life; nor yet is it clear whether their education ought to be with more concern for the intellect than for the character of the soul. . . . And it is by no means certain whether training should be directed at things useful in life, or at those conducive to virtue, or at exceptional accomplishments. (All these answers have been judged correct by somebody.) And there is no agreement as to what in fact does tend towards virtue. For a start, men do not all prize the same virtue, so naturally they differ also about the proper training for it. . . .

Roughly four things are generally taught to children, (a) reading and writing, (b) physical training, (c) music, and (d), not always included, drawing. Reading and writing and drawing are included as useful in daily life in a variety of ways, gymnastic as promoting courage. But about music there could be an immediate doubt. Most men nowadays take part in music for the sake of the pleasure it gives; but originally it was included in education on the ground that our own nature itself, as has often been said, wants to be able not merely to work properly but also to be at leisure in the right way. And leisure is the single fundamental principle of the whole business. . . .

If we need both work and leisure, but the latter is preferable to the former and is its end, we must ask ourselves what are the proper activities of leisure. Obviously not play; for that would inevitably be to make play our end in life, which is impossible. Play has its uses, but they belong rather to the sphere of work; for he who toils needs rest, and play is a way of resting. . . . We must therefore admit play, but keeping it to its proper uses and occasions, and prescribing it as a cure; such movement of the soul is a relaxation, and, because we enjoy it, rest. But leisure seems in itself to contain pleasure, happiness and the blessed life. This is a state attained not by those at work but by those at leisure, because he that is working is working for some hitherto unattained end, and happiness is an end, happiness which is universally regarded as concomitant not with pain but with pleasure. Admittedly men do not agree as to what that pleasure is; each man decides for himself following his own disposition. . . . Thus it becomes clear that, in order to spend leisure in civilized pursuits, we do require a certain amount of learning and education, and that these branches of education and these subjects studied must have their own intrinsic purpose, as distinct from those necessary occupational subjects which are studied for reasons beyond themselves.

Hence, in the past, men laid down music as part of education, not as being necessary, . . . nor yet as being useful in the way that a knowledge of reading and writing is useful for business or household administration, for study, and for many of the activities of a citizen, nor as a knowledge of drawing seems useful for the better judging of the products of a skilled worker, nor again as gymnastic is useful for health and vigour—neither of which do we see gained as a result of music. There remains one purpose—for civilized pursuits during leisure; and that is clearly the reason why they do introduce it, for they give it a place in what they regard as the civilized pursuits of free men. . . .

Clearly then there is a form of education which we must provide for our sons, not as being useful or essential but elevated and worthy of free men. . . .

It is also clear that there are some useful things, too, in which the young must be educated, not only because they are useful (for example they must learn reading and writing), but also because they are often the means to learning yet further subjects. Similarly they must learn drawing, not for the sake of avoiding mistakes in private purchases, and so that they may not be taken in when buying and selling furniture, but rather because it teaches one to be observant of physical beauty.

READING REVIEW

1. What four subjects were generally taught to children in the Greek city-states?
2. According to Aristotle why did the Greeks' ancestors make music a part of education?
3. What points about education raised by Aristotle are still debated by educators today?

---

23 THE MEDICAL APHORISMS OF HIPPOCRATES

Hippocrates, who lived from about 460 B.C. to 377 B.C., is considered the founder of medical science. Through scientific observation and experimentation, Hippocrates proved that illness was the result of natural causes and not, as had been believed, of punishment from the gods. Hippocrates wrote many of his observations and findings in aphorisms—short, concise statements. As you read the excerpt below from The Medical Works of Hippocrates, *consider which aphorisms might still be found in modern medical texts.*

Life is short, science is long; opportunity is elusive, experiment is dangerous, judgment is difficult. It is not enough for the physician to do what is necessary, but the patient and the attendants must do their part as well, and circumstances must be favorable.

. . . Do not allow the body to attain extreme thinness for that too is treacherous, but bring it only to a condition which will naturally continue unchanged, whatever that may be. . . .

Desperate cases need the most desperate remedies.

Old people bear fasting most easily, then adults, much less youths and least of all children. The more active they are, the less do they bear it.

Fluid diets are beneficial to all who suffer from fevers, but this is specially true in the case of children and [toothless people] who are accustomed to such kind of food.

In deciding whether food should be given once or twice a day, more often or less, in greater or in smaller quantities at a time, one must consider habit, age, place and season.

A disease in which sleep causes trouble is fatal. Where sleep is beneficial, it is not fatal.

Both sleep and wakefulness are bad if they exceed their due proportion.

Neither a surfeit of food nor of fasting is good, nor anything else which exceeds the measure of nature.

Unprovoked fatigue means disease.

It is unwise to prophesy death or recovery in acute diseases.

It is a bad thing if a patient does not put on weight when he is being fed up after an illness.

In every illness, a healthy frame of mind and an eager application to [food] is good. The reverse is bad.

Rest, as soon as there is pain, is a great restorative in all disturbances of the body.

The changes of the seasons are especially liable to beget diseases, as are great changes from heat to cold, or cold to heat in any season. Other changes in the weather have similar severe effects.

Some natures are naturally well-suited to summer and some to winter; others are ill-suited to one or the other.

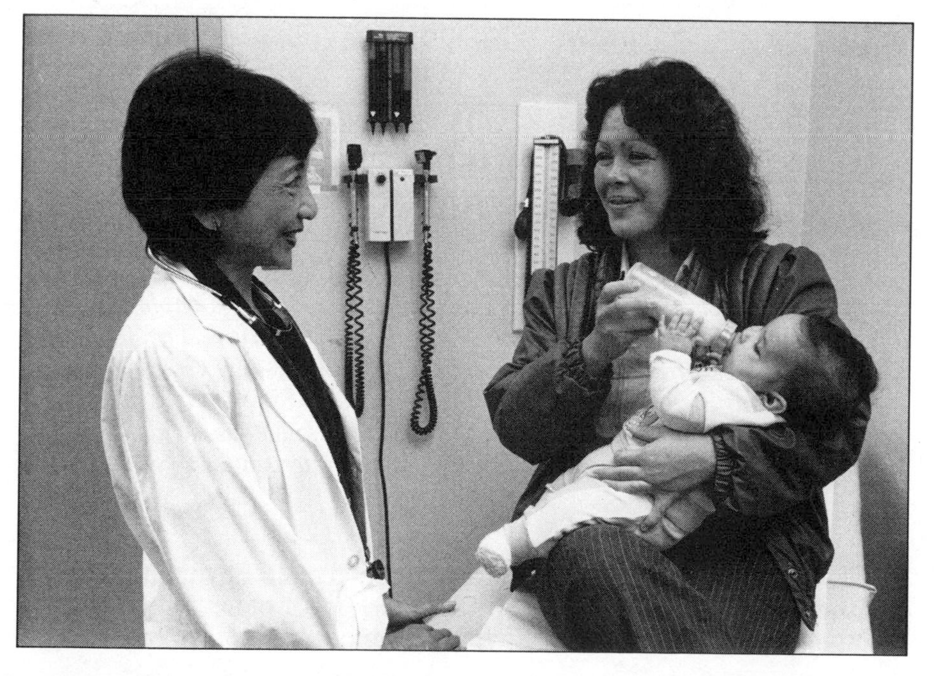

A pediatrician giving a young mother advice

Every disease occurs at all seasons of the year but some of them more frequently occur and are of greater severity at certain times.

In summer . . . we must . . . expect continued fevers, . . . vomiting, diarrhoea, ophthalmia, earache, . . . ulcers, . . . and heat spots.

During the winter season, pleurisy, pneumonia, lethargy, catarrh of the nose, hoarseness, cough, pain in the chest, pains in the side and loins, headaches, vertigo and apoplexy all occur.

. . . Care must also be exercised in giving drugs to infants and children.

The vomiting of blood of any kind is bad; its passage as excrement is not a good sign.

What drugs will not cure, the knife will; what the knife will not cure, the cautery will; what the cautery will not cure must be considered incurable.

READING REVIEW

1. According to Hippocrates, what kind of diet is good for someone suffering from a fever?
2. What does Hippocrates suggest are the best remedies to restore good health?
3. Which of the aphorisms in the excerpt might still be of use to physicians today?

---

24 ALEXANDER'S DEIFICATION AT THE TEMPLE OF ZEUS-AMMON

In 332 B.C. Alexander the Great confirmed his belief that he was the son of a god, when he consulted the oracle at the Temple of Zeus-Ammon deep in the Libyan Desert of North Africa. The following description of Alexander's journey to the temple—by Greek historian Diodorus Siculus in Volume 8 of Didorus of Sicily*—was written in the first century B.C. As you read the excerpt, note the incidents on the journey that the writer attributes to divine intervention.*

Alexander himself with all his army marched on to Egypt and secured the adhesion of all its cities without striking a blow.

Having settled the affairs of Egypt, Alexander went off to the Temple of [Zeus-]Ammon, where he wished to consult the oracle of the god. When he had advanced half way along the coast, he was met by envoys from the people of Cyrene, who brought him a crown and magnificent gifts, among which were three hundred chargers and five handsome four-horse chariots. He received the envoys cordially and made a treaty of friendship and alliance with them; then he continued with his travelling companions on to the temple. When he came to the desert and waterless part, he took on water and began to cross a country covered with an infinite expanse of sand. In four days their water had given out and they suffered from fearful thirst. All fell into despair, when suddenly a great storm of rain burst from the heavens, ending their shortage of water in a way which had not been foreseen, and which, therefore, seemed to those so unexpectedly rescued to have been due to the action of divine Providence. They refilled their containers . . . and again with a four days' supply in hand marched for four days and came out of the desert. At one point, when their road could not be traced because of the sand dunes, the guide pointed out to the king that crows cawing on their right were calling their attention to the route which led to the temple. Alexander took this for an omen, and thinking that the god was pleased by his visit pushed on with speed. . . . After a journey of one day, he approached the sanctuary. . . .

When Alexander was conducted by the priests into the temple and had regarded the god for a while, the one who held the position of prophet, an elderly man, came to him and said, "Rejoice, son; take this form of address as from god also." He replied, "I accept, father; for the future I shall be called thy son. But tell me if thou givest me the rule of the whole earth." The priest now entered the sacred enclosure and as the bearers now lifted the god and were moved according to certain prescribed sounds of the voice, the prophet cried that of a certainty the god had granted him his request, and Alexander spoke again: "The last, O spirit, of my questions now answer; have I punished all those who were the murderers of my father or have some escaped me?" The prophet shouted: "Silence! There is no mortal who can plot against the one [Zeus-Ammon] who begot him. All the murderers of Philip, however, have been punished. The proof of his divine birth will reside in the greatness of his deeds; as formerly he has been undefeated, so now he will be unconquerable for all time." Alexander was delighted with these responses. He honoured the god with rich gifts and returned to Egypt.

READING REVIEW

1. How long did it take for Alexander the Great and his companions to cross the desert?
2. According to the prophet, what was the proof of Alexander the Great's divine birth?
3. What two incidents in the desert did Alexander the Great and his companions interpret as good omens?

25 ROME'S PERFECT LOCATION

One reason Rome flourished was its sheltered location some 15 miles from the Mediterranean coast. In addition, it lay at one of the major crossing points on the Tiber River. In the excerpt below from On the Commonwealth, *Marcus Tullius Cicero, the first-century* B.C. *orator and philosopher, explains the importance of the city's geographic location. As you read the excerpt, note the advantages of Rome's location mentioned by Cicero.*

The location [Romulus] chose for the city . . . was unbelievably favorable. For he did not move his city down the coast, a step very easy for him to take with the forces at his command, either by invading the territory of the Rutuli or of the Aborigines, or by himself founding a city at the mouth of the Tiber. . . . But with singular foresight Romulus saw and divined that a location upon the seaboard was not the most advantageous for cities intended to enjoy permanence and imperial sway, chiefly because maritime cities are exposed to dangers both numerous and impossible to foresee. A city surrounded on all sides by land receives many warnings of an enemy's approach . . . such as the crashing [of the forest] and even the noise [of marching troops]. No enemy, in fact, can arrive by land without enabling us to know both his hostile intent and who he is and whence he comes. On the contrary, an enemy who comes by ships over the sea may arrive before anyone can suspect his coming; and indeed, when he appears, he does not show by any signs who he is, whence he comes, or even what he wants. . . .

In addition, cities located on the sea are subject to certain corrupting influences and to moral decline, for they are affected by alien forms of speech and by alien standards of conduct. Not only foreign merchandise is imported but also foreign codes of morals, with the result that nothing in the ancestral customs of a maritime people can remain unchanged. The inhabitants of the seaboard do not remain at home but are tempted far from their cities by the hope and dream of swiftly gained wealth; and even when they remain at home in body, they are exiles and wanderers in spirit. . . .

How, then, could Romulus with a more divine insight have made use of the advantages of a situation on the sea, while avoiding its disadvantages, than by placing his city on the banks of a river that flows throughout the year with an even current and empties into the sea through a wide mouth? Thus, the city could receive by sea the products it needed and also dispose of its superfluous commodities. By the river the city could bring up from the sea the necessaries of a civilized life as well as bring them down from the interior. Accordingly, it seems to me that even then Romulus foresaw that this city would sometime be the seat and home of supreme dominion. For practically no city situated in any other part of Italy could have been better able to command such economic advantages.

Is there, moreover, anyone so unobservant as not to have marked and clearly appraised the natural defenses of our city? Romulus and the other kings planned the extent and location of the city's wall with such wisdom that it followed everywhere the brink of the high steep hills; that the only access . . . was blocked by a great rampart and girt with a deep ditch; and that the citadel, thus fortified, rose from an ascent steep on every side and above a precipitous cliff. As a result, even at the terrible time when the Gauls attacked us, the citadel remained safe and uncaptured. In addition, the location which he chose is plentifully watered with streams; and although in an unhealthful region, the site is healthful because of hills, which are themselves cooled by the breezes and which also give shade to the valleys.

READING REVIEW

1. According to Cicero what led Romulus to choose this particular location for the city of Rome?
2. What three advantages of Rome's location does Cicero mention?
3. Why do you think geography is such an important factor in the development of cities?

The Roman Forum

26 CAESAR'S FUNERAL

One of the most powerful speeches in drama is Mark Antony's funeral oration from William Shakespeare's Julius Caesar. *In the excerpt below from* The Twelve Caesars, *Roman historian Suetonius—who lived from about* A.D. *69 to* A.D. *122—discusses the actual circumstances of Caesar's death and describes his funeral. As you read the excerpt, note how Suetonius' description differs from the way Caesar's funeral is presented in Shakespeare's play.*

When the funeral arrangements had been announced, [Caesar's] friends raised a pyre . . . near his daughter Julia's tomb, and a gilded shrine . . . resembling that of Mother Venus. In it they set an ivory couch, spread with purple and gold cloth, and from a pillar at its head hung the gown in which he had been murdered. Since a procession of mourners laying funeral gifts would have taken more than a day to file past the pyre, everyone was invited to come there by whatever route he pleased, regardless of precedence. . . . Mark Antony dispensed with a formal eulogy; instead, he instructed a herald to read, first, the recent decree simultaneously voting Caesar all divine and human honours, and then the oath by which the entire Senate had pledged themselves to watch over his safety. Antony added a very few words of comment. When the ivory funeral couch had been carried down into the Forum by a group of magistrates . . . , and a dispute arose as to whether the body should be cremated in the Temple of Capitoline Jupiter or in Pompey's Assembly Hall, two divine forms suddenly appeared, two javelins in their hands and sword at thigh, and set fire to the couch with torches. Immediately the spectators assisted the blaze by heaping on it dry branches and the judges' chairs, and the court benches, with whatever else came to hand. Thereupon the musicians and professional mourners, who had walked in the funeral train wearing the robes that [Caesar] had himself worn at his four triumphs, tore these in pieces and flung them on the flames—to which veterans who had assisted at his triumphs added the arms they had then borne. Many women in the audience similarly sacrificed their jewellery together with their children's breast-plaques and robes. Public grief was enhanced by crowds of foreigners lamenting in their own fashion, especially Jews, who came flocking to the Forum for several nights in succession.

As soon as the funeral was over, the populace, snatching firebrands from the pyre, ran to burn down the houses of Brutus and Cassius, and were repelled with difficulty. Mistaking Helvius Cinna for the Cornelius Cinna who had delivered a bitter speech against Caesar on the previous day, and whom they were out to kill, they murdered him and paraded the streets with his head stuck on the point of a spear. Later they raised a substantial, almost twenty-foot-high column of . . . marble in the Forum, and inscribed on it: "To the Father of His Country." For a long time afterwards they used to offer sacrifices at the foot of this column, make vows there and settle disputes by oaths taken in Caesar's name.

Some of [Caesar's] friends suspected that, having no desire to live much longer because of his failing health, he had taken no precautions against the conspiracy, and neglected the warnings of soothsayers and well-wishers. It has also been suggested that he placed such confidence in the Senate's last decree and in their oath of loyalty, that he dispensed even with the armed Spaniards who had hitherto acted as his permanent escort. A contrary view is that as a relief from taking constant precautions, he deliberately exposed himself, just this once, to all the plots against his life which he knew had been formed. Also, he is quoted as having often said: "It is more important for Rome than for myself that I should survive. I have long been sated with power and glory; but, should anything happen to me, Rome will enjoy no peace. A new Civil War will break out under far worse conditions than the last."

Almost all authorities agree on one thing, that he more or less welcomed the manner of his death. He had once read in Xenophon's *Boyhood of Cyrus* the paragraph about the funeral instructions given by Cyrus on his deathbed, and said how much he loathed the prospect of a lingering end—he wanted a sudden one. And on the day before his murder he had dined at Marcus Lepidus's house, where the topic discussed happened to be "the best sort of death"—and "Let it come swiftly and unexpectedly," cried Caesar.

He was fifty-five years old when he died, and his immediate deification, formally decreed, was more than a mere official decree since it reflected public conviction; if only because, on the first day of the Games given by his successor Augustus in honour of this apotheosis, a comet appeared about an hour before sunset and shone for seven days running. This was held to be Caesar's soul, elevated to Heaven. . . .

The Senate voted that the Assembly Hall where he fell should be walled up; that the Ides of March should be known ever afterwards as "The Day of Parricide"; and that a meeting of the Senate should never take place on it again.

Very few, indeed, of the assassins outlived Caesar for more than three years. . . . All were condemned, and all perished in different ways—some in shipwreck, some in battle, some using the very daggers with which they had murdered Caesar to take their own lives.

READING REVIEW

1. How does Suetonius' description of Caesar's funeral differ from William Shakespeare's description in the play, *Julius Caesar*?
2. What was the feeling of the crowd toward Caesar's assassins? Support your answer with an example from the excerpt.
3. What three explanations does Suetonius give as to why Caesar was so unprotected on the Ides of March?

27 CHRISTIANS IN THE ROMAN EMPIRE

Between the A.D. 100s and A.D. 200s, successive Roman emperors persecuted Christians and attempted to completely wipe out Christianity from the empire. At the end of the A.D. 300s, when Christianity became widely accepted throughout the Roman Empire, Christian emperors showed a similar lack of tolerance for pagan worship. In the two excerpts below, the first by Eusebius, discusses Emperor Diocletian's (reigned: 284–305) persecution of Christians in Palestine, while the second is from the law code of Emperor Theodosius I (reigned: 379–395). As you read the excerpts, ask yourself why the Roman emperors and Christians felt it necessary to persecute "unbelievers."

Persecution in Palestine

It was in the nineteenth year of the reign of Diocletian, in the month . . . called April by the Romans, about the time of the feast of our Saviour's passion, while Flavianus was governor of the province of Palestine, that letters were published everywhere, commanding that the churches be leveled to the ground and the Scriptures be destroyed by fire, and ordering that those who held places of honor be degraded, and that imperial freedmen, if they persisted in the profession of Christianity, be deprived of freedom.

Such was the force of the first edict against us. But not long after, other letters were issued, commanding that all the bishops of the churches everywhere be first thrown into prison, and afterward, by every artifice, be compelled to sacrifice [to the gods]. . . .

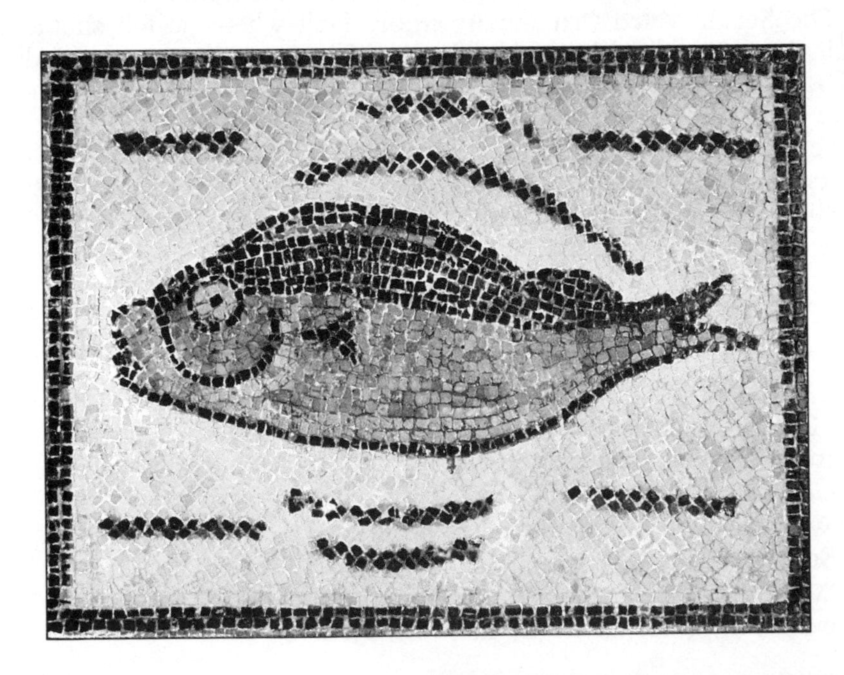

The fish, a traditional Christian symbol representing the Lord

In the course of the second year, the persecution against us increased greatly. And at that time, Urbanus being governor of the province, imperial edicts were issued to him, commanding by a general decree that all the people should sacrifice at once in the different cities, and offer libations to the idols.

Theodosius Against Heretics

It is our desire that all the various nations which are subject to our Clemency and Moderation, should continue in the profession of that religion which was delivered to the Romans by the divine Apostle Peter, as it hath been preserved by faithful tradition. . . . We authorize the followers of this [religion] to assume the title of Catholic Christians; but as for the others, since, in our judgement, they are foolish madmen, we decree that they shall be branded with the ignominious name of heretics. . . . They will suffer in the first place the chastisement of the divine condemnation, and in the second the punishment which our authority, in accordance with the will of Heaven, shall decide to inflict. . . .

Let them be entirely excluded even from the thresholds of churches, since we permit no heretics to hold their unlawful assemblies in the towns. If they attempt any disturbance, we decree that their fury shall be suppressed and that they shall be expelled outside the walls of the cities. . . .

READING REVIEW

1. What were the terms of Diocletian's first edict?
2. How did Theodosius characterize those who did not follow the Christian faith?
3. Why do you think both the Roman emperors and later Christians persecuted those who would not accept their respective religions?

---

28 A DESCRIPTION OF THE BARBARIANS

One group of barbarians, the Germans, had long been known to the Romans. The Germans, who lived beyond the Rhine and north of the Danube rivers, had been entering the empire peacefully since the time of Augustus. The description of the Germans in the excerpt below from Germania *was written by the Roman historian Tacitus in A.D. 98. As you read the excerpt, ask yourself what Tacitus' impression of these barbarians was.*

All [Germans] have fierce blue eyes, red hair, huge frames, fit only for a sudden exertion. They are less able to bear laborious work. Heat and thirst they cannot in the least endure; to cold and hunger their climate and their soil inure [accustom] them. . . .

... Few use swords or long lances. They carry a spear ... with a narrow and short head, but so sharp and easy to wield that the same weapon serves, according to circumstances, for close or distant conflict. As for the horse-soldier, he is satisfied with a shield and spear; the foot-soldiers also scatter showers of missiles, each man having several and hurling them to an immense distance. ... On the whole, one would say that their chief strength is in their infantry, which fights along with the cavalry; admirably adapted to the action of the latter is the swiftness of certain foot-soldiers, who are picked from the entire youth of their country, and stationed in front of the line. ... Their line of battle is drawn up in a wedge-like formation. To give ground, provided you return to the attack, is considered prudence rather than cowardice. The bodies of their slain they carry off even in indecisive engagements. To abandon your shield is the basest of crimes; nor may a man thus disgraced be present at the sacred rites, or enter their council; many, indeed, after escaping from battle, have ended their infamy [by suicide].

... They also carry with them into battle certain figures and images taken from their sacred groves. And what most stimulates their courage is, that their squadrons or battalions, instead of being formed by chance ... are composed of families and clans. Close by them, too, are those dearest to them, so that they hear the shrieks of women, the cries of infants. *They* are to every man the most sacred witnesses of his bravery—*they* are his most generous applauders. The soldier brings his wounds to mother and wife, who shrink not from counting or even demanding them and who administer both food and encouragement to the combatants. ...

They transact no public or private business without being armed. It is not, however, usual for anyone to wear arms till the state has recognized his power to use them. Then in the presence of the council one of the chiefs, or the young man's father, or some kinsman, equips him with a shield and a spear. These arms are ... the first honour with which the youth is invested. Up to this time he is regarded as a member of a household, afterwards as a member of the commonwealth. Very noble birth or great services rendered by the father secure for lads the rank of a chief; such lads attach themselves to men of mature strength and of long approved valour. It is no shame to be seen among a chief's followers. ...

When they go into battle, it is a disgrace for the chief to be surpassed in valour, a disgrace for his followers not to equal the valour of the chief. And it is an infamy and a reproach for life to have survived the chief, and returned from the field. To defend, to protect him, to ascribe one's own brave deeds to his renown, is the height of loyalty. The chief fights for victory; his vassals fight for the chief. If their native state sinks into ... prolonged peace and repose, many of its noble youths voluntarily seek those tribes which are waging some war ... because they win renown more readily in the midst of peril. ...

Whenever they are not fighting, they pass much of their time in the chase, and still more in idleness, giving themselves up to sleep and to feasting, the bravest and most warlike doing nothing, and surrendering the management of the household, of the home, and of the land, to the women, the old men, and all the weakest members of the family. . . .

No nation indulges more profusely in entertainments and hospitality. To exclude any human being from their roof is thought impious; every German, according to his means, receives his guest with a well-furnished table. When his supplies are exhausted, he who was but now the host becomes the guide and companion to further hospitality, and without invitation they go to the next house. It matters not; they are entertained with like cordiality. No one distinguishes between an acquaintance and a stranger, as regards the rights of hospitality. It is usual to give the departing guest whatever he may ask for, and a present in return is asked with as little hesitation. They are greatly charmed with gifts, but they expect no return for what they give, nor feel any obligation for what they receive.

READING REVIEW

1. According to Tacitus what was the chief strength of the German fighting force?
2. In your opinion what was the quality most valued by the Germans?
3. How do you think Tacitus felt about the Germans? Give examples to support your answer.

The World In Transition

29 JUSTINIAN'S CODE

The greatest contribution of the Byzantine emperor Justinian to civilization was in the field of law. Early in his reign, Justinian established a commission of legal scholars to organize and clarify all Roman law. After six years of work, the commission produced what is known as the Corpus Juris Civilis *("Body of Civil Law"), or Justinian's Code. In the excerpt below, the nature of the law is discussed. As you read, note the similarities between Justinian's Code and United States law.*

Justice is the constant and perpetual desire to give to each one that to which he is entitled.

Jurisprudence is the knowledge of matters divine and human, and the comprehension of what is just and what is unjust. . . .

The following are the precepts of the Law: to live honestly, not to injure another, and to give to each one that which belongs to him.

There are two branches of this study, namely, public and private. Public Law is that which concerns the administration of the Roman government; Private Law relates to the interests of individuals. Thus Private Law is said to be threefold in its nature, for it is composed of precepts of Natural Law, of those of the Law of Nations, and of those of the Civil Law.

Natural Law is that which nature has taught to all animals, for this law is not peculiar to the human race, but applies to all creatures which originate in the air, or the earth, and in the sea. Hence arises the union of the male and the female which we designate marriage; and hence are derived the procreation and the education of children; for we see that other animals also act as though endowed with knowledge of this law.

The Civil Law and the Law of Nations are divided as follows. All peoples that are governed by laws and customs make use of the law which is partly peculiar to themselves and partly pertaining to all men; for what each people has established for itself is peculiar to that State, and is styled the Civil Law; being, as it were, the especial law of that individual commonwealth. But the law which natural reason has established among all mankind and which is equally observed among all peoples, is called the Law of Nations, as being that which all nations make use of. The Roman people also employ a law which is in part peculiar to them, and in part common to all men. . . . Our Law, which

We make use of, is either written or unwritten, just as among the Greeks written and unwritten laws exist. The written law consists of the Statutes, the *Plebiscita,* the Decrees of the Senate, the Decisions of the Emperors, the Orders of the Magistrates and the Answers of Jurisconsults.

A Statute is what the Roman people have established as the result of [a formal proposal] of a senatorial magistrate, for example, a consul. The *Plebiscitum* is what the plebeians have established upon [a formal proposal] of a plebeian magistrate, for instance, a tribune. . . .

A Decree of the Senate is what the Senate orders and establishes, for since the Roman people have increased in numbers to such an extent that it is difficult for them to be convoked in an assembly for the purpose of adopting a law, it has seemed advisable for the Senate to be consulted instead of the people.

Whatever is approved by the sovereign has also the force of law, because by the *Lex Regia,* from when his power is derived, the people have delegated to him all their jurisdiction and authority. Therefore, whatever the Emperor establishes by means of . . . decrees, . . . [or] by an Edict, stands as law, and these are called Constitutions. . . .

The Answers of Jurisconsults are the decisions and opinions of persons upon whom has been conferred authority to establish laws; for it was decided in ancient times that the laws should be publicly interpreted by those to whom the right to answer had been granted by the Emperor,

The bustling great bazaar in Constantinople

and who were called jurisconsults, and the unanimous decisions and opinions of the latter had such force that . . . a judge was not permitted to deviate from what they had determined.

The unwritten law is that which usage has confirmed, for customs long observed and sanctioned by the consent of those who employ them, resemble law.

READING REVIEW

1. According to the Code, what are the precepts of the Law?
2. Why did the need for Decrees of the Senate develop?
3. How are Justinian's Code and United States law similar?

---

30 JUSTINIAN PUTS DOWN A REBELLION

In 532 a number of Byzantine senators, angered by the behavior of a corrupt tax officer, led a rebellion against Emperor Justinian. In an orgy of violence, the rebels killed any government officials they came upon and set fire to half of Constantinople. Afraid for their lives, Justinian and his advisers prepared to flee the city. But Justinian's wife, Theodora, shamed them into staying and fighting. The excerpt below from History of the Wars *by Procopius gives a brief account of the rebellion and its outcome. As you read the excerpt, note the arguments that Theodora used to persuade Justinian to stay.*

At this time an insurrection broke out unexpectedly in Byzantium among the populace, and, contrary to expectation, it proved to be a very serious affair, and ended in great harm to the people . . . , as the following account will show. In every city the population has been divided for a long time past into the Blue and the Green factions; but within comparatively recent times it has come about that, for the sake of these names . . . [the members of the factions] fight against their opponents knowing not for what end they imperil themselves. . . . So there grows up in them against their fellow men a hostility which has no cause, and at no time does it cease or disappear, for it gives place neither to the ties of marriage nor of relationship nor of friendship, and the case is the same even though those who differ with respect to these colours be brothers or any other kin. . . .

But at this time the officers of the city administration in Byzantium were leading away to death some of the rioters. But the members of the two factions, conspiring together and declaring a truce with each other, seized the prisoners and then straightway entered the prison and released all those who were in confinement there. . . . All the attendants in the service of the city government were killed . . . and fire was applied to the city as if it had fallen under the hand of an enemy. . . . During this time the emperor and [Theodora] with a few members of the senate shut themselves up in the palace and remained quietly there. Now the watchword which the populace passed around to one another was Nika ["conquer"], and the insurrection has been called by this name up to the present time. . . .

Now on the fifth day of the insurrection in the late afternoon the Emperor Justinian gave orders to Hypatius and Pompeius, nephews of the late emperor, Anastasius, to go home as quickly as possible . . . because he suspected that some plot was being matured by them against his own person. . . . But they feared that the people would force them to the throne (as in fact fell out), and they said that they would be doing wrong if they should abandon their sovereign when he found himself in such danger. When the Emperor Justinian heard this, he inclined still more to his suspicion, and he bade them quit the palace instantly. . . .

But on the following day at sunrise it became known to the people that both men had quit the palace. . . . So the whole population ran to them, and they declared Hypatius emperor and prepared to lead him to the market place to assume the power. . . . [So] he by no will of his own came to the Forum of Constantine, where they summoned him to the throne . . . and proclaimed him Emperor of the Romans. . . .

Now the emperor and his court were deliberating as to whether it would be better for them if they remained or if they took to flight in the ships. And many opinions were expressed favouring either course. And the Empress Theodora also spoke to the following effect: ". . . My opinion then is that the present time, above all others, is inopportune for flight, even though it bring safety. . . . For one who has been an emperor it is unendurable to be a fugitive. May I never be separated from this purple. . . . If, now, it is your wish to save yourself, O Emperor, there is no difficulty. For we have much money, and there is the sea, here the boats. However consider whether it will not come about after you have been saved that you would gladly exchange that safety for death. For as for myself, I approve a certain ancient saying that royalty is a good burial-shroud." When the queen had spoken thus, all were filled with boldness, and, turning their thoughts towards resistance, they began to consider how they might be able to defend themselves if any hostile force should come against them. Now the soldiers as a body . . . were neither well disposed to the emperor nor willing openly to take an active part in the fighting, but were waiting for what the future would bring forth. All the hopes of the emperor [therefore] centred upon [generals] Belisarius and Mundus, of whom the former, Belisarius, had recently returned from the Persian war bringing with him a following which was both powerful and imposing, and in particular he had a great number of spearmen and guards who had received their training in battles and the perils of warfare. . . .

When Hypatius reached the hippodrome, he went up immediately to where the emperor is accustomed to take his place and seated himself on the royal throne . . . And from the palace Mundus went out through the gate which, from the circling descent, has been given the name of the Snail. . . . Belisarius, with difficulty and not without danger and great exertion, made his way over ground covered by ruins and half-burned buildings, and ascended to the stadium. . . . Concluding . . . that he must go against the populace who had taken their stand in the hippodrome—a vast multitude crowding each other in great disorder—he drew his sword from its sheath and, commanding the others to do likewise, with a shout he advanced upon them at a run. But the populace, who were standing in a mass and not in order, at the sight of the armoured soldiers who had a great reputation for bravery and experience in war, and seeing that they struck out with their swords unsparingly, beat a hasty retreat. Then a great outcry arose, as was natural, and Mundus, who was standing not far away, was eager to join in the fight. . . . He straightway made a sally into the hippodrome through the entrance which they call the Gate of Death. Then indeed from both sides the partisans of Hypatius were assailed with might and main and destroyed. . . .There perished among the populace on that day more than thirty thousand. . . . And the soldiers killed both [Hypatius and Pompeius] on the following day and threw their bodies into the sea. . . . This was the end of the insurrection in Byzantium.

READING REVIEW

1. What were the Blues and the Greens?
2. Why did Justinian expel Hypatius and Pompeius from the palace?
3. How did Theodora persuade Justinian to stay in Constantinople?

---

31 THE *PRAVDA RUSSKAIA*

Kievan Rus reached the height of its power under the brillant reign of Yaroslav the Wise, who ruled from 1019 to 1054. Among the prince's greatest contributions was the establishment of a legal code—the Pravda Russkaia, *or "The Russian Justice." This code was a combination of Slavic tribal customs and Roman law. As you read the excerpt below, ask yourself how the* Pravda Russkaia *compares to other medieval legal codes.*

The Pravda Russkaia

1. If a man kills a man [the following relatives of the murdered man may avenge him]: the brother is to avenge his brother; the son, his father; or the father, his son; and the son of the brother [of the murdered man] or the son of his sister, [their respective uncle]. If there

is no avenger, [the murderer pays] 40 *grivna* [compensation]. Be [the murdered man] a [Kievan] Russian—a palace guard, a merchant, an agent, or a sheriff— . . . or a [Novgorodian] Slav, his [compensation] is 40 *grivna*.

2. If [a man injures a man, and the injured man] is smeared with blood or is blue from bruises, he needs no eyewitness [to prove the offense]; if there is no mark [of injury] upon him, let him produce an eyewitness; if he cannot, the matter ends there. If he is not able to avenge, he receives 3 *grivna* for the offense. . . .

3. If anyone hits another with a club, or a rod, or a fist, or a bowl, or a [drinking] horn . . . and [the offender] evades being hit, he has to pay 12 *grivna* and that ends the matter.

4. If [anyone] strikes [another] with a sword without unsheathing it, or with the hilt of a sword, 12 *grivna* for the offense.

5. If [anyone] cuts [another's] arm, and the arm is cut off or shrinks, 40 *grivna*.

6. If [anyone cuts another's leg and] the leg is cut off, or the [injured man] becomes lame, then the latter's sons have to chastise [the offender].

Kiev today

7. If a finger is cut off, 3 *grivna* for the offense.

8. And for the mustache, 12 *grivna;* and for the beard, 12 *grivna.*

9. He who unsheathes his sword, but does not strike, pays one *grivna.*

10. If a man pulls a man toward himself or pushes him, 3 *grivna,* but [the offended man] has to bring two eyewitnesses. . . .

11. If a slave runs away . . . and [the man who conceals that slave] does not declare him for three days, and [the owner] discovers him on the third day, he [the owner] receives his slave back and 3 *grivna* for the offense.

12. If anyone rides another's horse without asking the owner's permission, he has to pay 3 *grivna.*

13. If anyone takes another's horse, or weapon, or clothes, and [the owner] identifies [the object] within his township, he receives it back and 3 *grivna* for the offense.

14. If the owner identifies [his property outside of his town] he must not seize it outright; do not tell [the man who holds the property]: "This is mine," but tell him thus: "Come for confrontment to the place where you got it"; and if he does not come immediately he must produce two bails [to guarantee that he will come] within five days.

15. If a man [engaged in business] claims his share in the balance from his partner, and the latter balks, he has to go for an investigation by [a jury of] 12 men; if [it is established] that he [the partner] maliciously refused to refund [the first man's share], the man must receive his money and 3 *grivna* for the offense.

16. If anyone, having recognized his [runaway] slave [in another's possession] wants to take him, [the man who holds that slave] has to lead [the owner] to the party from whom he bought that slave, and that party has to lead [the owner] to the one [from whom he bought the slave], and [so they go eventually] even to the third party. Then tell the third party: "Give me the slave, and sue [the fourth party] for your money with [the help of] an eyewitness."

17. And if a slave strikes a freeman and hides in [his master's] house, and his master is not willing to give him up, the master has to pay 12 *grivna,* and the offended freeman beats the slave whenever he finds him.

18. And if anyone breaks [another's] spear, or shield, or [cuts his] clothes and wants to keep them, he must pay for them. And if he wants to return the damaged things he has to pay for the damage.

READING REVIEW

1. What in the excerpt suggests that Russian men placed a value on their beards?
2. What is interesting about the punishments established for murder?
3. What similarities are there between the *Pravda Russkaia* and other medieval legal codes?

32 IVAN THE TERRIBLE'S PUNISHMENT OF NOVGOROD

The ferocious acts of cruelty perpetrated by Ivan IV earned him the nickname "Ivan the Terrible." The excerpt below from Medieval Russia: A Source Book, 900–1700, *edited by Basil Dmytryshyn, describes Ivan's devastation of Novgorod and the massacre of tens of thousands of its inhabitants. The selection graphically shows that Ivan's nickname was appropriate. These barbarous actions were sparked by Ivan's unfounded suspicion that city leaders had shifted their allegiance to Poland. As you read the excerpt, try to think of reasons why Ivan behaved in such a manner.*

On Monday the 2d of January, in the year [1570], . . . the illustrious Tsar and Grand Prince Ivan Vasilevich, lord of All Russia, sent an advance guard of the army in forced march toward Great Novgorod. . . .

When these troops had arrived before Great Novgorod, . . . they established a great camp in the environs of the city, surrounded by strong posts with fortifications of every kind. They erected sentinel towers near the posts and decreed that the inhabitants of the city be closely watched in order that not one human being could escape from the city.

And other princes and nobles of the Tsar from the same advance guard rode in all directions in the area around Great Novgorod and sealed all the monasteries and money boxes of the Church. They captured the abbots, the . . . clergy, the deacons, and the elders from the monasteries, and took them, perhaps 500 or more persons, to Great Novgorod. They were brought to the place of execution where they were to wait until the arrival of the Tsar.

And other nobles of the Tsar . . . seized the priests and deacons of all the churches in Novgorod and also brought them to the execution site. Every ten prisoners were assigned a police officer. And these officers received orders to keep the prisoners in iron chains and to beat them mercilessly from morning to evening . . . until ransom was obtained. . . .

By order of the monarch, other nobles . . . arrested all the administrative officials and all the important merchants of Great Novgorod and placed them under guard. They were chained, their houses were sealed up with all their wealth, and their wives and children were ordered closely watched until the arrival of the sovereign.

On January 6th of the same year, 1570, . . . the illustrious Tsar and Grand Prince Ivan Vasilevich, lord of All Russia, arrived in Great Novgorod. He was accompanied by his son, the rightful heir to the throne, Prince Ivan Ivanovich, and an uncountable host. . . .

On . . . the day after his arrival, the illustrious Tsar and Grand Prince Ivan Vasilevich, lord of All Russia, gave the order that the abbots, clergy, and monks who had previously been brought to the place of execution should be beaten to death with clubs. . . .

"Tsar and Grand Prince Ivan Vasilevich, lord of All Russia, gave the order that the abbots, clergy, and monks who had previously been brought to the place of execution should be beaten to death with clubs."

The patriarch of the Russian Orthodox church warning Ivan the Terrible about the consequences of his sins

The Tsar ordered his steward . . . together with several *boyars*, to go into the Church of St. Sophia and to confiscate the treasures in the vestry as well as costly, sacred vessels, the holy miraculous ikons . . . , and paintings by Greek artists. In addition, the Tsar decreed that all holy church treasures, the holy, divine, costly, and wondrous ikons, and the chasubles used in celebrating mass, and the bells in all of Great Novgorod's churches be confiscated. . . .

Thereupon, the . . . Tsar . . . and his son . . . held court in the suburbs . . . where he had encamped upon his arrival. The Tsar commanded that the powerful *boyars*, the important merchants, the administrative officials, and the citizens of every rank be brought before him, together with their wives and children. The Tsar ordered that they be tortured in his presence in various spiteful, horrible, and inhuman ways. . . . He ordered that each man be tied to a sled, be dragged to the Volkhov bridge . . . , and be thrown into the Volkhov River from the bridge. The Tsar ordered that their wives and children be brought to the Volkhov bridge where a high platform had been erected. He commanded that they be chained on the arms and legs and that the children be tied to their mothers and then be thrown from the platform into the waters of the Volkhov River. . . . In [this] horrible manner they were submerged without mercy in the depths of the river, and abandoned to a terrible and bitter death.

Because of our sins, this unspeakable shedding of Christian blood, caused by the excessive anger of the Tsar, continued uninterrupted each day for five weeks or more. And every day perhaps a thousand human beings of all ages were thrown into the water and drowned; . . . and if perchance only five or six hundred people were thrown into the water, the day in question was considered an easy day, one deserving of thanks.

READING REVIEW

1. Why did Ivan's troops build sentinel towers around their camp?
2. What in the excerpt suggests that Ivan used the destruction of Novgorod as a way to swell the coffers of his treasury?
3. Why, in your opinion, did Ivan behave in this way?

---

33 THE MUSLIM CONQUEST OF SPAIN

In A.D. 711 Arab and Berber Muslims streamed across the narrow straits between North Africa and Spain in search of lands to conquer. By 719 they had driven as far north as the Pyrenees. Their conquests were made easier by the assistance of many Spaniards, who hated their Visigoth rulers. The excerpt below from the History of the Conquest of Spain *by Ibn-el-Hakem, was written in the mid-800s. The excerpt describes the first Muslim invasion of Spain led by the Berber general, Tariq. As you read the excerpt, ask yourself to what the author attributed Tariq's success.*

Musa Ibn Nosseyr [the Governor of North Africa] . . . appointed Tarik Ibn Zeiyad governor [of Tangier]. . . . Tarik remained some time in this district, waging a holy war. . . . The governor of the straits between this district and Andalus [Spain] was a foreigner called Ilyan, Lord of Septa. . . . Tarik put himself in communication with Ilyan, and treated him kindly, until they made peace with each other. Ilyan had sent one of his daughters to Roderic, the Lord of Andalus, for her improvement and education; but she became pregnant by him. Ilyan having heard of this, said, I see for him no other punishment or recompense, than that I should bring the Arabs against him. He sent to Oarik, saying, I will bring thee to Andalus. . . . Tarik went to Ilyan who was in Septa on the straits. The latter rejoicing at his coming, said, I will bring thee to Andalus. But there was a mountain called the mountain of Tarik [Gibraltar] between the two landing places, that is, between Septa and Andalus.

The Courtyard of Lions at the Moorish Alhambra Palace in Grenada, Spain

When the evening came, Ilyan brought him the vessels, in which he made him embark for that landing-place, where he concealed himself during the day, and in the evening sent back the vessels to bring over the rest of his companions. So they embarked for the landing-place, none of them being left behind: whereas the people of Andalus did not observe them, thinking the vessels crossing and recrossing were similar to the trading vessels which for their benefit plied backwards and forwards. . . . The news of Tarik and of those who were with him, as well as of the place where they were, [finally] reached the people of Andalus. Tarik, going along with his companions, marched over a bridge of mountains to a town called Cartagena. He [then] went in the direction of Cordova. . . .

As Abd-Errahman has related to us . . . : There was a house in Andalus, the door of which was secured with padlocks, and on which every new king of the country placed a padlock of his own, until the accession to power of the king against whom the Moslems marched. They therefore begged [Roderic] to place a padlock on it, as kings before him were wont to do. But he refused saying, I will place nothing on it, until I shall have known what is inside; he then ordered it to be opened; but behold inside were portraits of the Arabs, and a letter in which it was written: "When this door shall be opened, these people will invade this country."

When Tarik landed, soldiers from Cordova came to meet him; and seeing the small number of his companions they despised him on that account. They then fought. The battle with Tarik was severe. They were routed, and he did not cease from slaughter of them till they reached the town of Cordova. When Roderic heard of this, he came to their rescue from Toledo. . . . They fought a severe battle; but God, mighty and great, killed Roderic and his companions. . . . Tarik [passed] over to Toledo. He, then, entered it and asked for the table, having nothing else to occupy himself. This, as the men of the Bible relate, was the table of Suleyman Ibn Dawid [Solomon]. . . .

. . . Tarik was told that the table was in a citadel . . . two days' journey from Toledo, and the governor of this citadel was a nephew of Roderic. Tarik, then, wrote to him, promising safety both for himself and family. The nephew descended from the citadel, and Tarik fulfilled his promise with reference to his safety. Tarik said to him, deliver the table, and he delivered it to him. On this table were gold and silver, the like of which one had not seen. . . . The table was valued at two hundred thousand dinars, on account of the pearls that were on it. He took up the pearls, the armour, the gold, the silver, and the vases which he had with him, and found that quantity of spoils, the like of which one had not seen. He collected all that. Afterwards he returned to Cordova, and having stopped there, he wrote to Musa Ibn Nosseyr informing him of the conquest of Andalus, and of the spoils which he had found.

READING REVIEW

1. Why did the people of Andalus not take any notice of Tariq's invasion ships?
2. Why did the Visigoth soldiers from Cordova look upon Tariq's invasion force with disdain?
3. To what did the author attribute Tariq's success in conquering Spain?

---

34 MUSLIM TOWNS AND TRADE IN NORTH AFRICA

As their empire grew, the Muslims built fortified garrison towns in North Africa from which they controlled and administered their new conquests. In time these garrison towns became important centers of government, learning, commerce, and trade. The excerpt below provides a description of the Muslim towns of Kairouan and Sijilmasa, located in what is today Tunisia. As you read the excerpt, note the chief exports of the Maghrib region.

Kairouan, the largest town of the Maghrib, surpasses all others in its commerce, its riches, and the beauty of its buildings and bazars. It is the seat of government of the whole Maghrib, the center to which flows the wealth of the land, and the residence of the sultan of that country. I heard from Abu al-Hasan head of the [public] treasury in [A.D. 947–48], that the income of all provinces and localities of the Maghrib . . . was between seven hundred and eight hundred million dinars. . . .

The exports from the Maghrib to the East are fair mulatto girls, . . . young and handsome European slaves, amber, silks, suits of very fine woolen, fineries, woolen skirts, carpets, iron, lead, mercury, eunuchs from the countries of the Negroes and of the Slavs. People there possess excellent draft horses and camels innured to fatigue, which they procure from the Berbers. . . .

Kairouan and Sijilmasa are similar in salubrity of climate and in their nearness to the desert. Rich caravans constantly leave Sijilmasa for the Sudan and bring great profits to the inhabitants of that town. . . . The inhabitants of other towns in [the Maghrib] perhaps resemble those of Sijilmasa in their characteristics and the conditions of their existence, but they are inferior to the latter in wealth and comforts.

Devout Muslims at prayer

READING REVIEW

1. In what three things did Kairouan surpass all the other towns?
2. What were the similarities between Kairouan and Sijilmasa?
3. How would you characterize the major trade items of the Maghrib?

35 SOCIAL CLASSES IN MUSLIM INDIA

Indian Muslims believed that the ideal social order was the result of harmony among the four social classes, just as the physical world was the result of a balance among the four elements—earth, wind, fire, and water. The excerpt below from Sources of Indian Tradition, *compiled by William Theodore de Bary, provides a description of each of these four classes. As you read the excerpt, note the similarities between Muslim social order and the Hindu caste system.*

In order to preserve [the] political equipoise [balance], there is a correspondence to be maintained between the various classes. Like as the equipoise of bodily temperament is effected by intermixture and correspondence of four elements, the equipoise of the political temperament is to be sought for in the correspondence of four classes.

1. *Men of the pen,* such as lawyers, divines, judges, bookmen, statisticians, geometricians, astronomers, physicians, poets. In these and their exertions in the use of their delightful pens, the subsistence of the faith and of the world itself is vested and bound up. They occupy the place in politics that water does among the elements. Indeed, to persons of ready understanding, the similarity of knowledge and water is as clear as water itself, and as evident as the sun that makes it so.

2. *Men of the sword,* such as soldiers, fighting zealots, guards of forts and passes, etc.; without whose exercise of the impetuous and vindictive sword, no arrangement of the age's interests could be effected; without the havoc of whose tempest-like energies, the materials of corruption, in the shape of rebellious and disaffected persons, could never be dissolved and dissipated. These then occupy the place of fire, their resemblance to it is too plain to require demonstration; no rational person need call in the aid of fire to discover it.

3. *Men of business,* such as merchants, capitalists, artisans, and craftsmen, by whom the means of emolument [compensation] and all other interests are adjusted; and through whom the remotest extremes enjoy the advantage and safeguard of each other's most peculiar commodities. The resemblance of these to air—the auxiliary of growth and increase in vegetables—the reviver of spirit in animal life—the medium by the undulation and movement of which all sorts of rare and precious things traverse the hearing to arrive at the headquarters of human nature—is exceedingly manifest.

4. *Husbandmen,* such as seedsmen, bailiffs, and agriculturists—the superintendents of vegetation and preparers of provender; without whose exertions the continuance of the human kind must be cut short. These are, in fact, the only producers of what had no previous existence; the other classes adding nothing whatever to subsisting products, but only transferring what subsists already from person to person, from place to place, and from form to form. How close these come to the soil and surface of the earth—the point to which all the heavenly circles refer—the scope to which all the luminaries of the purer world direct their rays—the stage on which wonders are displayed—the limit to which mysteries are confined—must be universally apparent.

In like manner then as in the composite organizations the passing of any element beyond its proper measure occasions the loss of equipoise, and is followed by dissolution and ruin, in political coalition, no less, the prevalence of any one class over the other three overturns the adjustment and dissolves the junction.

READING REVIEW

1. What is the purpose of the men of the pen?
2. Which of the four classes produce things that had no previous existence?
3. From what you have read about India in your text, how are the Muslim social order and the Hindu caste system similar?

---

36 A DAY IN THE LIFE OF A MOGUL EMPEROR

Akbar, who ruled from 1556 to 1605, is considered the greatest of the Mogul emperors. An inquisitive, thoughtful, and learned man, he introduced religious tolerance to India and tried to develop a legal system in which all people, regardless of class or creed, were equal before the law. In the excerpt below from Akbar *by English writer Laurence Binyon, the author draws a picture of a typical day at Akbar's court. As you read the excerpt, ask yourself how Binyon felt about Akbar.*

Any day, then, our traveller might have seen Akbar holding a reception; for he holds audiences twice a day. The blaze of the Indian sun makes strong shadows from the verandah-pillars of the red sandstone palace, where Akbar receives one courtier or envoy after another. Peacocks sun themselves on the roof of the verandah; in the courtyard elephants are slowly led; a groom holds a cheetah in leash; an animated crowd of virile-looking men in dresses of fine silk and of various colours stand about. Akbar himself is dressed in a surcoat reaching to the knees (were he a stricter Muslim it would reach to the feet), and wears a closely-rolled turban hiding his hair; a rope of great pearls hangs from his neck. His manner has subtle changes. With the great he is great and does not unbend; to the humble he is kindly and sympathetic. It is noticeable how he makes more of the small presents of the poor (and he is very fond of presents) than of the costly gifts of the nobles, at which he will hardly glance. As a dispenser of justice he is famous; every one wronged (an observer has said) "believes the emperor is on his side."

Four times in twenty-four hours Akbar prays to God: at sunrise, at noon, at sunset, and midnight. But any one who tried to keep up with his daily activities would need to be of iron make. Three hours suffice for Akbar's sleep. He eats but one meal a day, and that at no fixed time. He eats but little meat, less and less as he grows older: "Why should we make ourselves a sepulchre for beasts?" is one of his sayings. Rice and sweetmeats are the chief of his diet, and fruit, of which he is extremely fond. His day is a long one, and he fills it full. Between state councils and conferences with ministers or generals he inspects his elephants—of which he has five thousand in his stables—his horses, and other animals. He knows them by name. He notes their condition; if any show signs of growing thin and poorly, the keeper responsible finds his salary docked. Presently he will repair to an upper terrace where are the dove-cotes, built of blue and white brick, and with infinite pleasure he watches the evolutions of the tumbler-pigeons, deploying and returning, massing or separating, to the sound of a whistle. . . . At another time he will be watching . . . gladiatorial combats, or fights between elephants, or between elephants and lions. But though entering with such zest on his amusements, his mind is occupied also with other things: for messengers arrive continually from every part of the empire and rapid decisions have to be taken. Another time he is inspecting his school of painters, passing quickly among them and appraising their work. Or he will go down to the workshop, and turn carpenter or stonemason. He is especially fond of the foundry, and loves to found a cannon with his own hands.

"Four times in twenty-four hours Akbar prays to God."

When at evening lights are lit in the great hall, the emperor takes his seat among his courtiers and has books read to him; or music is played, and Akbar himself joins in or he laughs at jests and stories. If there are foreigners present, he plies them with unceasing questions. He will sit far into the night absorbed in discussions on religion: this is one of his dear delights. He drinks wine, or wine mixed with opium, and sometimes falls into a stupor: but this does not affect his terrible energy. Yet this crowded, pulsing life does not wholly absorb him. Frequently he will disappear and sit apart in solitary meditation for hours at a time.

Such is Akbar's way of life at court.

READING REVIEW

1. What in the excerpt suggests that Akbar believed in equal justice for all?
2. How does the author illustrate Akbar's inquisitive nature?
3. Do you think that Binyon admired Akbar? Why or why not?

37 PEASANT LIFE DURING THE TIME OF CHARLEMAGNE

During the Middle Ages, the manor was the basis of economic life in Europe. Sometimes the land grant, or fief, of the manor was held by the church rather than by a noble. In the excerpt below from Medieval People *by Eileen Power, the fief of the Villaris manor was held by the Abbey of St. Germain, just outside Paris. Power, a modern historian, describes a typical day in the life of a peasant family who lived on the manor. As you read the excerpt, note the various obligations and rents the peasants owed to the lord of Villaris.*

The abbey [of St Germain] possessed a little estate called Villaris, near Paris, in the place now occupied by the park of Saint Cloud. When we turn up the pages in the estate book dealing with Villaris, we find that there was a man called Bodo living there. He had a wife called Ermentrude and three children called Wido and Gerbert and Hildegard; and he owned a little farm of arable and meadow land, with a few vines. . . . Let us try to imagine a day in his life. On a fine spring morning towards the end of Charlemagne's reign Bodo gets up early, because it is his day to go and work on the monks' farm, and he does not dare to be late, for fear of the steward. To be sure, he has probably given the steward a present of eggs and vegetables the week before, to keep him in good temper; but . . . Bodo knows that he will not be allowed to go late to work. It is his day to plough, so he takes his big ox with him and little Wido to run by its side with a goad, and he joins his friends from some of the farms near by, who are going to work at the big house too. They all assemble, some with horses and oxen, some with mattocks and hoes and spades and axes and scythes, and go off in gangs to work upon the fields and meadows and woods of the seigniorial manse, according as the steward orders them. . . . Bodo goes whistling off in the cold with his oxen and his little boy; and it is no use to follow him farther, because he ploughs all day long and eats his meal under a tree with the other ploughmen, and it is very monotonous.

Let us go back and see what Bodo's wife, Ermentrude, is doing. She is busy too; it is the day on which the chicken-rent is due—a fat pullet and five eggs in all. She leaves her second son, aged nine, to look after the baby Hildegard and calls on one of her neighbours, who has to go up to the big house too. The neighbour is a serf and she has to take the steward a piece of woollen cloth, which will be sent away to St Germain to make a habit for a monk. Her husband is working all day in the lord's vineyards, for on this estate the serfs generally tend the vines, while the freemen do most of the ploughing. Ermentrude and the serf's wife go together up to the house. There all is busy. In the men's workshop are several clever workmen—a shoemaker, a carpenter, a blacksmith, and two silversmiths; they are not more, because the best artisans on the estates of St Germain live by the walls of the abbey, so that they can work for the monks on the spot and save the labour of carriage. . . .

But Ermentrude does not stop at the men's workshop. She finds the steward, bobs her curtsy to him, and gives up her fowl and eggs, and then hurries off to the women's part of the house, to gossip with the serfs there. . . . Their quarter consisted of a little group of houses, with a workroom, the whole surrounded by a thick hedge with a strong bolted gate . . . so that no one could come in without leave. Their workrooms were comfortable places, warmed by stoves, and there Ermentrude (who, being a woman, was allowed to go in) found about a dozen servile women spinning and dyeing cloth and sewing garments. Every week the harassed steward brought them the raw materials for their work and took away what they made. . . . Ermentrude, however, has to hurry away after her gossip. . . . She goes back to her own farm and sets to work in the little vineyard; then after an hour or two goes back to get the children's meal and to spend the rest of the day in weaving warm woollen clothes for them. All her friends are either working in the fields on their husbands' farms or else looking after the poultry, or the vegetables, or sewing at home; for the women have to work just as hard as the men on a country farm. . . . Then at last Bodo comes back for his supper, and as soon as the sun goes down they go to bed; for their hand-made candle gives only a flicker of light, and they both have to be up early in the morning.

READING REVIEW

1. According to the excerpt, was Bodo a freeman or a serf? Explain your answer.
2. What were the obligations and rents owed by Bodo and his family?
3. Do you agree with the author that peasant life on a manor was monotonous? Explain your answer.

---

38 THE TABLE OF A THIRTEENTH-CENTURY ENGLISH LORD

During the Middle Ages, most nobles lived in fortified castles in which daily life usually centered on the meal table. In the excerpt below from Life in a Medieval Castle *by Joseph and Frances Gies, the authors describe the kinds of foods, the rituals, and the entertainment that could be found at the table of a typical lord in medieval England. As you read the excerpt, note how medieval table manners compared to table manners today.*

At mealtimes, servants set up the trestle tables and spread cloths, setting steel knives, silver spoons, dishes for salt, silver cups, and *mazers*—shallow, silver-rimmed wooden bowls. At each place was a trencher or *manchet*, a thick slice of day-old bread serving as a plate for the roast meat. Meals were announced by a horn blown to signal time for washing hands. Servants with ewers, basins, and towels attended the guests.

At the table, seating followed status: The most important guests were at the high table, with the loftiest place reserved for an ecclesiastical dignitary, the second for the ranking layman. After grace, the procession of servants bearing food began. First came the pantler with the bread and butter, followed by the butler and his assistants with the wine and beer. Wine, in thirteenth-century England mostly imported from English-ruled Bordeaux, was drunk young in the absence of an effective technique for stoppering containers. Wine kept a year became undrinkable. No attention was paid to vintage, and often what was served even at rich tables was of poor quality. Peter of Blois described in a letter wine served at Henry II's court: "The wine is turned sour or mouldy—thick, greasy, stale, flat and smacking of pitch . . . ."

The castle bought wine by the barrel and decanted it into jugs. Some was spiced and sweetened by the butlers to go with the final course. Ale, made from barley, wheat, or oats, or all three, was drunk mainly by the servants. A castle household brewed its own, hiring an ale-wife for the task and using grain from its own stores. At the royal court, according to Peter of Blois, the ale was not much better than the wine—it was "horrid to the taste and abominable to the sight."

Ceremony marked the service at table. There was a correct way to do everything, from the laying of cloths to the cutting of trenchers and carving of meat. Part of a squire's training was learning how to serve his lord at meals: the order in which dishes should be presented, where they should be placed, how many fingers to use in holding the joint for the lord to carve, how to cut the trenchers and place them on the table.

The solid parts of soups and stews were eaten with a spoon, the broth sipped. Meat was cut up with the knife and eaten with the fingers. Two persons shared a dish, the lesser helping the more important, the younger the older, the man the woman. The former in each case broke the bread, cut the meat, and passed the cup.

Etiquette books admonished diners not to leave the spoon in the dish or put elbows on the table, not to belch, not to drink or eat with their mouths full, not to stuff their mouths or take overly large helpings. Not surprisingly, in the light of finger-eating and dish-sharing, stress was laid on keeping hands and nails scrupulously clean, wiping spoon and knife after use, wiping the mouth before drinking, and not dipping meat in the salt dish.

The lord and lady were at pains to see their guests amply served. Bishop Robert Grosseteste advised the countess of Lincoln to make sure that her servants were judiciously distributed during dinner, that they entered the room in an orderly way and avoided quarreling. "Especially do you yourself keep watch over the service until the meats are placed in the hall, and then . . . command that your dish be so refilled and heaped up, and especially with the light dishes, that you may courteously give from your dish to all the high table on the right and the left." . . .

An everyday dinner, served between 10:00 A.M. and noon, comprised two or three courses, each of several separate dishes, all repeating the same kinds of food except the last course, which consisted of fruits, nuts, cheese, wafers, and spiced wine.

On such festive occasions as holidays and weddings, fantastic quantities of food were consumed. When Henry III's daughter married the king of Scotland on Christmas Day 1252 at York, Matthew Paris reported that "more than sixty pasture cattle formed the first and principal course at table . . . the gift of the archbishop. The guests feasted by turns with one king at one time, at another time with the other, who vied with one another in preparing costly meals." . . . Such feasts included

Knights in combat

boars' heads, venison, peacocks, swans, sucking pigs, cranes, plovers, and larks.

During dinner, even on ordinary days, the party might be entertained with music or jokes and stories. Many households regularly employed harpers and minstrels. . . . When the meal was over, one of the guests might regale the company with a song; many a knight and baron composed songs in the tradition of the trouveres, the knightly poets who were the troubadours of the North. . . . They might be accompanied by the harp, the lute, or the viele, ancestor of the violin. Sometimes the accompanist played chords as a prelude to the song and as background to an occasional phrase; sometimes the singer accompanied himself in unison on the viele. . . .

The meal finished, tables were cleared, the company washed hands again, and turned to the afternoon's tasks and amusements.

READING REVIEW

1. What determined seating at the lord's dinner table?
2. What determined the way guests were served at the lord's dinner table?
3. How do medieval table manners compare to modern table manners?

"The king William of whom we spoke was a very wise man, very powerful, and more worthy and stronger than any of his predecessors were."

39 A SAXON VIEW OF WILLIAM THE CONQUEROR

The entries in The Anglo-Saxon Chronicle, *a journal of English history that was kept for about 300 years, vary greatly. A whole decade might be covered in a sentence, while pages and pages might be given to a battle or the character of a king. One monarch the writers of the* Chronicle *had much to say about was William the Conqueror, as the excerpt below shows. As you read the excerpt, consider how the writers personally felt about William.*

[1086] . . . If any wishes to know what kind of man he was, or what honour he had, or of how many lands he was lord, then we will write of him just as we perceived him, who looked on him and at one time lived at his court. The king William of whom we spoke was a very wise man, very powerful, and more worthy and stronger than any of his predecessors were. He was mild with good men who loved God, and over all measure hard with men who spoke against his will. In the same place that God granted him that he obtain England he raised a great minster, set monks there and endowed it well. In his days the minster at Canterbury was built, and also many others all over England. Also this land was largely filled with monks, who lived their lives after the rule of St.

Benedict. And Christendom was such in his days that each man, whatever his state might happen to be, followed it if he wished. Also he was very dignified....

[1087] A hard man he was, and fierce; no man dared against his will. He had eorls in chains, who went against his will; bishops he deposed from their bishoprics and thanes he set in prison. Next, he did not spare his own brother, called Odo; he was a very powerful bishop in Normandy... and was the foremost man next to the king. He had an eorldom in England, and when the king was in Normandy he was the master of this land; and him he set in prison. Among other things it is not to be forgotten, that good peace he made in this land, so that a man of any account might fare over the kingdom with a bosom full of gold unmolested; and no man dared kill another man, even if he had done much evil to him....

He reigned over England, and so searched it through with his craft that there was not a hide of land in England that he knew not what he had from it and what its worth was, and after had it set down in his document. Wales was in his power; he built castles therein, and ruled all the people there. So also Scotland he subjected by his great strength. Normandy was his natural land, and over an eorldom called Maine he reigned. If he had lived two years yet he would have won Ireland with his cunning, and without any weapons. Truly, in his time men had much oppression and many injuries.

He had castles made and oppressed poor men;
the king was very hard
and took of his underlings many marks of gold,
and many more hundred pounds of silver,
that he took by weight, unjustly,
from his people for little need.
Into avarice was he fallen
and greediness he loved overall.
He set many deer free, and laid a law upon
  it, that whoever
slew hart or hind should be blinded.
As he forbade the killing of harts
he forbade the killing of boars,
and he loved the stags as if he were their father.
He decreed also that hares must go free.
The rich complained, the poor lamented;
but he was so hard he set their hate at naught,
but they must in all the king's will follow
if they would live or have land—
land, or goods, or have his good will.
Welaway! That any man should grow so proud,
to think himself lifted up over all men;
almighty God show his soul mildheartedness,
and forgive him for his sins.

These things we have written of king William, both good and evil, so that good men take after goodness and eschew all the evil, and go on that way that takes us to the heavenly kingdom.

READING REVIEW

1. According to the writers of the *Chronicle,* what positive actions did William take during his reign?
2. What is the "document" referred to in the second paragraph of the 1087 entry in the *Chronicle?*
3. How do you think the writers of the *Chronicle* felt about William? Explain your answer.

---

40 AN EXCHANGE BETWEEN POPE GREGORY VII AND EMPEROR HENRY IV

On becoming pope, Gregory VII attempted to restore the power of the papacy. His major opponent in this effort was the Holy Roman Emperor, Henry IV. In the first letter in the excerpt below, Gregory appeals to Henry to cease associating with five of his councilors who had been excommunicated for simony—the buying or selling of church offices—and to end the practice of lay investiture of bishops. The second letter contains Henry's harsh, unconciliatory reply. As you read note the arguments Gregory and Henry made to support their points of view.

Pope Gregory VII's Letter to Henry IV

December, 1075

Gregory, bishop, servant of the servants of God, to Henry, the king, greeting and apostolic benediction,—that is, if he be obedient to the apostolic see as is becoming in a Christian king:

It is with some hesitation that we have sent you our apostolic benediction, knowing that for all our acts as pope we must render an account to God, the severe judge. It is reported that you have willingly associated with men who have been excommunicated by decree of the Pope and sentence of a synod. If this be true, you are very well aware that you can receive the blessing neither of God nor of the Pope until you have driven them from you and have compelled them to do penance, and have also yourself sought absolution and forgiveness for your transgressions with due repentance and good works. Therefore we advise you that, if you realize your guilt in this matter, you immediately confess to some pious bishop, who shall absolve you with our permission, prescribing for you penance in proportion to the fault, and who shall faithfully report to us by letter, with your permission, the nature of the penance required.

We wonder, moreover, that you should continue to assure us by letter and messengers of your devotion and humility; that you should call yourself our son and the son of the holy mother Church, obedient in faith, sincere in love, diligent in devotion; and that you should commend yourself to us with all zeal of love and reverence—whereas in fact you are constantly disobeying the canonical and apostolic decrees in important matters of faith. . . . Since you confess yourself a son of the Church, you should treat with more honor the head of the Church, that is, St. Peter, the prince of apostles. If you are one of the sheep of the Lord, you have been entrusted to him by divine authority. . . . And since we, although an unworthy sinner, exercise his authority by divine will, the words which you address to us are in reality addressed directly to him. And although we read or hear only the words, he sees the heart from which the words proceed. Therefore your highness should be very careful that no insincerity be found in your words and messages to us; and that you show due reverence, not to us, indeed, but to omnipotent God, in those things which especially make for the advance of the Christian faith and the well-being of the Church. . . .

"Since you confess yourself a son of the Church, you should treat with more honor the head of the Church . . .

Now in the synod . . . to which the divine will has called us (at which some of your subjects also were present) we . . . decreed nothing new, nothing of our invention; but we decided that the . . . single primitive rule of ecclesiastical discipline and the familiar way of the saints should be again sought out and followed. . . . And we have decided that this decree—which some, placing human above divine honor, have called an unendurable weight and an immense burden, but which we call by its proper name, that is, the truth and light necessary to salvation—is to be received and observed not only by you and your subjects, but also by all princes and peoples of the earth who confess and worship Christ. . . .

Nevertheless, that this decree may not seem to you beyond measure grievous and unjust, we have commanded you . . . to send to us the wisest and most pious men . . . in your kingdom, so that if they show or instruct us in any way how we can temper the sentence promulgated by the holy fathers without offense to the eternal King or danger to our souls, we may consider their advice. But, even if we had not warned you in so friendly a manner, it would have been only right on your part, before you violated the apostolic decrees, to ask justice of us in a reasonable manner in any matter in which we had injured or affected your honor. But from what you have since done and decreed it is evident how little you care for our warnings, or for the observance of justice.

But since we hope that, while the long-suffering patience of God still invites you to repent, you may become wiser and your heart may be turned to obey the commands of God, we warn your with fatherly love that, knowing the rule of Christ to be over you, you should consider how dangerous it is to place your honor above His, and that you should not interfere with the liberty of the Church.

Henry IV's Reply to Pope Gregory's Letter

January, 1076

Henry, king not by usurpation, but by the holy ordination of God, to Hildebrand, not pope, but false monk.

This is the salutation which you deserve, for you have never held any office in the Church without making it a source of confusion and a curse to Christian men, instead of an honor and a blessing. To mention only the most obvious cases out of many, you have not only dared to lay hands on the Lord's anointed, the archbishops, bishops, and priests, but you have scorned them and abused them, as if they were ignorant servants not fit to know what their master was doing. . . . You have declared that the bishops know nothing and that you know everything; but if you have such great wisdom you have used it not to build but to destroy. . . . All this we have endured because of our respect for the papal office, but you have mistaken our humility for fear, and have dared to make an attack upon the royal and imperial authority which we received from God. You have even threatened to take it away, as if we had received it from you, and as if the Empire and the kingdom were in your disposal and not in the disposal of God. Our Lord Jesus Christ has called us to the government of the Empire, but He never called you to the rule of the Church. This is the way you have gained advancement in the Church: through craft you have obtained wealth; through wealth you have obtained favor; through favor, the power of the sword; and through the power of the sword, the papal seat, which is the seat of peace; and then from the seat of peace you have expelled peace. For you have incited subjects to rebel against their prelates by teaching them to despise the bishops, their rightful rulers. . . . You have attacked me, who, unworthy as I am, have yet been anointed of God, and who, according to the teaching of the fathers, can be judged by no one save God alone, and can be deposed for no crime except infidelity. . . . St. Paul, who said that even an angel from heaven should be accursed who taught any other than the true doctrine, did not make an exception in your favor, to permit you to teach false doctrines. . . . Come down, then, from that apostolic seat which you have obtained by violence; for you have been declared accursed by St. Paul for your false doctrines, and have been condemned by us and our bishops for your evil rule. Let another ascend the throne of St. Peter, one who will not use religion as a cloak of violence, but will teach the life-giving doctrine of that prince of the apostles. I, Henry, king by the grace of God, with all my bishops, say unto you: "Come down, come down, and be accursed through all the ages."

READING REVIEW

1. How does Gregory's letter indicate that he was open to discussion on Henry's position?
2. According to Henry, how did Gregory treat his bishops?
3. How does Gregory support the view that he had the right to exercise authority over Henry? What is Henry's reply?

41 SALADIN'S COURAGE AND STEADFASTNESS

The crusaders who fought in the Third Crusade found that the Muslim leader Saladin was not at all what they had been told to expect. He was honorable, trustworthy, courteous, generous, and courageous. In short, except for his religion, he was a perfect illustration of the chivalrous knight. In the excerpt below from Arab Historians of the Crusades, *Baha' ad-Din, one of Saladin's court officials, discusses his great courage. As you read the excerpt, consider the impact that Saladin's behavior had on the crusaders.*

The Prophet is reported to have said: "God loves courage, even in the killing of a serpent." Saladin was indeed one of the most courageous of men; brave, gallant, firm, intrepid in any circumstance. I remember when he was encamped facing a great Frankish army which was continuously growing with the addition of reinforcements and auxiliaries, and all the time his strength of will and tenacity of purpose increased. One evening more than seventy enemy ships arrived—I counted them myself—between the [early afternoon] prayer and sunset, and their only effect seemed to be to incense him the more. When winter came he had disbanded his army and faced the enemy with only a small detachment of troops. I asked Baliān ibn Barzān how many there were—he was one of the great Frankish kings of Palestine, and had an audience of the Sultan on the day when peace was signed—and he replied . . . : "The Prince of Sidon (another of their kings and commanders) and I came from Tyre to join our army. When we came within sight of them we laid a wager on the size of the army. He guessed 500,000, I guessed 600,000." "And how many of them are dead?" "Killed in battle, 100,000; died of sickness or drowned, God alone knows." And of all that multitude only a small minority returned home.

Every day for as long as we were in close contact with the enemy he made it an inflexible rule to make one or two circuits of the enemy camp; in the thick of battle he would move through the ranks, accompanied only by a page with a warhorse led on a bridle. He would traverse the whole army from the right wing to the left, creating a sense of unity and urging them to advance and to stand firm at the right time. He directed his troops from a commanding height and followed the enemy's movements from close at hand. He had certain sections of *hadīth* [sayings of the Prophet] read up and down the army's ranks. . . . A section of the *hadīth* was taken down to the troops, together with one who had made a regular study of them, and the reading was held while we were all in the saddle, sometimes advancing and sometimes at a halt between the ranks of the two armies.

I never saw him find the enemy too numerous or too powerful. He would ponder and deliberate, exposing each aspect of the situation and taking the necessary steps to deal with it, without becoming angry, for he was never irate. On the day of the great battle on the plain of Acre the centre of the Muslim ranks was broken, drums and flags fell to the ground, but he stood firm with a handful of men until he was able to withdraw all his men to the hill and then lead them down into battle again, shaming them into turning and fighting, so that although there were almost 7,000 infantry and cavalry killed that day God gave the Muslims victory over their enemies. He stood firm before overwhelming hordes of enemy soldiers until it became clear to him that the Muslims were exhausted, and then he agreed to a truce at the enemy's request. The Franks were also exhausted and had suffered even heavier losses than we, but they could expect reinforcements, as we could not, so that peace was in our interest. . . . When he was ill, which happened often, or throughout the most appalling crises he stayed firmly in camp; the camp-fires of each side could be seen clearly by the other; we heard the sound of their bells and they heard our call to prayer.

READING REVIEW

1. What effect did the arrival of more than 70 enemy ships have on Saladin?
2. How did Saladin rally his troops in the thick of battle?
3. If you had been a crusader, how would you have viewed Saladin? Explain your answer.

---

42 THE BLACK DEATH IN PARIS

In the late 1340s, an epidemic of bubonic plague, or the Black Death, broke out in Europe. In the next few years, the disease had a devastating effect on Europe, claiming the lives of at least one-third of the continent's population. In the excerpt below from Volume 2 of Western Awakening: Sources in Medieval History, *Jean de Venette, a Carmelite friar from Paris, discusses the arrival and impact of the plague in France. As you read the excerpt, note the causes of the disease that Jean de Venette mentions.*

In A.D. 1348, the people of France and of almost the whole world were struck by a blow . . . For in addition to the famine . . . and to the wars . . . pestilence and its attendant tribulations appeared again in various parts of the world. In the month of August, 1348, after Vespers when the sun was beginning to set, a big and very bright star appeared above Paris, toward the west. It did not seem, as stars usually do, to be very high above our hemisphere but rather very near. As the sun set and night came on, this star did not seem to me or to many friars who were watching it to move from one place. At length, when night had come, this big star, to the amazement of all of us who were watching, broke into many different rays and, as it shed these rays over Paris toward the east, totally disappeared and was completely annihilated. Whether it was a comet or not, . . . I leave to the decision of astronomers. It is, however, possible that it was a presage [omen] of the amazing pestilence to come, which, in fact, followed very shortly in Paris and throughout France and elsewhere. . . . All this year and next, the mortality of men and women, of the young even more than of the old, in Paris and in the kingdom of France, and also, it is said, in other parts of the world, was so great that it was almost impossible to bury the dead. People lay ill little more than two or three days and died suddenly, as it were in full health. He who was well one day was dead the next and being carried to his grave. Swellings appeared suddenly in the armpit or in the groin—in many cases both—and they were infallible signs of death. This sickness or pestilence was called an epidemic by the doctors. Nothing like the great numbers who died in the years 1348 and 1349 has been heard of or seen or read of in times past. This plague and disease came from . . . association and contagion, for if a well man visited the sick he only rarely evaded the risk of death. Wherefore in many towns timid priests withdrew, leaving the exercise of their ministry to such of the religious as were more daring. In many places not two out of twenty remained alive. So high was the mortality at the Hotel-Dieu in Paris that for a long time, more than five hundred dead were carried daily with great devotion in carts to the cemetery of the Holy Innocents in Paris for burial. A very great number of the saintly sisters of the Hotel-Dieu who, not fearing to die, nursed the sick in all sweetness and humility. . . .

The plague, it is said, began among the unbelievers, came to Italy, and then crossing the Alps reached Avignon, where it attacked several cardinals and took from them their whole household. Then it spread, unforeseen, to France, through Gascony and Spain, little by little, from town to town, from village to village, from house to house, and finally

Stained glass from Canterbury Cathedral, Canterbury, England, showing the funeral of a plague victim

from person to person. It even crossed over to Germany, though it was not so bad there as with us. . . .

Some said that this pestilence was caused by infection of the air and waters, since there was at this time no famine nor lack of food supplies, but on the contrary great abundance. As a result of this theory of infected water and air as the source of the plague the Jews were suddenly and violently charged with infecting wells and water and corrupting the air. The whole world rose up against them cruelly on this account. In Germany and other parts of the world where Jews lived, they were massacred and slaughtered by Christians, and many thousands were burned everywhere, indiscriminately. . . . It is said that many bad Christians were found who in a like manner put poison into wells. But in truth, such poisonings, granted that they actually were perpetrated, could not have caused so great a plague nor have infected so many people. There were other causes; for example, the will of God and the [body's] corrupt humors and evil inherent in air and earth. . . . The plague lasted in France for the greater part of the years 1348 and 1349 and then ceased. Many country villages and many houses in good towns remained empty and deserted. Many houses, including some splendid dwellings, very soon fell into ruins. . . .

READING REVIEW

1. What reason did Jean de Venette have for believing that the strange star was an omen?
2. What population was made a scapegoat for the bubonic plague?
3. The bubonic plague led to an upsurge in religious zeal. Why, in your opinion, was this so?

---

43 ROWDY PARIS STUDENTS

The University of Paris was one of the first major universities to develop in western Europe. Although theology was the major course of study at Paris, not all the students who attended the university were interested in religious devotion and learning. The excerpt below from University Records and Life in the Middle Ages *by Lynn Thorndike is from a proclamation issued by the religious court of Paris in 1268. The proclamation provides a vivid illustration of students not interested in religious studies. As you read the excerpt, note the kinds of punishment that religious courts were empowered to hand down.*

The official of the court of Paris to all the rectors of churches, masters and scholars residing in the city and suburb of Paris. . . . A frequent and continual complaint has gone the rounds that there are in Paris some

Students in traditional gowns

clerks and scholars, likewise their servants, trusting in the folly of the same clerks, unmindful of their salvation, not having God before their eyes, who, under pretense of leading the scholastic life, more and more often perpetrate unlawful and criminal acts, relying on their arms: namely, that by day and night they atrociously wound or kill many persons, rape women, oppress virgins, break into inns, also repeatedly committing robberies and many other enormities hateful to God. And since they attempt these and other crimes relying on their arms, we, having in mind the decree of the supreme pontiff in which it is warned that clerks bearing arms will be excommunicated, also having in mind that our predecessors excommunicated those who went about thus, and in view of the fact that this is so notorious and manifest that it cannot be concealed by any evasion and that their proclamation was not revoked, wishing to meet so great evils and to provide for the peace and tranquility of students and others who wish to live at peace, at the instance of many good men and by their advice do excommunicate in writing clerks and scholars and their servants who go about Paris by day or night armed, unless by permission of the reverend bishop of Paris or ourself. We also excommunicate in writing those who rape women, break into inns, . . . likewise all those who have banded together for this purpose. No less do we excommunicate all those who have known anything about the aforesaid, unless within seven days from the time of their information, after the proclamation issued against the aforesaid has come to their notice, they shall have revealed what they know to the said reverend bishop or ourselves and have submitted to fitting [correction]. Nevertheless we specially reserve to the lord bishop or ourselves the right to absolve clerks excommunicated for the aforesaid reasons.

READING REVIEW

1. Of what basic crime were the clerks, scholars, and their servants accused?
2. What punishment did the religious court hand down for all the crimes mentioned in the proclamation?
3. Why, in your opinion, did the religious court have jurisdiction in these matters?

---

44 THE PAPAL COURT AT AVIGNON

In 1309, the seat of the papacy was moved from Rome to the southern French town of Avignon as a result of a coup by Philip IV of France. This began a 70-year period known in papal history as the Babylonian Captivity. The Avignon popes seemed to be interested only in their own comforts, and in time the papal court became more luxurious than any of the secular courts of Europe. In the excerpt below from Volume 3 of Translations and Reprints From the Original Sources of European History, *the Italian poet Petrarch records his reaction to the papal court at Avignon. As you read the excerpt, note the comparisons Petrarch made between the apostles and the Avignon popes.*

I have a double Parnassus [the mountain sacred to Apollo], one in Italy, the other in France. . . . I was very happy in my [Italian one]. . . . But now I am living in France, in the Babylon of the West. The sun, in its travels sees nothing more hideous than this place on the shores of the wild Rhone, which suggests the hellish streams of Cocytus and Acheron [the rivers of Hades]. Here reign the successors of the poor fishermen of Galilee; they have strangely forgotten their origin. I am astounded, as I recall their predecessors, to see these men loaded with gold and clad in purple, boasting of the spoils of princes and nations; to see luxurious palaces and heights crowned with fortifications, instead of a boat turned downwards for shelter. We no longer find the simple nets which were once used to gain a frugal sustenance from the Lake of Galilee, and with which, having labored all night and caught nothing, they took, at day break, a multitude of fishes, in the name of Jesus. One is stupified nowadays to hear the lying tongues, and to see worthless parchments, turned by a leaden seal, into nets which are used, in Christ's name, but by the arts of [the Devil], to catch hordes of unwary Christians. These fish, too, are dressed and laid on the burning coals of anxiety before they fill the insatiable maw of their captors. Instead of holy solitude we find a criminal host and crowds of the most infamous [hangers-on]; instead of soberness, [depraved] banquets; instead of pious pilgrimages, [abnormal] and foul sloth; instead of the bare feet of the apostles, the snowy coursers of brigands fly past us, the horses decked in gold and fed on gold, soon to be shod with gold, if the Lord does not check this slavish luxury. In short, we seem to be among . . . kings . . . before whom we must fall down and worship, and who cannot be approached except presents be offered. O, ye unkempt and emaciated old men, is it for this you labored? Is it for this that you have sown the field of the Lord and watered it with your holy blood?

READING REVIEW

1. To what did Petrarch compare the Rhone River?
2. What do you think the "worthless parchments" that Petrarch referred to were?
3. According to Petrarch, how did the Avignon popes compare to the apostles?

---

45 A WOMAN'S HUNDRED YEARS

One kind of literature that flourished during the Tang dynasty was the popular song. Inspired by the basic ideas of Buddhism, most popular songs frequently offered some kind of religious message. The excerpt below contains a popular song, titled A Woman's Hundred Years, *that discusses the changes a woman goes through as she grows older. As you read the excerpt, ask yourself which theme of Buddhism might have inspired this song.*

At ten, like a flowering branch in the rain,
She is slender, delicate, and full of grace.
Her parents are themselves as young as the rising moon
And do not allow her past the red curtain without a reason.

At twenty, receiving the hairpin, she is a spring bud.
Her parents arrange her betrothal; the matter's well done.
A fragrant carriage comes at evening to carry her to her lord.
Like Hsiao-shih and his wife, at dawn they depart with the clouds.

At thirty, perfect as a pearl, full of the beauty of youth,
At her window, by the gauze curtain, she makes up in front of the mirror.
With her singing companions, in the waterlily season,
She rows a boat and plucks the blue flowers.

At forty, she is mistress of a prosperous house and makes plans.
Three sons and five daughters give her some trouble.
With her [lyre] not far away, she toils always at her loom,
Her only fear that the sun will set too soon.

At fifty, afraid of her husband's dislike,
She strains to please him with every charm,
Trying to remember the many tricks she had learned since
the age of sixteen.
No longer is she afraid of mothers- and sisters-in-law.

At sixty, face wrinkled and hair like silk thread,
She walks unsteadily and speaks little.
Distressed that her sons can find no brides,
Grieved that her daughters have departed for their husbands'
homes.

At seventy, frail and thin, but not knowing what to do about it,
She is no longer able to learn the Buddhist Law even if she
tries.
In the morning a light breeze
Makes her joints crack like clanging gongs.

At eighty, eyes blinded and ears half-deaf,
When she goes out she cannot tell north from east.
Dreaming always of departed loves,
Who persuade her to chase the dying breeze.

At ninety, the glow fades like spent lightning.
Human affairs are no longer her concern.
Lying on a pillow, solitary on her high bed,
She resembles the dying leaves that fall in
autumn.

At a hundred, like a cliff crumbling in the wind,
For her body it is the moment to become dust.
Children and grandchildren will perform sacrifices to her
spirit,
And clear moonlight will forever illumine her patch of earth.

READING REVIEW

1. In which decade does a woman first start to notice she is growing older?
2. What comparisons does the song make between a woman and a tree to show youth and age?
3. Which of the Four Noble Truths do you think inspired this song? Why?

Marco Polo

46 KUBLAI KHAN'S GREAT PARK AT SHANGDU

Under Mongol rule, China increased its contacts with the outside world. Many European merchants and adventurers traveled through China during this time. Perhaps the most famous of these travelers was Marco Polo, a young Venetian merchant. He recorded the highlights of his 17 years in China in a book titled Descriptions of the World. *In the excerpt below, Polo describes Kublai Khan's magnificent palace and park at Shangdu, some 200 miles north of Beijing. As you read the excerpt, consider how Polo reacted to the opulence of Kublai Khan's palaces.*

Proceeding three days' journey in a north-easterly direction, you arrive at a city called [Shangdu], built by the Grand Khan Kublai, now reigning. In this he caused a palace to be erected, of marble and other handsome stones, admirable as well for the elegance of its design as for the skill displayed in its execution. The halls and chambers are all gilt, and very handsome. It presents one front towards the interior of the city, and the other towards the wall; and from each extremity of the building runs another wall to such an extent as to enclose sixteen miles in circuit of the adjoining plain, to which there is no access but through the palace. Within the bounds of this royal park there are rich and beautiful meadows, watered by many rivulets, where a variety of animals of the deer and goat kind are pastured, to serve as food for the hawks and other birds employed in the chase, whose mews are also in the grounds. The number of these birds is upwards of two hundred; and the grand khan goes in person, at least once in the week, to inspect them. Frequently, when he rides about this enclosed forest, he has one or more small leopards carried on horseback, behind their keepers; and when he pleases to give direction for their being slipped, they instantly seize a stag, or goat, or fallow deer, which he gives to his hawks, and in this manner he amuses himself. In the centre of these grounds, where there is a beautiful grove of trees, he has built a royal pavilion, supported upon a colonnade of handsome pillars, gilt and varnished. Round each pillar a dragon, likewise gilt, entwines its tail, whilst its head sustains the projection of the roof, and its talons or claws are extended to the right and left along the entablature. The roof is of bamboo cane, likewise gilt, and so well varnished that no wet can injure it. The bamboos used for this purpose are three palms in circumference and ten fathoms in length, and being cut at the joints, are split into two equal parts, so as to form gutters, and with these (laid concave and convex) the pavilion is covered; but to secure the roof against the effect of wind, each of the bamboos is tied at the ends to the frame. The building is supported on every side (like a tent) by more than two hundred very strong silken cords, and otherwise, from the lightness of the materials, it would be liable to oversetting by the force of high winds. The whole is constructed with so much ingenuity of contrivance that all the parts may be taken asunder, removed, and again set up, at his majesty's pleasure. This spot he has selected for his recreation on account of the mild temperature and salubrity of the air, and he accordingly makes it his residence during three months of the year, namely, June, July, and August; and every year, on the twenty-eighth day of the moon, in the last of these months, it is his established custom to depart from thence.

READING REVIEW

1. What in Marco Polo's description suggests that the park was strictly for the use of Kublai Khan?
2. Why did Kublai Khan select Shangdu for his summer residence?
3. How do you think Marco Polo felt about Kublai Khan's palace at Shangdu? Support your answer with evidence from the excerpt.

47 DRINKING TEA FOR LONG LIFE

A Zen Buddhist monk named Eisai was the first to bring tea from China to Japan in the late 1100s. He actively advocated the drinking of tea, largely to alter the Japanese nobility's taste for alcohol. Such was Eisai's influence that tea soon became Japan's national beverage. This drink also became the center piece of one of Zen Buddhism's most beautiful and refined rituals—the tea ceremony. In the excerpt below from Sources of Japanese Tradition, *compiled by Ryusaku Tsunoda, Eisai discusses the wonderful qualities of tea. As you read the excerpt, note the impact Eisai suggests that drinking tea has on health.*

Traditional Japanese tea ceremony

Tea is the most wonderful medicine for nourishing one's health; it is the secret of long life. On the hillsides it grows up as the spirit of the soil. Those who pick and use it are certain to attain a great age. India and China both value it highly, and in the past our country too once showed a great liking for tea. Now as then it possesses the same rare qualities, and we should make wider use of it. . . .

Of all the things which Heaven has created, man is the most noble. To preserve one's life so as to make the most of one's allotted span is prudent and proper [considering the high value of human life]. The basis of preserving life is the cultivation of health, and the secret of health lies in the well-being of the . . . organs. Among these . . . the heart is sovereign, and to build up the heart the drinking of tea is the finest method. When the heart is weak, the other organs all suffer. . . .

When the heart becomes sick, all organs and tastes are affected. Then, eat as one may, one will have to vomit and stop eating. But if one drinks tea, the heart will be strengthened and freed from illness. It is well to know that when the heart is ailing, the skin has a poor color, a sign that life is ebbing away. I wonder why the Japanese do not care for bitter things. In the great country of China they drink tea, as a result of which there is no heart trouble and people live long lives. Our country is full of sickly-looking, skinny persons, and this is simply because we do not drink tea. Whenever one is in poor spirits, one should drink tea. This will put the heart in order and dispel all illness. . . .

Drink lots of tea, and one's energy and spirits will be restored to full strength.

READING REVIEW

1. According to Eisai, where does the secret of good health lie?
2. What symptom of heart disease does Eisai note?
3. How, according to Eisai, is the drinking of tea beneficial to health?

---

48 ACTORS AND ENTERTAINERS IN FEUDAL JAPAN

Actors and entertainers, because of their way of life and the profession they followed, were considered outsiders by traditional Japanese society. They were strictly segregated from the rest of society, having to live along the banks of rivers. In fact, the name by which they were generally known was the "river-bank people." In the excerpt below from Everyday Life in Traditional Japan *by C. J. Dunn, the author discusses the social status and typical day-to-day lives of actors and entertainers are discussed. As you read the excerpt, consider why people in entertainment were considered social outcasts.*

These people were deliberately excluded [from society], either because of some personal disqualification, or on account of the trade or profession that they followed. . . . Some, like actors . . . , were precluded because they took part in entertainment; such people were supposed to be unacceptable only while pursuing their trade, but in practice for them admittance into respectable society was difficult. . . .

There were, of course, many sorts of actors. Those who entertained the warriors, and even taught them their art, had respectability as part of their reward. . . . Their status was considerably higher than that of the performers in what had become the aristocratic drama, the *nō* plays. Actors of *nō* were tightly organised into families, either by birth or adoption, and their status within their profession was well defined, depending upon clearly understood precedences. The public of the artisan and merchant classes may not have seen them very often. The Shogun, however, sometimes admitted the townsfolk to performances given in Edo, and there was a certain amount of interchange with *kabuki* actors [performers in the live popular drama] in Osaka. *Kabuki* and *nō* actors had much the same public status. . . .

An actor's life was arduous. It is true that he usually had the evenings to himself, for it was exceptional to have performances after dark. However, they started early in the morning and went on all day. Runs were short, depending upon the success of the piece, and, even though rehearsals were sketchy by modern Western standards, there was nearly always some new piece being prepared. . . . The actor had no life apart from the theatre, and this was especially true of the *omnagata* player of female roles. Apart from a short time in the early seventeenth century, women had not been allowed to appear on the public stage, and actors who took female parts were expected, if they were to be accepted by the public and the critics . . . to live as women even outside of the theatre, and to keep any male characteristics, not to mention a wife and family, very much out of the public view.

Entry into the profession might be by following one's father, and making a first appearance in a child's part, or by being adopted by an actor, or by coming up through the arduous profession of a child entertainer. Alternatively, just as a British actor might start his career in the provinces and achieve fame by getting a part in a London West-End production, so some actors in Japan began in the country, . . . then were fortunate enough to obtain employment in Edo, Kyoto or Osaka, where the great theatres were to be found. Such local talent might be spotted by actors from the great theatres during their own visits to the provinces. . . .

Kabuki actors . . . were only the apex of a pyramid of entertainers of all sorts. Some of these led a comparatively sheltered life in the restaurants and other places of entertainment. Such were the male jesters whose function it was to do comic dances and sing comic songs and generally make the party go. Their female colleagues lived in their own strictly stratified society. . . .

There were also a great number of wandering entertainers who had no such comfortable abodes. The better of these overlapped with the lowest grades of actors. They were the conjurers, the dancers, the singers, the puppet-men, and street-corner men and women of all sorts, whose ranks included the semi-religious bell-ringers, chest-beaters and others reminiscent of some of the holy men of India. They collected alms but were barely distinguishable from pure beggars.

READING REVIEW

1. Why was life especially arduous for actors who took female roles?
2. How did people normally enter the acting profession?
3. Why do you think actors and entertainers were looked upon as outsiders? Explain your answer.

---

49 BLIND MAN AND LAME MAN

The peoples of Africa have a strong oral tradition, passing on by word of mouth their history through stories, poems, and songs. In some areas of the continent, oral tradition has been used to pass on more than tales of the past. One kind of story, called the dilemma tale, teaches ethical behavior by setting a moral problem for listeners. The excerpt below from The Intimate Folklore of Africa *by Alta Jablow is taken from the Gio people of West Africa. The problem presented is: who should get the monkey stew, the lame man who shot and cooked the monkey, or the blind man who carried the lame man on his back to hunt the monkey? As you read the excerpt, ask yourself how the tale might be applied to modern-day Africa.*

This did not happen in my town, nor did it happen in your town, but it did happen and in some other town.

There were two men who lived together in one hut; one was blind and the other was lame. It was a time of famine and all the people suffered hunger. These two were hungry also. As they sat in their hut, Lame Man saw a troupe of monkeys in their yard. He thought of monkey stew and smacked his lips. Then he groaned.

"What is it with you, friend? Are you not well?" asked Blind Man.

Lame Man answered, "Oh, I am well enough, but hungry. If I could only walk, I would shoot a monkey and cook a fine stew to eat."

Blind Man laughed. "I laugh so that I will not cry. My belly is empty, too. And the bush is empty of game. The hunters in our village go out each day and find nothing to shoot. Where would you find monkeys?"

"Right in the yard of our hut," said Lame Man. "Because you cannot see them there, don't think I am blind, too. There are monkeys outside!"

This convinced Blind Man and he said, "Climb onto my shoulders, and tell me where to walk and where to stop. I will carry you and the gun to shoot the game."

Lame Man got on Blind Man's shoulders and directed his steps. They came so outside, where the monkeys were in the pawpaw trees. Boom! Lame Man fired his gun and a monkey fell. The others fled speedily out of range.

They carried the game inside and Lame Man built the fire up and began to prepare the stew. As he stirred the pot, Blind Man asked, "Is it ready?"

"Not yet."

Lame Man added the palm oil and the pepper and continued stirring. And the other asked again, "Is it ready?"

"Not yet."

All the while he was cooking the stew, Lame Man kept tasting it for flavor, and because he was so hungry. And each time Blind Man asked, "Is it ready?" Lame Man had just taken a large mouthful of the hot stew and had to swallow hastily to answer his companion. Before long there was nothing left in the pot but bones and a weak soup.

This time when Blind Man asked, "Is it ready?" the answer was, "Yes, it is ready," and he was given a bowlful of bones and soup.

"What is this? Bones? Ah, you wretched fellow! You have taken advantage of my blindness and eaten all the meat. Did I not share equally with you in its capture? Should I not then have equal share to eat? Without my legs you would not have shot anything at all."

Lame Man answered, "I saw the game. I shot it. I cooked it. This is the larger part of the work, and hence I should get the larger portion of food. You used only your physical strength. I used my eyes, my skill as a hunter, and my talent as a cook. This is certainly more! If I had not first seen the monkeys there would be nothing in the pot at all."

Thus they disputed and grew very vexed with each other. Blind Man went from the house and stood on the road, stopping all the people to listen to his account and beseeching them to judge and punish Lame Man. From the hut, Lame Man shouted his arguments and besought the people to judge him right.

The people were not able to judge. Can you tell, of the two, who was right?

"The people were not able to judge. Can you tell, of the two, who was right?"

READING REVIEW

1. How did Blind Man solve the problem of Lame Man not being able to walk to hunt the monkeys?
2. Who do you think was right, Blind Man or Lame Man? Give reasons for your answer.
3. How might the tale of Blind Man and Lame Man be applied to modern-day Africa?

50 MANSA MUSA'S PILGRIMAGE

Great kingdoms flourished in West Africa for hundreds of years. However, knowledge of these kingdoms did not reach a wide audience in the outside world until the 1300s, when Mansa Musa, the king of Mali, made his pilgrimage to Mecca. Soon, people throughout North Africa and southern Europe were aware of the generous, noble leader from the "land of the gold mines." In the excerpt below from The Splendor That Was Africa *by Ricky Rosenthal, a modern historian tells the story of Mansa Musa's journey to and from Mecca. As you read the excerpt, note the impact that the pilgrimage had on the economy of Cairo.*

The bazaars of Cairo could not be quieted—the least bit of gossip sprints from market to market stall in record time under any condition. There was no doubt about it, something extraordinary had captured the attention of the great city which served as an important caravan terminus. Reports of Mansa Musa's entrance into Cairo in 1324, seventeen years after his ascent to the throne was nothing short of spell-binding. For his own part, Mansa Musa was on his way to the holy city of Mecca. It was said that when this remarkable sight came into view that 60,000 men were counted, including a personal retinue of 12,000 slaves, dressed in the most sumptuous silks and brocades. This must be war, people thought, as 500 slaves each carrying a staff of gold weighing about 6 pounds were observed, and later this was noted down. This was an invasion surely—word darted from person to person! When the curtain of dust that had enveloped the caravan had cleared, it was learned that there was a baggage train of 80 camels carrying 300 pounds of gold dust each. The guardians of the caravan let this be known among the townspeople.

This was no invasion—impressions clarified, the air was clearing amid coughs and sneezes, but no violence was taking place, so fear was brushed aside as quickly as the handkerchief could remove dust from the eyes. It was learned that there was nothing to fear, no secret could be kept within the confines of the caravan for long. Word circulated through the market and wound round through the cool alleys . . . that this grand visitor was Mansa Musa! Such good behavior, such fine clothes. . . . This must be the caravan of a rich man, perhaps a Moslem, oh joy! it was learned he was also a pious Moslem. They could not know that this man was to elevate the city of Timbuktu to the point where it would become a great center of Islamic culture. It was difficult for those, that observed him that day, to know what aspirations this man had among this finery; for in fact, they had very little actual knowledge or contact with the "country of the black people" which is what the Sudan means.

Mansa Musa had no political motives, oh! relief! word swept through the city. Where had he come from was the question of the day. This

African dancers from Mali.

immense caravan had made its way from Niani on the upper Niger to Walata, to Tuat, and then to Cairo. Such a lengthy journey crossed the unrelieved dunes of the Sahara. . . . The very name Sahara, legendary as a lure to men of all races, is an Arabic word symbolizing wilderness or emptiness, the word having the hot sound of a man gasping for breath. What these travellers endured, the terrible monotony! . . . With the end of the day's heat, as surely came the sudden cold of the desert night. The nights in the desert have a virtue of their own. Brilliant night skies seem to remove the haze of fine dust that half obscures the merciless daytime sun. This caravan, like many others, must have camped gratefully near the spiky desert date . . . huddling near the lines of doum palms. . . . These oases of rest are almost sacred to the traveller. These patches of green growth in the desert are designed by the whim of nature. When the rare, but awesome rain storm falls, water collects in hollows and water-courses and soaks into beds of silt and sand. It is here that the perennial plants and trees can live and man can take his respite—Mansa Musa felt such a journey worth it in the performance of his religious duties.

He could not stop in Cairo, for he must complete his religious devotions. He was slightly standoffish, and it was only through the persistence of his advisers that he called upon the Sultan of Egypt.

It was of this journey that El-Omari, 12 years later, heard in Cairo. It was through a conversation that he had had with a lawyer, that we learn that Mansa Musa described the length and breadth of his country as a year's journey across. It was more sensibly ascertained that it could have been four months journey each way. This state pilgrimage literally put Mali on the map. A map made in Majorca in 1331 by one Abraham Cresques, pictures Rex Melli, "the king of the gold mines."

Mansa Musa's veritable army of people, some for protection, others taken along for political reasons, also included doctors, chiefs, servants and family. This massive entourage caused so much gold to be put in circulation, that El-Omari's ears rang from the complaints of how the price of everything had gone up since the visit of that splendid and pious emperor. He was always referred to in a most respectful manner, though a conversation concluded with a complaint. Mansa Musa's charitable nature caused him to distribute gifts of gold in the holy cities, sending the price of this precious metal plunging.

Completing his religious duties in Mecca, his mind became restless. He felt that he must do something that would add to the splendor of his empire. Yes, he would do it, by some miracle he persuaded Es-Saheli, known as the poet-architect of Granada to accompany him home. Following this accomplishment, he received a message that Gao had been captured. Gao, a strategically located town had risen from Berber beginnings, and . . . [now was] a city of the Songhai people. . . . The capture of Gao extended the Mali Empire for a thousand miles. Overjoyed by this news he was determined to visit this new captive of his on the middle Niger. This he did. . . .

Gao, he noted, had no buildings really suitable, at least to his eye, for the worship of God. Who could he trust he thought, smiling to himself. Who possessed the appropriate artistic sense, who possessed a cultured enough mind for such an important task? He knew the answer, of course; Es-Saheli could be trusted with the task. Es-Saheli was eminently successful in behalf of his patron, he built Mosques of burnt brick, using the crenelated wall and enhanced the design of the roof with a pyramidal minaret. He also designed several receiving houses for the king when he was in residence. This architecture was extended through the Western Sudan, where heretofore only cylindrical huts and conical roofs had been built. This style of architecture was admired as late as the 17th century. . . .

Traveling with Mansa Musa was a rich merchant from Cairo. This is how he came to have this guest. It was inevitable that Mansa Musa should run out of gold. His generosity, alas! had overflowed into lavishness, and a steady depletion of funds followed. In Cairo he was forced to borrow money from a merchant. This man was not only skeptical but curious as to Mansa Musa's destination; and being only familiar by rumor with the interior of West Africa, he went with him. If the truth were to be known, payment of the debt was probably uppermost in his mind. This merchant's curiosity was probably more alive than the man himself, and the journey under the fierce and compelling sun was probably too much for him, and he died at Timbuktu. This was by no means the close of the transaction. The Emperor upon his arrival home sent a special courier across the desert to the man's children in Alexandria. With the money, he sent a greeting.

READING REVIEW

1. What did the people of Cairo first think Mansa Musa's great caravan was?
2. (**a**) What evidence in the excerpt suggests that Mansa Musa was a devout man? (**b**) What evidence in the excerpt suggests that he was honest?
3. How did Mansa Musa's pilgrimage affect the economy of Cairo?

---

51 WOMEN LEADERS IN NORTH AMERICAN INDIAN SOCIETIES

It has been a widely accepted view that North American Indian women occupied the lower levels of society, being completely subordinate to men. In most traditional Indian societies it was certainly true that few women held office or sat on the tribal council. Even so, women were able to exercise considerable authority in day-to-day tribal life. The ways in which women exercised power in a number of Indian societies is discussed in the excerpt below from Daughters of the Earth: The Lives and Legends of American Indian Women *by Carolyn Neithammer. As you read the excerpt, compare how women attained power in the four societies mentioned.*

While there has never been a true matriarchy in ancient or modern times, the Iroquois did come as close to it as any other society. The Iroquois were a woodland culture and inhabited the area that is now New York.

Women in that society had the upper hand economically because they owned the fields, crops, and houses. Descent was traced through the women and all titles, rights, and property passed through the female line. While this still left power in the hands of men, it gave the women a great deal of control over the exercise of that power.

Although Iroquois women did not actually hold the position of chief (called a sachem in that tribe), it was they who not only chose the leaders but also decided if the men they selected were doing a creditable job. Each clan was divided into lineages, and at the head of each lineage was an older woman—the matron—who derived her position from her age and her qualities of leadership and diplomacy. One of her duties was the coordination of the economic activities of the female clan members—not only their work in the fields, but also their contributions of food for charity and public festivals.

When one of the sachems died, it was up to the matron of his lineage, in consultation with her female relatives, to select his successor. If the new sachem's conduct was not satisfactory, the matron would warn him three times, giving him a chance to improve. After that the matron would ask the council to depose him. Because of her position, it was necessary for the matron to always conduct herself with great decorum, so that when she had to admonish an erring chief her warnings were respected. . . .

Women also played a very important role among the Natchez, who lived along the lower Mississippi River and had an unusual system of government. The society was divided into several classes, with the Suns being the chiefs, followed by Nobles and Honored People, who were also considered aristocracy. The rest of the people were called Stinkards.

The principal leader, or Great Sun, was always a male; because nobility was transferred only through the female line, this ruler was succeeded not by one of his sons but by the son of the woman most closely related to him. This woman was also considered a Sun, or White Woman. While the women Suns generally did not meddle in governmental affairs, they did command great respect from the rest of the populace, who were

An Indian village

expected to supply them with the best products of their farming, hunting, or fishing endeavors. These aristocrats also had the power of life and death over their subjects; if anyone displeased them they had only to command, "Rid me of that dog," and they were instantly obeyed by their guards.

The Suns, both men and women, were not allowed to intermarry and were required to take mates from the Stinkard class. Husbands of White Women functioned more as servants than partners—they were not allowed to eat with their wives, they were required to stand at attention when in their wives' presence, they even had to salute in the same manner as the rest of the servants. Their only privileges were freedom from labor and a chance to exercise authority over the other servants. . . .

In some tribes on the western side of the continent we also find women in leadership roles. . . .

In northern California, the Nisenan sometimes had a woman at their head. The chieftainship was primarily hereditary, and, if on the death of a chief, there was no male relative competent to fill the position, the deceased's widow, daughter, or niece might be chosen to succeed him. A woman in this office had no actual power, although she was always consulted by the leading men; the measure of strength she held depended on the degree of support she had from the populace. Besides advising the council, her duties included planning community activities and food gathering, arbitrating disputes, acting as official hostess, and arranging "big times" or celebrations.

In the southwestern groups, where women often have high status and command considerable respect, we find several tribes in which there were specific positions of leadership filled by women. . . .

The leader of a Hopi town was usually assisted in his duties by a woman relative, who was called "Keeper of the Fire." She was chosen for this honor on the basis of her wisdom, intelligence, and interest in religious ceremony. The male head priest or chief kept his office in this woman's home and consulted her on many decisions, drawing on her experience and knowledge of precedents.

Every clan in a Hopi village was also headed by a matriarch, or clan mother, who enjoyed certain privileges as a result of her seniority. The clan mother was always consulted by her male relatives on any matter which fell within her realm of competence or sphere of influence, for example, family quarrels or other such disputes. The matriarch of the leading clan did not necessarily hold the position of Keeper of the Fire—sometimes a younger woman was felt to be more suited to the job.

READING REVIEW

1. How did Iroquois women have the upper hand economically?
2. Among the Hopi, why was the matriarch of the clan not always chosen as the Keeper of the Fire?
3. What similarities can you see among the four societies mentioned in the excerpt in terms of women's power?

52 THE INCAS: WORSHIPPERS OF THE SUN

Although the most important of the Inca gods was the creator, known as Viracocha and Pachayachachic—meaning "lord" and "instructor of the world"—the Incas reserved their most impressive rituals for the sun. In fact, the Inca royal family claimed the sun as an ancestor—the word Inca *means "children of the sun." In the excerpt below from* Latin American Civilization: The Colonial Origins, *edited by Benjamin Keen, Bernabe Cobo (1582–1657), a Jesuit priest, records how the Incas felt about the sun god. As you read the excerpt, consider whether Cobo respected the religion of the Incas.*

The god most respected by them after Viracocha was that most excellent of material creations, the sun; and the Inca, who boasted that they were the Children of the Sun, bent all their efforts toward exalting its authority and endowing it with a magnificent ritual, numerous priests, and frequent offerings and sacrifices. Not that much had to be done to inspire esteem for the sun among their people; they respected the objects of Nature in accord with the benefits that they obtained from them, and since the beneficial effects produced by this planet were so manifest and excellent, they held it in great regard. The authority and example of the Inca only served to make the external displays of worship more costly and elaborate. They believed that the Pachayachachic had given the sun power to create all the foods, together with the earth, whence came their regard for it as the greatest guaca of all after the Viracocha; and so they called it *Apu-Inti,* which means "My Lord Sun": they visualized it in the likeness of a man, and consequently they used to say that the moon was his wife and the stars their children.

They held the sun in such reverence throughout this kingdom of the Inca that I question whether in any other part of the world there ever prevailed a cult so respected and well served. This may be seen from the fact that to no other god did they dedicate so many and such magnificent temples; for there was not an important town where the sun did not have a temple with numerous priests and *mamaconas* and ample revenues for its maintenance. And the wealthiest and most sumptuous temple of all was that which the Inca kings had erected to the sun in their court, the temple called Coricancha, where they kept their principal and most venerated idol. It was an impressive image, called *Punchau,* which means "the day," all worked in finest gold with a wealth of precious stones, in the likeness of a human face, surrounded by rays, as we depict the sun; they placed it so that it faced the east, and when the sun rose its rays fell on it; and since it was a sheet of finest metal the rays were reflected from it so brightly that it actually seemed to be the sun. The Indians were wont to say that the sun lent this image both its light and its power. From the spoils which the Spaniards obtained in the beautiful temple of Coricancha there fell to the lot of a soldier this splendid sheet of gold, and since at that time gambling was the popular pastime he lost it one night at play; from this came the saying used in Peru about heavy gamblers: "He gambles the sun away before it rises." . . .

They regarded the eclipse of the sun as a grave matter, and when it occurred they consulted the diviners about its meaning; and having been told what it denoted, they made great and costly sacrifices, offering up various gold and silver figures, and killing a large number of sheep as well as many boys and girls. The sorcerers commonly asserted that the eclipse portended the death of some prince, and that the sun had gone into mourning for the loss that the world would suffer; when this happened all the women dedicated to the sun fasted for many days, wore mourning garments, and offered frequent sacrifices. The Inca retired to a secret spot, and there, having dealings with none, he fasted many days; during all this time no fire was lighted in the whole city.

READING REVIEW

1. According to Cobo why did Inca priests not have to do much to inspire esteem for the sun god among the Inca people?
2. According to Inca sorcerers, what did an eclipse of the sun mean?
3. How do you think Cobo felt about the Incas' worship of the sun? Explain your answer.

The Emergence of Modern Nations

53 ADVICE TO PRINCES

Niccolò Machiavelli

Niccolò Machiavelli's best known work, The Prince, *recorded the rules of the game of power politics. To stay in power, Machiavelli said, rulers would have to ignore the lofty ideals of politics—honesty, justice, honor, magnanimity, and so on—and adopt whatever means necessary. In the excerpt below, Machiavelli offers advice on the kinds of qualities a prudent ruler should possess. As you read the excerpt, ask yourself how useful Machiavelli's advice would be to rulers in today's world.*

Chapter XIV
How a ruler should act concerning military matters

A ruler, then, should have no other objective and no other concern, nor occupy himself with anything else except war and its methods and practices, for this pertains only to those who rule. And it is of such efficacy that it not only maintains hereditary rulers in power but very often enables men of private status to become rulers. On the other hand, it is evident that if rulers concern themselves more with the refinements of life than with military matters, they lose power. The main reason why they lose it is their neglect of the art of war; and being proficient in this art is what enables one to gain power.

Because Francesco Sforza was armed, from being a private citizen he became Duke of Milan; since his descendants did not trouble themselves with military matters, from being dukes they became private citizens. For being unarmed (apart from other bad consequences) results in your being despised, which is one of those disgraceful things against which a ruler must always guard. . . . There is an enormous difference between an armed man and an unarmed man; and it cannot be expected that a man who is armed will obey willingly a man who is unarmed, or that an unarmed man can be safe among armed servants. Since the latter will be contemptuous and the former suspicious and afraid, they will not be able to work well together. Therefore, apart from the other disadvantages already mentioned, a ruler who does not understand military matters cannot be highly regarded by his soldiers, and he cannot trust them.

Chapter XVII
Whether it is better to be loved than feared

A controversy has arisen about this: whether it is better to be loved than feared, or vice versa. My view is that it is desirable to be both loved and feared; but it is difficult to achieve both and, if one of them has to be lacking, it is much safer to be feared than loved.

For this may be said of men generally: they are ungrateful, fickle, feigners and dissemblers, avoiders of danger, eager for gain. While you benefit them they are all devoted to you: they would shed their blood for you; they offer their possessions, their lives, and their sons . . . when the need to do so is far off. But when you are hard pressed, they turn away. A ruler who has relied completely on their promises, and has neglected to prepare other defences, will be ruined, because friendships that are acquired with money, and not through greatness and nobility of character, are paid for but not secured, and prove unreliable just when they are needed.

Men are less hesitant about offending or harming a ruler who makes himself loved than one who inspires fear. For love is sustained by a bond of gratitude which, because men are excessively self-interested, is broken whenever they see a chance to benefit themselves. But fear is sustained by a dread of punishment that is always effective. Nevertheless, a ruler must make himself feared in such a way that, even if he does not become loved, he does not become hated. For it is perfectly possible to be feared without incurring hatred. And this can always be achieved if he refrains from laying hands on the property of his citizens and subjects, and on their womenfolk. If it is necessary to execute anyone, this should be done only if there is a proper justification and obvious reason. But, above all, he must not touch the property of others, because men forget sooner the killing of a father than the loss of their patrimony [property].

Chapter XVIII
How rulers should keep their promises

Everyone knows how praiseworthy it is for a ruler to keep his promises, and live uprightly and not by trickery. Nevertheless, experience shows that in our times the rulers who have done great things are those who have set little store by keeping their word, being skilful rather in cunningly confusing men; they have got the better of those who have relied on being trustworthy.

You should know, then, that there are two ways of contending: one by using laws, the other, force. The first is appropriate for men, the second for animals; but because the former is often ineffective, one must have recourse to the latter. Therefore, a ruler must know well how to imitate beasts as well as employing properly human means. . . .

Since a ruler, then, must know how to act like a beast, he should imitate both the fox and the lion, for the lion is liable to be trapped, whereas the fox cannot ward off wolves. One needs, then, to be a fox to recognise traps, and a lion to frighten away wolves. Those who rely merely upon a lion's strength do not understand matters.

Therefore, a prudent ruler cannot keep his word, nor should he, when such fidelity would damage him, and when the reasons that made him promise are no longer relevant. This advice would not be sound if all men were upright; but because they are treacherous and would not keep their promises to you, you should not consider yourself bound to keep your promises to them.

Moreover, plausible reasons can always be found for such failure to keep promises. One could give countless modern examples of this, and show how many peace treaties and promises have been rendered null and void by the faithlessness of rulers; and those best able to imitate the fox have succeeded best. But foxiness should be well concealed: one must be a great feigner and dissembler. And men are so naive, and so much dominated by immediate needs, that a skilful deceiver always finds plenty of people who will let themselves be deceived. . . .

A ruler, then, should be very careful [about] everything he says . . . : to those who see and hear him, he should seem to be exceptionally merciful, trustworthy, upright, humane and devout. And it is most necessary of all to seem devout. In these matters, most men judge more by their eyes than by their hands. For everyone is capable of seeing you, but few can touch you. Everyone can see what you appear to be, whereas few have direct experience of what you really are; and those few will not dare to challenge the popular view, sustained as it is by the majesty of the ruler's position.

READING REVIEW

1. According to Machiavelli why is it safer for a ruler to be feared than loved?
2. What advice does Machiavelli give about why a prudent ruler should not keep promises?
3. Do you think that today's world leaders should follow the rules Machiavelli set down in *The Prince?* Why or why not?

---

54 LUTHER'S REFUSAL AT THE DIET OF WORMS

After he had been excommunicated by Pope Leo X, Martin Luther was summoned by the Holy Roman Emperor, Charles V, to appear before the Imperial Diet at Worms in 1521. There, he was given an opportunity to renounce his ideas. However, in a dramatic encounter with imperial rulers and church theologians, Luther refused to recant. The excerpt below from Documents of the Christian Church, *edited by Henry Bettenson, contains part of this exchange between Luther and his opponents. As you read the excerpt, consider whether there was any way for Luther to recant in good faith.*

Do you wish to defend the books which are recognized as your work? Or to retract anything contained in them? . . .

. . . [Luther replied:] Most Serene Lord Emperor, Most Illustrious Princes, Most Gracious Lords . . . I beseech you to grant a gracious hearing to my plea, which, I trust, will be a plea of justice and truth; and if through my inexperience I neglect to give to any their proper titles or in any way offend against the etiquette of the court in my manners or behaviour, be kind enough to forgive me, I beg, since I am a man who has spent his life not in courts but in the cells of a monastery; a man who can say of himself only this, that to this day I have thought and written in simplicity of heart, solely with a view to the glory of God and the pure instruction of Christ's faithful people. . . .

. . . Your Imperial Majesty and Your Lordships: I ask you to observe that my books are not all of the same kind.

There are some in which I have dealt with piety in faith and morals with such simplicity and so agreeably with the Gospels that my adversaries themselves are compelled to admit them useful, harmless, and clearly worth reading by a Christian. Even the [Excommunication] Bull, harsh and cruel though it is, makes some of my books harmless, although it condemns them also, by a judgement downright monstrous. If I should begin to recant here, what, I beseech you, should I be doing but condemning, alone among mortals, that truth which is admitted by friends and foes alike. . . .

The second kind consists in those writings levelled against the papacy and the doctrine of the papists, as against those who by their wicked doctrines and precedents have laid waste Christendom by doing harm to the souls and the bodies of men. No one can either deny or conceal this, for universal experience and worldwide grievances are witnesses to the fact that through the Pope's laws and through man-made teachings the consciences of the faithful have been most pitifully ensnared, troubled, and racked in torment, and also that their goods and possessions have been devoured (especially amongst this famous German nation) by unbelievable tyranny, and are to this day being devoured without end in shameful fashion. . . . If then I recant these, the only effect will be to add strength to such tyranny, to open not the windows but the main doors to such blasphemy, which will thereupon stalk farther and more widely than it has hitherto dared. . . .

The third kind consists of those books which I have written against private individuals, so-called; against those, that is, who have exerted themselves in defense of the Roman tyranny and to the overthrow of that piety which I have taught. . . . It is not in my power to recant them, because that recantation would give that tyranny and blasphemy an occasion to lord it over those whom I defend and to rage against God's people more violently than ever.

However, since I am a man and not God, I cannot provide my writings with any other defence than that which my Lord Jesus Christ provided for his teaching. When he had been interrogated concerning his teaching . . . and had received a buffet from a servant, he said: "If I have

"However, since I am a man and not God, I cannot provide my writings with any other defence than that which my Lord Jesus Christ provided for his teaching."

spoken evil, bear witness of the evil." If the Lord himself, who knew that he could not err, did not refuse to listen to witness against his teaching, even from a worthless slave, how much more ought I, scum that I am, capable of naught but error, to seek and to wait for any who may wish to bear witness against my teaching.

And so, through the mercy of God, I ask Your Imperial Majesty, and Your Illustrious Lordships, or anyone of any degree to bear witness, to overthrow my errors, to defeat them by the writings of the Prophets or by the Gospels; for I shall be most ready, if I be better instructed, to recant any error, and I shall be the first in casting my writings into the fire. . . .

Thereupon the Orator of the Empire, in a tone of upbraiding, said that his answer was not to the point. . . . He was being asked for a plain reply . . . to this question: Was he prepared to recant, or no?

Luther then replied: Your Imperial Majesty and Your Lordships demand a simple answer. Here it is, plain and unvarnished. Unless I am convicted of error by the testimony of Scripture or (since I put no trust in the unsupported authority of pope or of councils, since it is plain that they have often erred and often contradicted themselves) by manifest reasoning I stand convicted by the Scriptures to which I have appealed, and my conscience is taken captive by God's word, I cannot and will not recant anything, for to act against our conscience is neither safe for us, nor open to us.

On this I take my stand. I can do no other. God help me. Amen.

READING REVIEW

1. What three kinds of books did Luther admit to writing?
2. Under which conditions did Luther say he would recant?
3. Do you think there was any way for Luther to recant in good faith? Why or why not?

---

55 SPORTS IN ENGLAND

In medieval times most sports played in England—jousting, swordfighting, archery, wrestling, and so on—were related to military competition. Competing in such sports provided preparation and training for wartime. By the 1500s, however, sports that were played purely for recreation had developed. The excerpt below from The English *by Christopher Hibbert describes some of these sports. As you read the excerpt, note the early beginnings of soccer.*

While hunting remained the favourite pastime of the healthy, the adventurous and energetic, most gentlemen enjoyed quieter sports and games as well. Nearly everyone played bowls, and few country

The World Cup soccer match

houses were without their bowling-greens or bowling-alleys. The game was still played much as it had been in the time of Edward II, but the introduction of the bias, a heavy metal weight inserted into one side of the bowl, demanded much greater skill in play. Some houses also had courts for the playing of tennis, a game introduced from France where it seems to have originated as a sort of handball played in cathedral cloisters. There the game was known as *jeu de paume*, "palm game," the ball being struck with the palm of the hand, and its English name was probably derived from the French players' call of "Tenez!," "Watch out!," before serving. By the middle of the sixteenth century the game was being played in roofed courts with rackets and with harder balls made of bits of cloth tightly wadded together. . . . King Henry VII had had courts constructed at Blackfriars, Greenwich, Westminster and elsewhere; and his son, Henry VIII, a skilful player in his youth, had built tennis courts also at Whitehall, St James's and Hampton Court. By Elizabeth I's day fives, a form of handball played in a walled court with a gloved hand, was also popular; and fencing was becoming as widely practised among the upper classes . . . as archery and wrestling.

A kind of cricket was being played by the end of the century; but it had not yet caught the general fancy, whereas football had been played by the common people for centuries. With no generally accepted rules, it was a violent game in which "young men propel a huge ball not by throwing it into the air, but by striking and rolling it along the ground with their feet." It frequently led to quarrels and fights, sometimes to riot and murder. Constant efforts were made to control it. In the fourteenth and fifteenth centuries several proclamations were issued banning it . . . and imposing fines and even imprisonment on those who continued to play it. But it proved impossible to suppress and by the sixteenth century had become established as part of the social life of the country, being played everywhere on public holidays and on Sundays. The way in which it was played varied from place to place but in most there were no regulations as to the number of players on each side, no boundaries and no time limit. At Ashbourne in Derbyshire the goals were three miles apart and the game lasted all day. In Pembrokeshire . . . it was played with a wooden ball ("boyled in tallow to make it slipperye") by men stripped to the waist and with hair and beards so short their opponents could not get a grip on them. As many as 2000 players took part; and the confusion and violence was so great that a visitor who chanced upon the scene in 1588 observed, "If this be but playe, I cold wishe the Spaniardes were here to see our plaies in England. Certes they would be oodielye feare of our warre."

Football, indeed, according to [one Elizabethan spectator], was "a bloody and murderous practice."

> Doth not everyone lie in wait for his adversary, seeking to overthrow him and pitch him on the nose, though it be upon hard stones, in ditch or dale, in valley or hill, or what place soever it be? He careth not so he have him downe. . . . Sometimes their necks are broken, sometimes their backs, sometime their legs, sometime their arms; sometime one part thrust out of joint, some time another; sometime the noses gush out with blood, sometime their eyes start out. . . .

There were a few who saw good in the game. Richard Mulcaster, headmaster of St Paul's School, thought that the game "strengtheneth and brawneth the whole body." . . . But Mulcaster had to agree that as usually played in England, "with bursting of shins and breaking of legs, it be neither civil, [nor] worthy." If it were to become a game for gentlemen, rules would have to be made and referees introduced to enforce them.

READING REVIEW

1. What sports had developed by the 1500s?
2. What, according to the author, was the origin of the name *tennis*?
3. Why do you think football, or soccer, was such a violent game?

56 ON THE MOTION OF THE HEART AND BLOOD

William Harvey (1578–1657), the personal physician of James I and Charles I of England, published his revolutionary work On the Motion of the Heart and Blood *in 1628. He first described the circulation of the blood, however, to a group students at the London College of Physicians some 12 years earlier. In the excerpt below, Harvey describes the circular flow of the blood and the importance of the heart to the functioning of the body. As you read the excerpt, consider how important Harvey's breakthrough was to medical science.*

When I surveyed my mass of evidence, whether derived from vivisections, and my various reflections on them, or from the ventricles of the heart and the vessels that enter into and issue from them, the symmetry and size of these conduits—for nature doing nothing in vain would never have given them so large a relative size without a purpose—or from the arrangement and intimate structure of the valves in particular, and of the other parts of the heart in general, with many things besides, I frequently and seriously bethought me, and long revolved in my mind, what might be the quantity of blood which was transmitted, in how short a time its passage might be effected, and the like; and not finding it possible that this could be supplied by the juices of the ingested aliment without the veins on the one hand becoming drained, and the arteries on the other getting ruptured through the excessive charge of blood, unless the blood should somehow find its way from the arteries into the veins, and so return to the right side of the heart; I began to think whether there might not be *a motion, as it were, in a circle*. Now this I afterwards found to be true; and I finally saw that the blood, forced by the action of the left ventricle into the arteries, was distributed to the body at large, and its several parts, in the same manner as it is sent through the lungs, impelled by the right ventricle into the pulmonary artery, and that it then passed through the veins and along the vena cava, and so round to the left ventricle in the manner already indicated. Which motion we may be allowed to call circular. . . . The various parts are nourished, cherished, quickened by the warmer, more perfect, vaporous, spirituous, and, as I may say, alimentative blood; which, on the contrary, in contact with these parts becomes cooled, coagulated, and, so to speak, effete; whence it returns to its sovereign the heart, as if to its source, or to the inmost home of the body, there to recover its state of excellence or perfection. . . . The heart, consequently, is the beginning of life; the sun of the microcosm, even as the sun in his turn might well be designated the heart of the world; for it is the heart by whose virtue and pulse the blood is moved, perfected, made apt to nourish, and is preserved from corruption and coagulation.

READING REVIEW

1. On what did Harvey base his ideas on the flow of the blood?
2. To what celestial body did Harvey compare the heart? Why?
3. In your opinion, how important was Harvey's discovery to medical science? Explain your answer.

---

57 FIRST IMPRESSIONS OF THE NEW WORLD

After a two-month voyage across the Atlantic, Christopher Columbus made landfall in the West Indies on October 12, 1492. He spent the next three months exploring a number of islands in the Caribbean Sea. In February 1493, just before he began his homeward voyage, he sent a letter to the secretary of the Spanish treasury detailing his impressions of the land and people. As you read the excerpt of the letter from Renaissance and Reformation: 1300–1648, *edited by G. R. Elton, note Columbus's observations of the "Indians," as he called them, of the New World.*

European ships of the 1500s

Sir,—Believing that you will take pleasure in hearing of the great success which our Lord has granted me in my voyage, I write you this letter, whereby you will learn how in thirty-seven days' time I reached the Indies with the fleet which the most illustrious King and Queen, our sovereigns, gave to me, where I found very many islands thickly peopled, of all which I took possession without resistance for their Highnesses by proclamation made and with the royal standard unfurled. . . . When I reached Juana [Cuba], I followed its coast to the westward, and found it so large that I thought it must be the mainland,—the province of Cathay [China]; and, as I found neither towns nor villages on the sea-coast, but only a few hamlets, with the inhabitants of which I could not hold a conversation because they all immediately fled, I kept on the same route, thinking that I could not fail to light upon some large cities and towns. At length . . . I . . . returned to a certain harbour which I had remarked, and from which I sent two men ashore to ascertain whether there was any king or large cities in that part. They journeyed for three days and found countless small hamlets with numberless inhabitants, but with nothing like order; they therefore returned. In the meantime I had learned from some other Indians whom I had seized, that this land was certainly an island. . . . The lands are high and there are many very lofty mountains. . . . [The islands] are all most beautiful, of a thousand different shapes, accessible, and covered with trees of a thousand kinds of such great height that they seemed to reach the skies. . . . The nightingale was singing as well as other birds of a thousand different kinds; and that, in November, the month in which I myself was roaming amongst them. There are palm-trees of six or eight kinds, wonderful in their beautiful variety; but this is the case with all the other trees and fruits and grasses; trees, plants, or fruits filled us with admiration. It contains extraordinary pine groves, and very extensive plains. There is also honey, a great variety of birds, and many different kinds of fruits. In the interior there are many mines of metals and a population innumerable. . . . The inhabitants of this and of all the other islands I have found or gained intelligence of, both men and women, go as naked as they were born. . . . They have neither iron, nor steel, nor arms, nor are they competent to use them, not that they are not well-formed and of handsome stature, but because they are timid to a surprising degree.

On my reaching the Indies, I took by force, in the first island that I discovered, some of these natives that they might learn our language and give me information in regard to what existed in these parts; and it so happened that they soon understood us and we them, either by words or signs, and they have been very serviceable to us. They are still with me, and, from repeated conversations that I have had with them, I find that they still believe that I come from heaven. And they were the first to say this wherever I went, and the others ran from house to house and to the neighbouring villages, crying with a loud voice: "Come, come, and see the people from heaven!" And thus they all, men as well as women, after their minds were at rest about us, came, both large and small, and brought us something to eat and drink, which they gave us with extraordinary kindness. . . .

They assure me that there is another island larger than [Hispaniola] in which the inhabitants have no hair. It is extremely rich in gold; and I bring with me Indians taken from these different islands, who will testify to all these things. Finally, and speaking only of what has taken place in this voyage . . . their Highnesses may see that I shall give them all the gold they require, if they will give me but a little assistance; spices also, and cotton, as much as their Highnesses shall command to be shipped; and mastic, hitherto found only in Greece . . . ; slaves, as many of these idolators as their Highnesses shall command to be shipped. I think also I have found rhubarb and cinnamon, and I shall find a thousand other valuable things.

READING REVIEW

1. Where did Columbus think he had landed when he reached Cuba?
2. What was Columbus's impression of the lands he had found?
3. How do you think Columbus felt about the "Indians" he met? Explain your answer.

---

58 REVOLT IN BOHEMIA

When the Protestants of Bohemia refused to abide by his edicts, Holy Roman Emperor Matthias ordered the use of force against them. Two Catholic deputy-governors of Bohemia, Slavata and Martinitz, complied by imprisoning dozens of local government officials. In response, a mob of Bohemian Protestants, led by Count Matthias von Thurn, stormed the royal palace in Prague and tossed the two governors out of a window, thus beginning the first stage of the Thirty Years' War (1618–48). In the excerpt below from The Thirty Years' War, *historian C.V. Wedgwood describes the events that took place in May 1618. As you read the excerpt, consider why such a local affair led to a major war.*

Thurn called a meeting of Protestant officials and deputies from all over Bohemia and appealed for the release of the prisoners. When this demonstration proved useless, he urged . . . a yet larger assembly of Protestants. This second meeting was fixed for May 1618; it was now March. In the intervening time both parties set themselves to work up the feelings of the people and of the townsfolk of Prague in particular. In spite of Catholic propaganda the Protestant meeting assembled on May 21st, a formidable gathering of noblemen, gentry and burghers from all over the province. The imperial governors in vain commanded them to dissolve. Only then did Slavata and Martinitz grasp the danger in which they stood, and on the evening of the 22nd a secretary of state escaped in disguise towards Vienna to implore immediate help [from the Holy Roman Emperor].

It was too late. That very night Thurn called on the leading nobility to form a plan of action. . . . He demanded death for Slavata and Martinitz and the establishment of a Protestant emergency government. The city was already alive with excitement and when on the following morning the Protestant deputies were seen making their way towards the royal castle . . . an immense crowd followed in their wake. Through the portals surmounted by the outspread eagle of the Hapsburg they surged into the courtyard; up the staircase the deputies led the way, through the audience hall and into the small room where the governors sat. Trapped between the council table and the wall, the crowd before and the blank stones behind, Slavata and Martinitz stood at bay. Neither doubted that his last hour had come.

A hundred hands dragged them towards the high window, flung back the casement and hoisted them upwards. Martinitz went first. 'Jesu Maria! Help!' he screamed and crashed over the sill. Slavata fought longer, calling on the Blessed Virgin and clawing at the window frame under a rain of blows until someone knocked him senseless and the bleeding hands relaxed. Their shivering secretary clung to [one of the deputies] for protection; out of sheer intoxication the crowd hoisted him up and sent him to join his masters.

One of the rebels leant over the ledge, jeering: "We will see if your Mary can help you!" A second later, between exasperation and amazement, "By God, his Mary has helped," he exclaimed, for Martinitz was already stirring. Suddenly a ladder protruded from a neighbouring window; Martinitz and the secretary made for it under a hail of misdirected missiles. Some of Slavata's servants, braving the mob, went down to his help and carried him after the others, unconscious but alive.

The extraordinary chance which had saved three lives was a holy miracle or a comic accident according to the religion of the beholder, but it had no political significance. Martinitz fled that night in disguise and Slavata continued, ill and a prisoner, in the house whither he had been carried. That evening his wife knelt before the Countess Thurn entreating some guarantee for her husband's life, a request which the lady granted with the pessimistic stipulation that the Countess Slavata should do her a like service after the next Bohemian revolution.

Murder or no murder, the *coup d'état* was complete, and since Thurn had overruled many of his supporters in demanding death it was as well for the conscience of his allies that a pile of mouldering filth in the courtyard of the [royal palace] had made soft falling for the governors.

READING REVIEW

1. What demands did Thurn make on the night of May 22?
2. What saved Slavata and Martinitz from death?
3. Why do you think this incident led to the outbreak of war?

59 A DAY IN THE LIFE OF LOUIS XIV

For much of his reign, Louis XIV resided at the palace of Versailles. There he established a lavish court, which the country's leading nobles were expected to attend. Life at Versailles revolved around the king, and the simplest events of his day, such as getting dressed or going to bed, were accompanied by pomp and ceremony in which the court was required to take part. In the excerpt below from The Memoirs of Saint-Simon, *one of Louis' courtiers, the Duc de Saint-Simon, describes a typical day at Versailles. As you read the excerpt, consider what the day's activities tell you about the character of Louis XIV.*

At eight o'clock every morning the King was awoken by his First *Valet-de-Chambre*, who slept in the room with him. At the same time the First Physician and First Surgeon were admitted; and as long as she lived the King's former wet-nurse also came in and would kiss him. He would then be rubbed down, because he perspired a great deal. At a quarter past eight the Great Chamberlain was admitted, together with those members of the court who had the *grandes entrées*. The Great Chamberlain then opened the curtains round the bed . . . and offered him holy water from a stoup at the head of the bed. This was the chance for any courtier who wished to ask a favor or to speak to the King, and if one did so the others withdrew to a distance.

The Chamberlain then handed the King the book of the Office of the Holy Ghost, and having done so retired to the next room with everyone else. The King said the Office . . . and then, putting on his dressing-gown, summoned them back into the room; meanwhile the second *entrée* was admitted and, a few minutes later, the body of the court. By the time they came in the King was getting into his breeches (for he put on nearly all his clothes himself), which he accomplished with considerable grace. He was shaved every other day, with the court watching; while it was being done he wore a short wig, without which he never allowed himself to be seen. . . . While his barber was at work he sometimes talked to those around him, about hunting or some other light topic. He had no dressing-table at hand, only a servant who held up a glass for him.

"He was shaved every other day, with the court watching."

When he had finished dressing he knelt down at the side of his bed and said his prayers. . . . Next the King went into his study, followed by those permitted to do so—which, as a number of appointments carried this privilege, amounted to quite a gathering. He then announced his appointments for the day, so that everyone knew what he would be doing every quarter of an hour. Then the room was cleared. . . .

The courtiers waited in the Gallery until the king was ready to go to Mass, at which the choir always sang a motet. The Ministers were told as soon as he had gone to the chapel, and they then gathered in the King's study. . . . As soon as Mass was over the Council met, and that was the last engagement for the morning. One or other of the Councils met every day except Thursdays and Fridays—Thursday was kept free, and the few private audiences which the King very occasionally granted took place then; on Friday he used to make his confession, and his confessor would often stay with him until dinner-time. Dinner was [usually] at one. . . .

Dinner was always *au petit couvert*—that is to say, the King ate alone in his bedroom. . . . The meal was substantial whether he had ordered *petit couvert* or *trés-petit couvert,* for even the latter consisted of three courses, each made up of several different dishes. . . . Monsieur [the King's brother] often attended, and when present always handed the King his napkin and then remained standing. If the King saw that he intended to remain, he would ask him if he wished to be seated: Monsieur would bow . . . and sit down. He would remain seated until the end of the meal, when he would again hand the King his napkin. . . .

As soon as he had finished his dinner the King rose from the table and went into his study, where he spent time feeding his pointers and playing with them. Then he changed . . . after which he went down to the Marble Court by his own private staircase. . . . He liked fresh air, and if he could not get it he suffered from headaches and vapours, which had originally been caused by too much perfume—with the consequence that for years he had not cared for anything except orange water, and anyone who was going to approach him had to be very careful about this.

He felt neither heat nor cold, and wet weather affected him very little—it had to be very bad indeed to stop him from going out. At least once a week, and more if he were at [his estates at] Marly or Fontainebleau, he went stag-hunting. Once or twice a week he shot his own coverts, usually choosing Sundays or feast-days when there were no works for him to inspect; he was a first-class shot. Most other days he would walk round having a look at whatever building was in progress. Occasionally he would take ladies out and have a picnic in the forests of Marly or Fontainebleau. . . .

If there was no Council he often went over to Marly or Trianon for dinner. . . . After dinner one of the Ministers usually came in with some work, and when that was done he would pass the rest of a summer afternoon strolling with the ladies or playing cards. Sometimes he would get up a lottery in which there were no blanks, and every ticket drew a prize of plate, jewellery, or a dress length of rich material, which was a delicate way of making presents to the ladies about him. . . .

The King's supper was served, always *au grand couvert,* at ten o'clock, and the entire Royal Family sat down with him. [A frequent complaint was that the King was late and the meal often did not start until eleven-thirty.] The meal was attended by a large number of people, both those who were entitled to be seated and those who were not. . . .

After supper the King would stand by the balustrade at the foot of his bed for a few minutes, with the whole court about him; then he would bow to the ladies and retire into his study, where he played for an hour or so with his children and grandchildren. . . .

Before he retired to bed the King went to feed his dogs; then he said good-night and, going into his room, knelt down at his bedside to say his prayers. After he had undressed he would bow, which meant 'Good-night,' and at that sign all the court retired. As they filed out he, standing by the fire-place, gave the password to the Captain of the Guard. It was the last opportunity for the day of speaking to the King, and if anyone stepped forward the others withdrew at once and left him alone with the King.

READING REVIEW

1. What normally was the king's last official engagement of the morning?
2. What in the excerpt suggests that Louis XIV enjoyed outdoor life?
3. What does the routine of life at Versailles tell you about Louis XIV's character?

60 THE GREAT CZAR

When Peter the Great died, many Russians felt they had lost a leader of incredible brilliance and perception. One such person was the Archbishop of Novgorod, Feofan Prokopovich (1681–1736), a trusted and loyal adviser to Peter on religious affairs. In the excerpt below, taken from the oration he delivered at Peter's funeral, Prokopovich underscores Peter's greatness by comparing him to great Biblical figures. As you read the excerpt, ask yourself whether Prokopovich's opinion of Peter can be trusted.

What is this? O Russians, what have we lived to witness? What do we see? What are we doing? We are burying Peter the Great! Is it not a dream, an apparition? Alas, our sorrow is real, our misfortune certain! Contrary to everybody's wishes and hopes he has come to his life's end, he who has been the cause of our innumerable good fortunes and joys; who has raised Russia as if from among the dead and elevated her to such heights of power and glory; or better still, he who—like a true father of the fatherland—has given birth to Russia and nursed her. Such were his merits that all true sons of Russia wished him to be immortal; while his age and solid constitution gave everyone the expectation of seeing him alive for many more years; he has ended his life—o, horrible wound!—at a time when he was just beginning to live after many labors, troubles, sorrows, calamities, and perils of death. . . . But why intensify our complaints and pity which we ought to assuage. How can we do it? For if we recall his great talents, deeds, and actions we shall feel the wound from the loss of such great good, and we shall burst into tears. Alone a kind of lethargy or a death-like sleep can make us forget this truly great loss.

What manner of man did we lose? He was your Samson, Russia. No one in the world expected his appearance among you, and at his appearance the whole world marveled. He found but little strength in you, and on the model of his name he made your power strong like a rock and diamond. Finding an army that was disorderly at home, weak in the field, the butt of the enemy's derision, he created one that was useful to the fatherland, terrible to the enemy, renowned and glorious everywhere. In defending his fatherland he at the same time returned to it

Peter the Great disguised as a carpenter

lands that had been wrested from it and augmented it by the acquisition of new provinces. Destroying those who had arisen against us, he at the same time broke and destroyed those who had evil designs on us; and closing the mouth of envy, he commanded the whole world to glorify him.

Russia, he was your first Japhet! He has accomplished a deed heretofore unheard of in Russia: the building and sailing of ships, of a new fleet that yields to none among the old ones. It was a deed beyond the whole world's expectation and admiration, and it opened up to thee, Russia, the way to all corners of the earth and carried thine power and glory to the remotest oceans, to the very limits set by thy own interests and by justice. Thine power which had been based on land he also has established on the sea, firmly and permanently.

He was your Moses, o Russia! For are not his laws like the strong visor of justice and the unbreakable fetters of crime! And do not his clear regulations illuminate your path, most high governing Senate, and that of all principal and particular administrations established by him! Are they not beacons of light in your search for what will be useful and what will avoid harm, for the security of the law-abiding and the detection of criminals. In truth, he has left us wondering wherein he has been best and most deserving of praise; was he loved and caressed more by good and honest men than hated by unrepentant sycophants and criminals?

O Russia, he was your Solomon, who received from the Lord reason and wisdom in great plenty. This is proven by the manifold philosophic disciplines introduced by him and by his showing and imparting to many of his subjects the knowledge of a variety of inventions and crafts unknown to us before his time. To this also bear witness the ranks and titles, the civil laws, the rules of social intercourse, propitious customs, and codes of behavior, and also the improvement of our external appearance. We see and marvel then at our fatherland; it has changed externally and internally, and it has become immeasurably better than it had been previously. . . .

Most distinguished man! Can a short oration encompass his immeasurable glory? . . . Probably, in course of time, the thorns that butt our heart will dull, and then we shall speak of his deeds and virtues in fuller detail, even though we shall never be able to praise him adequately enough. But at this time, even remembering him but briefly, as if only touching on the edges of his mantle, we see, my poor and unfortunate hearers, we see who has left us and whom we have lost.

READING REVIEW

1. According to Prokopovich why did Peter's death come as a surprise?
2. Which of Peter's accomplishments did Prokopovich mention in his funeral oration?
3. Should we trust Prokopovich's opinion of Peter's greatness? Why or why not?

61 THE GUNPOWDER PLOT

English Catholics were involved in a number of attempts to assassinate Protestant monarchs and to place a person of their own faith on the throne. Perhaps the most spectacular of these conspiracies was the Gunpowder Plot of 1605, which was designed to blow up Parliament while King James I was in attendance. The excerpt below from A Jacobean Journal *by G. B. Harrison details the discovery of the conspiracy. The conspirator John Johnson's real name was Guy Fawkes, and to this day, effigies of Fawkes—commonly called "Guys"—are burnt to commemorate the foiling of the plot on November 5. As you read the excerpt, consider how and why the plot was discovered.*

[1605] 5th November (Tuesday).
A Most Horrible Conspiracy Discovered.

Very early this morning a most horrible conspiracy of the Papists against the King and the whole realm was discovered, being no less than to destroy the Parliament House and all therein by gunpowder this day.

About ten days since, the Lord Mounteagle . . . , being in his lodging in the Strand ready to go to supper about 7 of the clock, one of his footmen was met in the street by an unknown man who delivered him a letter, charging him to put it straightway into his lord's hands. The Lord Mounteagle, perceiving it to be in an unknown and somewhat unlegible hand, called one of his men to help him to read it, the tenor whereof was that my Lord should devise some excuse to shift off his attendance of this Parliament, "for," said this unknown writer, "God and men have concurred to punish the wickedness of this time; and think not slightly of this advertisement, but retire yourself into your country, where you may expect the event in safety; for though there be no appearance of any stir, yet I say, they shall receive a terrible blow this Parliament, and yet they shall not see who hurts them. This counsel is not to be [scorned], because it may do you good, and can do you no harm; for the danger is past as soon as you have burnt the letter."

Hereupon my Lord was greatly perplexed what construction to make thereof, whether it was a matter of great consequence, or some foolish [lampoon] (such as at this time abound), or some device of his enemies. Nevertheless, notwithstanding the darkness of the night, he went straightway to the Court at Whitehall and delivered the letter to the Earl of Salisbury, who gave him [suitable] thanks and encouragement. So the Earl of Salisbury showed the letter to the Lord Chamberlain, and to the Lord Admiral, and the Earls of Worcester and Northampton, who all agreed to acquaint the King withal when he should return from Royston, which was on Friday last.

Therefore the Earl of Salisbury alone in the Privy Gallery acquainted the King with all their proceeding. The King having read the letter once, paused awhile and read it again, and said he thought it was not to be

British women preparing to celebrate Guy Fawkes Day on November 5

[scorned], for the style seemed to be more quick and pithy than is usual in [lampoons] and libels or superfluities of idle brains. . . . [And he] conjectured that the danger should be some sudden danger by blowing up with powder, for it was not possible for them to endanger the King and State either by insurrection, invasion, rebellion or any other of like nature that might be suddenly attempted in this time of Parliament. The King was not in any way amazed, but wished that a very secret and exact search should be made in the Parliament House and all rooms and lodgings adjoining. . . .

. . . The next day (which was Saturday) the Earl renewed the matter with the King, the Lord Chamberlain being then present, and it was determined that the Lord Chamberlain . . . should view the Parliament House and all other places adjoining, and should do it with such [stealth] as would prevent idle rumours, or giving of any suspicion to the workers of this mischievous mystery.

Yesterday therefore in the afternoon the Lord Chamberlain, accompanied with the Lord Mounteagle, entering the cellar under the upper

House [of Parliament], found great store of [firewood] and coals, which he learnt were Master Thomas Percy's, who is kinsman to my Lord of Northumberland. As the Lord Chamberlain looked about him . . . he espied a fellow standing in a corner who said that he was Percy's man and keeper of the house for him. So the Lord Chamberlain went back to the King . . . to whom he made report, adding further that when the Lord Mounteagle heard the fellow (whose name is John Johnson) declare himself to be Mr. Thomas Percy's man, remembering Percy's backwardness in religion and his friendship to himself, he thought that he was a very desperate fellow and would have the chamber very narrowly searched.

The King instantly agreed to search thoroughly. . . . And Sir Thomas Knivett was selected for the business, accompanied with a small number specially fit for that employment.

At midnight therefore Sir Thomas went about the search, and coming before the entry to Percy's house, he perceived the pretended servant standing without the door, booted and spurred, whom he apprehended and was very desirous to search; but this Johnson, being wondrously unwilling to be searched, violently gripped one Mr. Doubleday by his fingers of the left hand, who would have drawn his dagger, but bethought himself and did not; and in the heat he struck up the fellow's heels, fell upon him and searched him, and in his pocket found . . . some touchwood, a tinder box and a match. Within the house, when they had removed some [firewood] and coals, they found a small barrel of powder, and afterwards many others, great and small, to the number of thirty-six, with other instruments fit for the purpose.

When Johnson saw his treasons discovered, he instantly confessed his own guiltiness, saying that if he had been within the house when they first laid hands upon him, he would have blown up them, himself and all.

So Sir Thomas Knivett comes to the Lord Chamberlain and the Earl of Salisbury, who forthwith draw together all the rest of Council which lay within the Court, and this morning about 4 of the clock they come to the King's bedchamber, where the Lord Chamberlain, in a confused haste, tells the King that all is discovered, and the traitor taken. Immediately upon this all the Council that lay abroad were summoned to Court, where they sit in council and examine the fellow, who will acknowledge no other name but John Johnson, flatly denying to know any other [plotters] in this treason, justifying the deed, and denying the King to be his liege Lord or God's anointed. He is quick and careless in his answers unto all objections, [sneering] and scoffing [at] all that mislike him, repenting only that the deed was not done.

Hereupon order is given to the Lord Mayor of London, and the City of Westminster to set a civil watch at the gates; and a proclamation is set forth for the apprehending of Thomas Percy.

It is not as yet known how far this treason may extend, though it is well perceived to be practised and commenced by some discontented papists, and everywhere there is a general jealousy. The common people mutter and imagine many things, and the nobles know not whom to clear or whom to suspect. The King hath deferred his coming to Parliament till Saturday next.

This night there were as many bonfires in and about London as the streets could permit, the people praising God for His mercy, and wishing that the day may for ever be held festival.

READING REVIEW

1. Why was Lord Mounteagle perplexed as to the importance of the letter?
2. Why did the search of Parliament need to be done with as much stealth as possible?
3. **(a)** Who do you think the unknown man was who delivered the letter to Lord Mounteagle? **(b)** Why do you think Lord Mounteagle was warned of the plot?

---

62 CHARLES I'S SPEECH ON THE SCAFFOLD

During his trial and judgment, Charles I was given no real opportunity to answer the charges brought against him. His first chance to comment publicly came on the day of his execution—January 30, 1649. The excerpt below is taken from his speech on the scaffold, which was published just a few hours after the execution. As you read the excerpt, note the advice Charles gave to those who had condemned him.

I shall be very little heard of anybody here, I shall therefore speak a word unto you. Indeed I could hold my peace very well, if I did not think that holding my peace would make some men think I did submit to the guilt as well as to the punishment. But I think it is my duty to God first and to my country for to clear myself both as an honest man and a good King, and a good christian. I shall begin first with my innocency. In truth I think it not very needful for me to insist long upon this, for all the world knows that I never did begin a war with the two Houses of Parliament. And I call God to witness, to whom I must shortly make an account, that I never did intend to encroach upon their privileges. They began upon me.... And, to be short, if any body will look to the dates of Commissions, of their commissions and mine, and likewise to the Declarations, will see clearly that they began these unhappy troubles, not I. So that as the guilt of these enormous crimes that are laid against me I hope in God that God will clear me of it.... God forbid that I should lay it upon the two Houses of Parliament; there is no necessity of either, I hope that they are free of this guilt.... Yet, for all this, God forbid that I should be so ill a christian as not to say God's judgments are just upon me. Many times he does pay justice by an unjust sentence, that is ordinary. I will only say this that an unjust sentence that I suffered for

The execution of Charles I

to take effect, is punished now by an unjust sentence upon me. That is, so far as I have said, to show you that I am an innocent man.

Now for to show you that I am a good christian. I hope there is a good man that will bear me witness that I have forgiven all the world, and even those in particular that have been the chief causes of my death. Who are they, God knows, I do not desire to know, God forgive them. But this is not all, my charity must go further. I wish that they may repent, for indeed they have committed a great sin in that particular. . . . Nay, not only so, but that they may take the right way to the peace of the kingdom, for my charity commands me not only to forgive particular men, but my charity commands me to endeavour to the last gasp the Peace of the Kingdom. So, sirs, I do wish with all my soul, and I do hope there is some here that will carry it further, that they may endeavour the peace of the Kingdom.

Now, Sirs, I must show you both how you are out of the way and will put you in a way. First, you are out of the way, for certainly all the way you have ever had yet, as I could find by anything, is by way of conquest. Certainly this is an ill way, for conquest, Sir, in my opinion is never just. . . . And so, Sir, I do think you the way that you are in is much out of the way. Now, Sir, for to put you in the way. Believe it you will never do right, nor God will never prosper you, until you give God his due, the King his due (that is, my successors) and the people their due, I am as much for them as any of you. You must give God his due by regulating rightly His Church (according to the Scripture) which is now out of order. For to set you in a way particularly now I cannot, but only this. A national synod freely called, freely debating among themselves, must settle this, when that every opinion is freely and clearly heard.

For the King, . . . the laws of the land will clearly instruct you for that. Therefore because it concerns my own particular, I only give you a touch of it.

For the people. And truly I desire their liberty and freedom as much as anybody whomsoever. But I must tell you that their liberty and freedom consists in having of government; those laws by which their life and their goods may be most their own. It is not for having share in government, Sir, that is nothing pertaining to them. A subject and a sovereign are clean different things, and therefore until they do that, I mean, that you do put the people in that liberty as I say, certainly they will never enjoy themselves.

Sirs. It was for this that now I am come here. If I would have given way to an arbitrary way, for to have all the laws changed according to the power of the sword I needed not to have come here. And, therefore, I tell you, and I pray God it be not laid to your charge, that I am the martyr of the people.

"That in truth I could have desired some little time longer. . .

In truth, Sirs, I shall not hold you much longer, for I will only say thus to you. That in truth I could have desired some little time longer, because I would have put then that I have said in a little more order, and a little better digested than I have done. And, therefore, I hope that you will excuse me.

I have delivered my conscience. I pray God that you do take those courses that are best for the good of the Kingdom and your own salvations.

READING REVIEW

1. Why did Charles choose not to hold his peace?
2. What, according to Charles, was the right course for his accusers to take?
3. What in Charles's speech suggests that he had not changed his ideas about absolutism?

63 THE FALL OF JAMES II

Many people in Great Britain found James II's open practice of the Catholic faith threatening and distasteful. His efforts to win freedom of worship for his fellow Catholics through the Declaration of Liberty of Conscience were met with opposition from Parliament and the Anglican church. Then, when James's Catholic wife gave birth to a son, a number of leaders in Parliament took steps to ensure the Protestant succession, inviting Prince William of Orange to take the throne. The excerpt below, taken from the diary of John Evelyn, discusses the events of the last few months of James's reign. As you read the excerpt, ask yourself what public opinion was of the events of 1688.

1688

18th May. The King enjoining the ministers to read his Declaration for giving liberty of conscience (as it was styled) in all the churches of England, this evening, six Bishops . . . in the name of all the rest of the Bishops, came to his Majesty to petition him, that he would not impose the reading of it . . . ; not that they were averse to the publishing it for want of due tenderness towards Dissenters, in relation to whom they should be willing to come to such a temper as should be thought fit, when that matter might be considered and settled in Parliament and Convocation; but that, the Declaration being founded on such a dispensing power as might at pleasure set aside all laws ecclesiastical and civil, it appeared to them illegal. . . .

The King was so far incensed at this address, that he with threatening expressions commanded them to obey him in reading it at their perils, and so dismissed them. . . .

8th June. This day, the Archbishop of Canterbury, with the Bishops of Ely, Chichester, St. Asaph, Bristol, Peterborough, and Bath and Wells, were sent from the Privy Council prisoners to the Tower, for refusing to give bail for their appearance, on their not reading the Declaration for liberty of conscience. . . .

10th June. A *young Prince* born, which will cause disputes.

About two o'clock, we heard the Tower-ordnance discharged, and the bells ring for the birth of a Prince of Wales. . . .

29th June. [The Bishops] appeared [in court]; the trial lasted from nine in the morning to past six in the evening, when the Jury retired to consider of their verdict, and the Court adjourned to nine the next morning. The Jury were locked up till that time, eleven of them being for an acquittal; but one (Arnold, a brewer) would not consent. At length he agreed with the others. . . . When this was heard, there was great rejoicing; and there was a lane of people from the King's Bench to the waterside, on their knees, as the Bishops passed and repassed, to beg their blessing. Bonfires were made that night, and bells rung, which was taken very ill at Court. . . .

10th August. Dr. Tenison now told me there would suddenly be some great thing discovered. This was the Prince of Orange intending to come over. . . .

18th September. I went to London, where I found the Court in the utmost consternation on report of the Prince of Orange's landing; which put Whitehall into [such] panic [and] fear, that I could hardly believe it possible to find such a change.

Writs were issued in order to a Parliament. . . .

30th September. The Court in so extraordinary a consternation, on assurance of the Prince of Orange's intention to land, that the writs sent forth for a Parliament were recalled. . . .

14th October. The King's Birthday. No guns from the Tower as usual. The sun eclipsed at its rising. This day signal for the victory of William the Conqueror against Harold, near Battel, in Sussex. The wind, which had been hitherto west, was east all this day. Wonderful expectation of the Dutch fleet. Public prayers ordered to be read in the churches against invasion.

28th October. A tumult in London on the rabble demolishing a Popish chapel that had been set up in the City. . . .

5th November. I went to London; heard the news of the Prince having landed at Torbay, coming with a fleet of near 700 sail, passing through the Channel with so favourable a wind, that our navy could not intercept, or molest them. This put the King and the Court into great consternation, they were now employed in forming an army to stop their further progress, for they were got into Exeter, and the season and ways very improper for his Majesty's forces to march so great a distance. . . .

14th November. The Prince increases every day in force. Several Lords go in to him. Lord Cornbury carries some regiments, and marches to Honiton, the Prince's headquarters. The City of London in disorder; the rabble pulled down the nunnery . . . at St. John's. . . .

2nd December. . . . The great favourites at Court, Priests and Jesuits, fly or abscond. . . . The Papists in offices lay down their commissions and fly. Universal consternation amongst them; it looks like a revolution. . . .

9th December. . . . The rabble demolished all Popish chapels, and several Papist lords' and gentlemen's houses, especially that of the Spanish Ambassador, which they pillaged, and burnt his library.

13th December. The King flies to sea, puts in at Faversham for ballast; is rudely treated by the people; comes back to Whitehall. . . .

18th December. I saw the King take barge to Gravesend at twelve o'clock—a sad sight! The Prince comes to St. James's, and fills Whitehall with Dutch guards. . . .

All the world [went] to see the Prince at St. James's, where there is a great Court. There I saw him. . . . He is very stately, serious, and reserved. . . .

24th December. The King passes into France, whither the Queen and child were gone a few days before.

26th December. The Peers and such Commoners as were members of the Parliament at Oxford, being the last of Charles II's meeting, desire the Prince of Orange to take on him the disposal of the public revenue till a convention of Lords and Commons should meet in full body.

READING REVIEW

1. Why did the bishops refuse to read the Declaration of Liberty of Conscience?
2. To what other invasion did Evelyn compare the coming of Prince William of Orange?
3. Based on the entries in Evelyn's diary, how would you describe the feelings of the general public about the events of 1688? Explain your answer.

---

64 THE COLONISTS' VIEW OF TAXATION

After the passage of the Stamp Act, the Massachusetts legislature called for all colonies to attend a meeting to discuss the attack on their liberties by the British government. This meeting, called the Stamp Act Congress, took place in New York in the fall of 1765. The delegates issued a Declaration of Rights and Grievances, *which outlined their view of taxation and called for the repeal of the hated act. The excerpt below contains sections of the Declaration. As you read the excerpt, consider which fundamental right the colonists thought the Stamp Act violated.*

The members of this Congress, sincerely devoted, with the warmest sentiments of affection and duty to his majesty's person and government, inviolably attached to the present happy establishment of the protestant succession and with minds deeply impressed by a sense of the present and impending misfortunes of the British colonies on this continent, having considered as maturely as time would permit, the circumstances of the said colonies, esteem it our indispensable duty to make the following declarations, of our humble opinion respecting the most essential rights and liberties of the colonists, and of the grievances under which they labor, by reason of several late acts of parliament.

1st. That his majesty's subjects in these colonies owe the same allegiance to the crown of Great Britain, that is owing from his subjects born within the realm, and all due subordination to the august body, the parliament of Great Britain.

2d. That his majesty's subjects in these colonies are entitled to all the inherent rights and privileges of his natural born subjects within the kingdom of Great Britain.

3d. That it is inseparably essential to the freedom of the people, and the undoubted rights of Englishmen, that no taxes should be imposed on them, but with their own consent, given personally, or by their representatives.

4th. That the people of these colonies are not, and from their local circumstances, cannot be, represented in the House of Commons in Great Britain.

5th. That the only representatives of the people of the colonies, are persons chosen therein, by themselves; and that no taxes ever have been, or can be constitutionally imposed on them, but by their respective legislatures.

6th. That all supplies to the crown, being free gifts of the people, it is unreasonable and inconsistent with the principles and spirit of the British constitution, for the people of Great Britain to grant his majesty, the property of the colonies. . . .

8th. That the late act of parliament, entitled, An act for granting and applying certain stamp duties, and other duties in the British colonies and plantations in America, etc. by imposing taxes on the inhabitants of these colonies, and the said act, and several other acts, by extending the jurisdiction of the courts of admiralty beyond its ancient limits, have a manifest tendency to subvert the rights and liberties of the colonists. . . .

12th. That the increase, prosperity, and happiness of these colonies depend on the full and free enjoyment of their rights and liberties, and an intercourse with Great Britain, mutually affectionate and advantageous. . . .

Lastly, That it is the indispensable duty of these colonies to the best of sovereigns, to the mother country, and to themselves, to endeavor by a loyal and dutiful address to his majesty, and humble application to both houses of parliament, to procure the repeal of the act for granting and applying certain stamp duties [and] of all clauses of any other acts of parliament, whereby the jurisdiction of the admiralty is extended as aforesaid, and of the other late acts for the restriction of the American commerce.

READING REVIEW

1. According to the Declaration, how did the colonists compare to the King's subjects born in Great Britain?
2. Who, according to the Declaration, were the only representatives of the people in the colonies?
3. Which famous slogan used by the colonists in their struggle with Great Britain best sums up the Declaration?

65 THE PEOPLE STATE THEIR GRIEVANCES

In the late 1780s, the Third Estate of France reeled under the weight of excessive taxes. When it became clear that Louis XVI would call a meeting of the Estates-General, many members of the Third Estate petitioned the assembly for tax relief. The excerpt below from The French Revolution, *edited by Philip Dawson, lists the grievances of the people of Arceville, a small village about 25 miles north of Orleans. As you read the excerpt, note the changes in the tax system proposed by the people of Arceville.*

Parisian flower sellers protesting the Old Regime

The said inhabitants hope that the goodness of the King, in whom they put all their confidence, and the enlightenment of the Estates-General will reform the abuses which have crept into the finances up to the present time, so that the money collected from them no longer passes through so many hands, in which it is diminished, but goes directly to the treasury to provide for the needs of the State, to which they are always ready to contribute, like His Majesty's other subjects; and as it is with confidence that they hope for the reform of abuses, they propose their particular grievances as follows:

1. The said inhabitants observe that they alone have been charged with the mass of the taxes, while their seigneur, who farms much of the land in the parish, enjoys total exemption, although he has had a great part of the land planted with woods, which are populated by game that devastates the rest of the countryside; and that the woods, as well as the avenues he has had planted in great quantity, damage and almost destroy the neighboring lands, so that these lands, even in better years, yield no harvest. Wherefore they ask that, concurrently with them and without any distinction of title or rank, the said seigneur be taxed like them, as well as all the other seigneurs who possess property in this parish . . . and that everyone be permitted to destroy the game which ruins his crop.

2. They complain that the tithe and the *champart* take a large part of the compost from their lands, so that, far from being able to improve their lands, they sadly watch them deteriorate annually through the removal of straw and fodder that would serve not only for the enrichment of their lands but also for the nourishment of their cattle. Wherefore they ask that the tithe and the *champart* be abolished, or at least converted into an annual payment in money.

3. That in this province there is a tax that perhaps does not exist elsewhere, which is the tax on importation and exportation of wine. . . . Wherefore they petition that the said tax on wines and other drinks be abolished as to importation, or at least made similar to those in the other provinces of the kingdom. . . .

5. The said inhabitants observe that they pay an infinity of taxes although knowing neither their origin nor the laws in virtue of which they pay them: among others, a tax of one per cent on the stipulated value of the rings and jewels provided for the bride in a marriage contract; a tax which was never asked for, which has only been required for about six months, and which occasions scandalous investigations into all the marriage contracts in the last twenty years and more. Wherefore they petition that all the taxes be abolished which presently exist and were not consented to by the Nation assembled, . . . and that in the future no tax can be established, either permanently or temporarily, without the consent of the whole Nation assembled in Estates-General.

As for the rest, the said inhabitants declare that they leave it to what is to be decided in the assembly of the Estates-General.

Done and adopted in the general assembly of all the inhabitants of the said parish of Arceville, this day, March 3, 1789.

READING REVIEW

1. What was the major grievance of the people of Arceville?
2. What impact did the payment of the tithe and the *champart* have on the farms of Arceville?
3. According to the people of Arceville, how should the French tax system be changed?

---

66 THE SENTENCING OF LOUIS XVI

In January 1793, after finding Louis XVI guilty of treason and of threatening the security of France, the National Convention went on to debate and vote on his fate. The excerpt below from Voices of the French Revolution, *edited by Richard Cobb, contains part of the debate. The excerpt shows that voting went along party lines. The conservative Girondins were against executing the king, whereas the radical Montagnards—so named because they occupied the seats in the Montagne, or "mountain", high up on the left side of the assembly hall—demanded that Louis pay with his life. Members of the moderate Plain party—who sat in the central, lower-level seats—were fairly evenly split on the issue. As you read the excerpt, consider whether the National Convention was justified in sentencing Louis to death.*

The Debate

VERGNIAUD (Girondin): I voted that the decree or verdict of the National Convention should be put to the people for approval. The National Convention decided otherwise. I obey; my conscience is clear. It is now a matter of ruling on Louis' punishment. The law says death, but as I utter this terrible word I fear for the fate of my country, the dangers which threaten even freedom, and all the blood which may be shed.

GUADET (Girondin): Louis is guilty of conspiring against liberty and the general security of the state. I have only to look at the penal code to see the death penalty there; but I demand the Convention's permission to consider whether the verdict should be carried out immediately, or delayed. I vote, provisionally, for death.

GENSONNE (Girondin): I vote for the application of the penalty for conspiracy. But so as to prove to Europe and the entire world that we are not the passive tools of one faction, I vote that you command the Ministry of Justice to bring the murderers of [the September Massacres] to justice.

LACAZE (Girondin): Citizens, Louis has spilt much blood; but will not this war which he has brought upon us shed more? Should we not use Louis' life to prevent it? From the depths of my conscience I vote for imprisonment until there is peace, and until such time as foreign powers have recognized the republic; and then for exile.

GARRAU (Montagnard): Citizens, Louis is convicted of conspiracy against national safety. The statute book shows the death penalty for all conspirators; I vote for death.

Marie Antoinette on the way to the guillotine

CAMBON (Montagnard): The will of the whole French nation is perfectly clear: to abolish all privilege. Today I am to pass judgement on one of the privileged who has been convicted of treason, and I would consider myself guilty under national justice if I restricted myself to deportation. I vote for death.

CAMBACERES (Plain): In my opinion the National Convention should decree that Louis has incurred the penalties for conspiracy, but it should suspend execution of the decree until the cessation of hostilities. Until that time he should remain in prison; if the enemies of the republic should invade French territory, the decree should be carried out.

LANJUINAIS (Girondin): As an individual I would vote for the death for Louis; but as legislator, mindful only of the nation's welfare and the interests of freedom, I vote for imprisonment until the restoration of peace, and then for exile, under pain of death if he should return to France.

AMAR (Montagnard): Louis has been found guilty of assault on the general security of the nation, and of conspiring against freedom; his existence is odious, his death is necessary to consolidate a Revolution to which he will always be opposed. I am resolved for his death.

DARTIGOEYTE (Montagnard): As a judge, I must avenge the blood of citizens spilt by the orders of the tyrant; as a statesman, I must do what seems in the best interests of the republic: I myself fear the return of tyranny if Louis lives. I vote for his immediate death.

CHABOT (Montagnard): I vote for death because Louis was, and still is, a tyrant, and because he may act as such again. I vote for death.

FOUCHE (Montagnard): Death.

JEAN-BON SAINT-ANDRE (Montagnard): Any nation which has sought freedom has achieved it only through the death of tyrants. I vote for death.

DROUET (Montagnard): Louis has conspired against the state. He opened the gates of the kingdom to our enemies. I condemn him to death.

ANACHARSIS CLOOTS (Montagnard): Louis is guilty of [treason]. How should his crimes be punished? In the name of humanity I answer, death.

ROBESPIERRE (Montagnard): [From a long speech] I am no lover of long speeches on obvious matters; they augur ill for freedom. I vote for death.

DANTON (Montagnard): One must never compromise with tyrants. One can only strike at kings through the head; nothing can be expected from European kings except by force of arms. I vote for the death of the tyrant.

BILLAUD-VARENNES (Montagnard): Death within twenty-four hours.

MARAT (Montagnard): From my profound conviction that Louis is the principal protagonist behind the spilling of so much blood . . . and all the killing which has disfigured France since the Revolution, I vote for the tyrant's death within twenty-four hours.

LEGENDRE (Montagnard): Since the Revolution I have devoted myself to hunting down tyrants. I vote for death. I respect the opinion of my colleagues who have voted for a different penalty, through political considerations. It is this same policy which makes me vote for death.

DAVID (Montagnard): Death.

PHILIPPE EGALITE [Formerly the duc d'Orléans] (Montagnard): In my conviction that all those who have attacked the sovereignty of the people deserve death, I vote for death.

THOMAS PAINE (Girondin): I vote that Louis be imprisoned until the end of the war, and exiled for life thereafter.

BARERE (Montagnard): The law proclaims death, and I am here as a servant of the law.

CREUZE-LATOUCHE (Plain): It seems unfortunate to me that those who create the law are able to command a man's death. I vote for prison until peace and then exile.

THIBADEAU (Plain): I vote for death.

JEAN DEBRY (Montagnard): Until the very moment when I stepped up to this desk I was in doubt; my unease is coming to an end. You have made me a judge, I have consulted the law, the inexorable law tells me Death: I speak for the law, for death.

SAINT-JUST (Montagnard): Since Louis XVI was the enemy of his people and their freedom and their happiness, I vote for death.

LAKANAL (Plain): A true republican needs few words. The motives of my decision are here [gesturing with his hand towards his heart]; I vote for death.

BRISSOT (Girondin): [From a long speech] I vote for death, the sentence to be suspended until the constitution has been ratified by the people.

The Vote

16–17 January 1793: What penalty should be suffered by Louis, former king of the French?

361: death
26: death, but with consideration for a reprieve
288: imprisonment, detention, banishment
28: absent

19 January 1793: Should there be a reprieve in carrying out the verdict of Louis Capet?

310: yes
380: no

The Formal Verdict

20 January 1793: The National Convention declares Louis Capet, last king of the French, guilty of conspiracy against national liberty and assault against national security.

The National Convention decrees that Louis Capet must suffer the death penalty.

READING REVIEW

1. How would you characterize the arguments of the Girondins against execution?
2. How would you characterize the arguments of the Montagnards for execution?
3. Do you think the execution of Louis XVI was justified? Why or why not?

---

67 ROBESPIERRE AND SAINT-JUST DEFEND THE ARREST OF DANTON

On March 31, 1794, four members of the National Convention—Danton, Desmoulins, Lacroix, and Phillipeaux—were arrested for antirevolutionary activities by orders of the Committee of Public Safety. Louis Legendre, speaking for their friends and colleagues, demanded that they be given the right to defend themselves before the National Convention. In the excerpt below, Robespierre and Saint-Just, both members of the Committee, answer Legendre's demand. The excerpt is taken from the play, Danton's Death, *by Georg Buechner, written some 30 years after the incident. As you read the excerpt, note how Saint-Just characterized revolution.*

ROBESPIERRE: The confusion in this assembly has suggested for some time that a great business is in hand. The question appears to be whether a handful of men shall be allowed to defeat the will of the people.—How can you so despise your principles as to grant today to some individuals what yesterday you denied to . . . so many others? What is this discrimination in favor of a few men? Some deputies in this assembly lavish speeches of praise on each other. What do they mean?—these self-congratulations. The history of the Revolution has taught us very clearly what to make of the cult of particular personalities. We may not ask if a man has done this or that patriotic action; we examine his entire political life and loyalty.—Legendre . . . named only

Danton, because he believes that to this name is attached some privilege.—No! We want no privileges! We want no idols!
[Cheers]
Some deputies in this assembly will try to frighten you. They will tell you that the powers that you yourselves exercise are being misused. They will cry out against "the despotism of the Committee [of Public Safety]"—as if the trust which the people have placed in you and you have vested in your Committee were not a sure guarantee of its patriotism.

Is there any deputy in this assembly who is frightened of our justice? I say to you, whoever trembles at this moment is guilty! For innocence never trembles before our vigilance.
[Great cheering]

Some people have tried to frighten *me*. They have told me that the danger which threatened Danton might one day threaten me. They have appealed to me, saying that some of Danton's friends were mine. Did they hope that memories of old friendship might weaken my passion for freedom? Let me say now that nothing shall make me weaken, nothing shall frighten me, even if Danton's danger shall be my own. We all have need of courage and greatness of soul. Only criminals and common souls tremble when their fellows fall from their sides. For when no crowd of accomplices surrounds them, they feel the light of truth shine full upon them. There may be some such feeble souls in this assembly. But the Republic stands by souls that are heroic. The number of cowards among us is not great—a few heads still shall fall, and France shall be saved.
[Cheers]
I demand that Legendre's motion be withdrawn.
ST. JUST: There appear to be a few sensitive ears in this assembly that cannot bear the word *blood*. A few general observations may persuade them that we are no more terrible than nature and our time. Nature calmly and irresistibly follows its laws. The man who comes into conflict with them is destroyed. A change in the composition of the air, a flare-up of the fires in the centre of the earth, a fluctuation in the poise of a mass of water, and a plague, a volcanic eruption, a flood, bury thousands of men. What is the result? An insignificant, in the larger sense quite unremarkable, change in physical nature, which would have passed unnoticed if corpses did not lie in its wake. I ask you: shall spiritual nature be more considerate in its revolutions than physical nature? Shall we not expect an idea to destroy what opposes it as well as a law of science? Shall an event take place which revolutionizes the entire shape of moral nature . . . and shed no blood? The footsteps of mankind are slow. They can only be counted in centuries, behind each of which stretch the graves of generations. The success of our simplest discoveries and principles has annihilated some millions of human beings, who died on the way. Is it not obvious that a Revolution, where the rush of history is bold and implacable, which must accomplish in four years the achievement of a century, shall be punctuated with more fervent celebrations of slaughter? Moses led his people through the Red Sea and the wilderness until the old and decadent generation was destroyed, before he founded the new city.

Legislators! We have neither the Red Sea nor the wilderness, but we have the guillotine. The Revolution dismembers mankind for its rebirth. Humanity shall rise up from the cauldron of blood in all the strength and purity of the first creation.
[Sustained cheering. . . .]

READING REVIEW

1. What arguments did Robespierre offer against Legendre's demand?
2. Why did Robespierre's speech prove to be ironic?
3. The Russian Communist leader Nikolai Lenin, in describing revolution, said that if you want an omelette you have to break some eggs. Do you think Saint-Just would have agreed with Lenin? Explain your answer.

68 A VIEW OF NAPOLEON'S CHARACTER

On meeting Napoleon most people had the same reaction. They were fascinated, yet uneasy. One person who strongly experienced this reaction was Madame Germaine de Staël, the daughter of Jacques Necker—the former finance minister of Louis XVI. In the excerpt below from The French Revolution, *edited by Philip Dawson, Madame de Staël describes Napoleon's character as she saw it. As you read the excerpt, consider how Napoleon's character might have contributed to his rise to power.*

Bonaparte made himself remarkable by his character and capacity as much as by his actions. . . . In [the] style [of the proclamations he issued in Italy] there reigned a spirit of moderation and dignity, which formed a contrast with the revolutionary bitterness of the civil leaders of France. He was said to be much attached to his wife, whose character was full of gentleness; people took delight in ascribing to him all the generous qualities which give a pleasing relief to extraordinary talents. Besides, the nation was so weary of oppressors who borrowed the name of liberty, and of oppressed persons who regretted the loss of arbitrary power, that admiration knew not what to attach itself to, and Bonaparte seemed to unite all that was fitted to take it captive.

It was with this sentiment, at least, that I saw him for the first time at Paris [in 1797]. I could not find the words to reply to him. . . . But, when I was a little recovered from the confusion of admiration, a strongly marked sentiment of fear followed. Bonaparte, at that time, had no power; . . . so that the fear which he inspired was caused only by the singular effect of his person on almost all who approached him. I had seen men highly worthy of esteem; I had likewise seen monsters of ferocity: there was nothing in the effect which Bonaparte produced on me, that could bring back to my recollection either the one or the other. I soon perceived, in the different opportunities which I had of meeting him during his stay at Paris, that his character could not be defined by the words we commonly use; he was neither good, nor violent, nor gentle, nor cruel, after the manner of individuals of whom we have knowledge. Such a being had no fellow. His cast of character, his understanding, his language, were stamped with the impress of an unknown nature. . . .

Far from recovering my confidence by seeing Bonaparte more frequently, he intimidated me more and more. I had a confused feeling that no emotion could influence him. . . . He never believed in exalted sentiments either in individuals or in nations: he considered the expression of these sentiments as hypocrisy. . . .

He regarded a human being as an action or a thing, not as a fellow creature. He did not hate any more than he loved; for him nothing existed but himself; all other creatures were cyphers. He was an able chess-player, and the human race was the opponent to whom he proposed to give check-mate. His successes depended as much on the qualities which he lacked as on the talents which he possessed. Neither pity, nor religion, nor attachment to any idea whatsoever, could [deflect] him from his principal direction. He was for his self-interest what the just man should be for virtue; if the end had been good, his perseverance would have been noble.

Every time that I heard him speak, I was struck with his superior [qualities. . . . His conversation] indicated a fine perception of circumstances, such as the sportsman has of the game which he pursues; sometimes he related the events of his life in a very interesting manner; he had even somewhat of the Italian imagination in narratives which allowed of gaiety. Yet nothing could triumph over my invincible aversion for what I perceived in him. I felt in his soul a cold sharp-edged sword, which froze the wound that it inflicted; I perceived in his understanding a profound irony, from which nothing great or beautiful, not even his own glory, could escape; for he despised the nation whose votes he wanted, and no spark of generous enthusiasm was mingled with his desire to astonish the human race.

READING REVIEW

1. Why, when she first met Napoleon, did Madame de Staël feel that the fear he generated was purely a product of his personality?
2. What do you think Madame de Staël meant when she said that Napoleon's successes depended as much on the qualities he lacked as much as on those he possessed?
3. How might Napoleon's character have helped him in his rise to power?

69 THE TREATY OF NANJING, 1842

The Treaty of Nanjing ended the Opium War between China and Great Britain, which had lasted from 1839 to 1842. In the past Chinese emperors had refused to negotiate on equal terms with foreign governments. At Nanjing, however, the Qing emperor was forced to accept British terms, and largely surrendered control over British activities in China. The most important clauses of the Treaty of Nanjing are included in the excerpt below from China: Selected Readings, *edited by Hyman Kublin. As you read the excerpt, consider whether the clauses appear fair to both sides involved.*

Whereas a Treaty between Us and Our Good Brother The Emperor of China, was concluded and signed in the English and Chinese Languages, on board Our Ship the *Cornwallis,* at [Nanjing], on the Twenty-ninth day of August, in the Year of Our Lord One Thousand Eight Hundred and Forty Two. . .

Article I. There shall henceforward be Peace and Friendship between Her Majesty the Queen of the United Kingdom of Great Britain and Ireland, and His Majesty the Emperor of China, and between their respective Subjects, who shall enjoy full security and protection within the Dominions of the other.

Article II. His Majesty the Emperor of China agrees that British Subjects, with their families and establishments, shall be allowed to reside, for the purpose of carrying on their Mercantile pursuits, without molestation or restraint at the Cities and Towns of Canton, Amoy, Foochow-fu, Ningpo, and Shanghai, and Her Majesty the Queen of Great Britain, etc., will appoint Superintendents or Consular Officers, to reside at each of the above-named Cities or Towns, to be the medium of communication between the Chinese Authorities and the said Merchants, and to see that the just Duties and other Dues of the Chinese Government . . . are duly discharged by her Britannic Majesty's Subjects.

Article III. It being obviously necessary and desirable that British Subjects should have some Port whereat they may careen and refit their Ships, when required, and keep Stores for that purpose, His Majesty the Emperor of China cedes to Her Majesty the Queen of Great Britain, etc., the Island of Hong Kong, to be possessed in perpetuity by Her Britannic Majesty, Her Heirs and Successors. . . .

Article IV. The Emperor of China agrees to pay the sum of Six Millions of Dollars as the value of Opium which was delivered up at Canton in the month of March 1839, as a Ransom for the lives of Her Britannic Majesty's Superintendent and Subjects, who had been imprisoned and threatened with death by the Chinese High Officers.

Article V. The Government of China having compelled the British Merchants trading at Canton to deal exclusively with certain Chinese Merchants called Hong Merchants (or Cohong) who had been licensed by the Chinese Government for that purpose, the Emperor of China agrees to abolish that practice in future at all Ports where British Merchants may reside, and to permit them to carry on their mercantile transactions with whatever persons they please; and His Imperial Majesty further agrees to pay to the British Government the sum of Three Millions of Dollars, on account of debts due to British Subjects by some of the said Hong Merchants (or Cohong), who have become insolvent, and who owe very large sums of money to Subjects of Her Britannic Majesty.

Article VI. The Government of Her Britannic Majesty having been obliged to send out an Expedition to demand and obtain redress for the violent and unjust proceedings of the Chinese High Authorities towards Her Britannic Majesty's Officers and Subjects, the Emperor of China agrees to pay the sum of Twelve Millions of Dollars on account of the Expenses incurred. . .

Article X. His Majesty the Emperor of China agrees to establish at all Ports which are by the 2nd Article of this Treaty to be thrown open for the resort of British Merchants, a fair and regular Tariff of Export and Import Customs and other Dues . . . and the Emperor further engages, that when British Merchandise shall have once paid at any of the said ports the regulated Customs and Dues . . . such Merchandise may be conveyed by Chinese Merchants, to any Province or City in the interior of the Empire of China on paying a further amount as Transit Duties. . .

Article XII. On the assent of the Emperor of China to this Treaty being received and the discharge of the first installment of money, Her Britannic Majesty's Forces will retire from [Nanjing] and the Grand Canal, and will no longer molest or stop the Trade of China. . . .

Article XIII. The Ratification of this Treaty by Her Majesty the Queen of Great Britain, etc., and His Majesty the Emperor of China shall be exchanged as soon as the great distance which separates England from China will admit; but in the meantime . . . all its provisions and arrangements shall take effect.

READING REVIEW

1. How much money in ransom, debts, and reparations did the treaty require the Emperor of China to pay Great Britain?
2. Which section of the treaty played a part in British foreign affairs in the 1980s?
3. The Opium War began a period in Chinese history that is known as the "era of unequal treaties." Based on the Treaty of Nanjing, do you think this is an accurate name? Give reasons for your answer.

70 YOSHIDA SHOIN: PHILOSOPHER OF THE MEIJI RESTORATION

Yoshida Shoin was a follower of Sakuma Shozan, who believed that Japan would advance only if it merged Eastern philosophy with Western technology. Taking Shozan's teaching to heart, Shoin tried to learn more about the West by stowing away on one of Commodore Perry's ships in 1854. In time, Shoin opened his own school, teaching his pupils—many of whom were involved in the Meiji Restoration—a philosophy of fierce nationalism, hatred for the shogun, and reverence for the emperor. Shoin was executed in 1859 for attempting to assassinate a shogunate official. The excerpt below from Sources of the Japanese Tradition, *compiled by Ryusaku Tsunoda, contains some of Shoin's philosophical writings. As you read the excerpt, ask yourself what is the main theme of Shoin's writings.*

On Leadership

What is important in a leader is a resolute will and determination. A man may be versatile and learned, but if he lacks resoluteness and determination, of what use will he be?

Once the will is resolved, one's spirit is strengthened. Even a peasant's will is hard to deny, but a samurai of resolute will can sway ten thousand men.

One who aspires to greatness should read and study, pursuing the True Way with such a firm resolve that he is perfectly straightforward and open, rises above the superficialities of conventional behavior, and refuses to be satisfied with the petty or commonplace.

Once a man's will is set, he need no longer rely on others or expect anything from the world. His vision encompasses Heaven and earth, past and present, and the tranquility of his heart is undisturbed.

Life and death, union and separation, follow hard upon one another. Nothing is steadfast but the will, nothing endures but one's achievements. These alone count in life.

To consider oneself different from ordinary men is wrong, but it is right to hope that one will not remain like ordinary men.

On Being Direct

In relations with others, one should express resentment and anger openly and straightforwardly. If one cannot express them openly and straightforwardly, the only thing to do is forget about them. To harbor

Samurai on horseback

grievances in one's heart, awaiting some later opportunity to give vent to them, is to act like a weak and petty man—in truth, it can only be called cowardice. The mind of the superior man is like Heaven. When it is resentful or angry, it thunders forth its indignation. But once having loosed its feelings, it is like a sunny day with a clear sky: within the heart there remains not a trace of a cloud. Such is the beauty of true manliness.

Facing Death

From the beginning of the year to the end, day and night, morning and evening, in action and repose, in speech and in silence, the warrior must keep death constantly before him and have ever in mind that the one death [which he has to give] should not be suffered in vain. In other words [he must have perfect control over his own death] just as if he were holding an intemperate steed in rein. Only he who truly keeps death in mind this way can understand what is meant by "preparedness."

If the body dies, it does no harm to the mind, but if the mind dies, one can no longer act as a man even though the body survives.

If a general and his men fear death and are apprehensive over possible defeat, then they will unavoidably suffer defeat and death. But if they make up their minds, from the general down to the last footsoldier, not to think of living but only of standing in one place and facing death together, then, though they may have no other thought than meeting death, they will instead hold on to life and gain victory.

Selfishness and Heroism

Nowadays everyone lives selfishly and seeks only the leisure in which to indulge his own desires. They look on all the beauties of nature—the rivers and mountains, the breeze and the moon—as their own to enjoy, forgetting what the shrine of the Sun Goddess stands for [i.e., that everything is held in trust from Heaven]. The common man thinks of his life as his own and refuses to perform his duty to his lord. The samurai regards his household as his own private possession and refuses to sacrifice his life for his state. The feudal lords regard their domains as their own and refuse to serve King and Country. Unwilling to serve King and Country, at home they cherish only the objects of desire and abroad they willingly yield to the foreign barbarian, inviting defeat and destruction. Thus the scenic beauties they enjoy will not long remain in their possession.

. . . Neither the lords nor the shogun can be depended upon [to save the country], and so our only hope lies in grass-roots heroes.

When I consider the state of things in our fief, I find that those who hold official positions . . . are incapable of the utmost in loyalty and patriotic service. Loyalty of the usual sort—perhaps, but if it is true loyalty and service you seek, then you must abandon this fief and plan a grass-roots uprising.

. . . To wear silk brocades, eat dainty food, hug beautiful women, and fondle darling children are the only things hereditary officials care about. To revere the emperor and expel the barbarian is no concern of theirs. If . . . it should be my misfortune to die, may my death inspire at least one or two men of steadfast will to rise up and uphold this principle after my death.

READING REVIEW

1. According to Shoin, how should one express resentment and anger?
2. According to Shoin, how must the warrior face death?
3. In your opinion, what is the basic message of Shoin's writings?

---

71 SÜLEYMAN THE MAGNIFICENT CAPTURES BELGRADE

Under Süleyman the Magnificent (1520–1566), considered the greatest of the Ottoman sultans, the Ottoman Empire expanded, taking in much of the old Islamic Empire and a large part of southeastern Europe. The first of Süleyman's major conquests was the Hungarian city of Belgrade. In the excerpt below from Suleiman the Magnificent 1520–1566 *by Roger Bigelow Merriman, the author describes Süleyman's campaign in Hungary. As you read the excerpt, consider the importance of the capture of Belgrade for the Ottomans.*

Hungary's . . . Council of State convened on April 24 [1521]. The defence of her two border fortresses of Belgrade and Sabač (on the south bank of the Save [River], some sixty miles to the westward) was obviously the first problem to be solved. But both were commanded by proud Hungarian noblemen, who stoutly refused to hand over their charges to any officer appointed by the crown. They declared that they were quite competent to perform their duties alone, provided only that they were furnished with money, provisions, ammunition, and cannon; and when the Council became importunate they withdrew to their own estates. . . .

Meanwhile Suleiman had left Constantinople on February 16. At Sophia, whence definite news of his advance first reached Hungary, he was joined by Ferhad Pasha with three thousand camels carrying ammunition; thirty thousand more camels which had been collected in Asia and were now laden with grain followed on, a day's journey behind. . . . There were three hundred cannon, and forty ships were equipped on the Danube. At Nish the army was divided. One part, commanded by Ahmed Pasha, . . . and followed a few days later by Suleiman himself, moved against Sabac; the Grand Vizir Piri Pasha with another force marched on Belgrade. . . .

Sabač defended itself with fruitless heroism. Ahmed Pasha captured it before Suleiman arrived, and the western flank of Belgrade had been turned. We may follow the events of the next three weeks in excerpts from the diary of the Sultan:

> On July 7, came news of the capture of Sabač; a hundred heads of the soldiers of the garrison, who had been unable like the rest to escape by the river, were brought to the Sultan's camp. July 8 these heads are placed on pikes along his route. . . . Suleiman visits the fort, and orders the construction of a bastion with a moat; he also commands that a bridge be built over the Save, so that his army may cross to the northern bank. . . . July 18. Day of rest. The bridge is finished; but the Save is flooded. July 19. The water covers the bridge so it can no longer be used. Orders to cross by boats. Provisions sent overland to Belgrade. . . . July 29. Suleiman sets forth for Belgrade along the Save. July 31. He arrives before the walls of Belgrade amid the cheers of his army.

The Grand Vizir had already been there for a month, and had captured Semlin; the south side of the Danube was now completely blocked from the westward. Suleiman spent the first of August in surveying the situation; on the second a general assault was launched, but was repulsed with a loss of five or six hundred men. The next day heavy cannon were planted on the island in the Danube, and the city was bombarded from that point. . . . August 8 . . . was a "black day" for the besieged. A triple attack was delivered. "The enemy," continues the [Sultan's] diary, "abandoned the defence of the town and set fire to it; they retired to the citadel." There they held out for three weeks more, but the Hungarians, now reduced to less than half their original number, had begun to quarrel with the Serbian mercenaries; finally, after one of the great towers had been blown up by a mine, the latter forced their masters to surrender on August 28. The Hungarians had been promised that they should have leave to depart unmolested, and the Sultan's diary would lead us to believe that the promise was kept; it seems more probable, however, that most of them were massacred. The Serbians, on the other hand, were transplanted to the environs of Constantinople. . . . Two days after the capitulation, the Sultan went to say his prayers in the lower town, in a church which had been converted into a mosque. The troops were rewarded, an administration was installed, and three thousand Janissaries were left behind as a garrison.

On October 19, Suleiman reentered Constantinople, where the inhabitants came out, rejoicing, to receive him. . . . His success had already been announced to all the magistrates and governors of his realms, and a special envoy was despatched to the Venetians, who received him on October 28 in solemn audience, and rewarded him with a present of five hundred ducats. The Doge [of Venice] wrote the same day to his ambassador in England to tell him that the Sultan's messenger had also "declared that his master had left all his artillery . . . [at Belgrade] for the purpose of returning in the spring to follow up the victory. This news is lamentable, and of importance to all Christians."

"Thus one of the two great outposts of Christendom had fallen into the hands of the Ottomans."

Thus one of the two great outposts of Christendom had fallen into the hands of the Ottomans. Within a year of his accession the new Sultan had successfully carried through an enterprise in which two of his most distinguished predecessors had failed. The last important barrier had been removed from the Danube route into the northwest.

READING REVIEW

1. What evidence in the excerpt suggests that Süleyman did not make a habit of taking prisoners?
2. Why did the Hungarians surrender at Belgrade?
3. Why, in your opinion, was the capture of Belgrade important for the Ottomans?

---

72 THE SIEGE AT LUCKNOW

After a disastrous attempt to destroy mutinous Indian forces at Chinhat in June 1857 during the Sepoy Rebellion, British troops fell back to the fortress at Lucknow, where the mutineers put them under siege. For the next few months, the people trapped at Lucknow had to combat hunger, disease, and other privations, as well as attacks by the mutineers. The excerpt below from Annals of the Indian Rebellion 1857–58, *compiled by N. A. Chick, offers an eyewitness account of the first few weeks of the siege. As you read the excerpt, consider the problems faced by the British at Lucknow.*

It is difficult to chronicle the proceedings of these few days, for everywhere confusion reigned supreme. That unfortunate day of Chinhat precipitated everything, inasmuch as we were closely shut up several days before anything of the kind was anticipated. People had made no arrangement for provisioning themselves; many, indeed, never dreamt of such a necessity; and the few that had were generally too late. Again, many servants were shut out the first day, and all attempts to approach us were met by a never ceasing fusillade. But though they could not get in, they succeeded in getting out; and after a few days, those who could boast of servants or attendants of any kind formed a very small and envied minority. The servants, in many instances, eased their masters of any superfluous articles of value easy of carriage. In fact, the confusion can be better imagined that described.

The head of the Commissariat had, most unfortunately for the garrison, received a severe wound at Chinhat, which effectively deprived them of his valuable aid. His office was all broken up . . . and the officers

Sikh troops dividing the spoils taken from rebels during the Sepoy Rebellion

appointed to assist him were all new hands. Besides all this, the first stores open were approachable only by one of the most exposed roads, and very many of the camp-followers preferred going without food to the chance of being shot. Some did not know where to apply, so that for three or four days many went without rations; and this in no small degree added to the number of desertions. Owing to these desertions, the commissariat and battery bullocks had no attendants to look after them, and went wandering all over the place looking for food; they tumbled into wells, were shot down in numbers by the enemy, and added greatly to the labour which fell on the garrison, as fatigue parties of civilians and officers after being in the defences all day repelling the enemy's attack, were often employed six and seven hours burying cattle killed during the day, and which, from the excessive heat, became offensive in a few hours. The artillery and other horses were everywhere to be seen loose, fighting and tearing at one another, driven mad for want of food and water; the garrison being too busily employed in the trenches to be able to secure them. . . .

There is no doubt that one great cause of the desertion of the native servants was the insufficient care bestowed upon them. It was difficult to shelter all the Europeans; and the native servants were, therefore, necessarily greatly exposed. Constantly in danger of being struck down by the bullets or shot of the enemy, and ill supplied with food, it is not surprising that many deserted. . . .

For some time before the siege our supplies had, however, been husbanded. . . . Our regular meals had . . . been diminished from three to two. A cold luncheon only was served, and we made an early dinner at four. By these timely precautions the supplies which we had were husbanded, and the wants of our numerous guests were provided for during the whole siege. Besides, we were often able to render assistance to persons in other garrisons who urgently needed aid, and to the wounded in hospital. After the siege had begun, and the commissariat arrangements got into train, rations were issued of beef or mutton, with flour or rice, and salt, to Europeans, according to a fixed scale. . . . Additions [were] made to the meal as our store-room afforded. These, however, besides the daily addition of spices, and sugar, were limited to a few canisters of preserved salmon, and a few of carrots. . . . When the sheep were all used up, beef only was served out in rations, which was usually made into stews, in consequence of our rarely getting a piece that could be boiled or roasted.

At dinner, our chief luxury were rice puddings, of which two daily appeared on table. The eggs for these were derived from a few poultry which we had managed to preserve; and the milk from goats and two cows belonging to our guests, which were half starved during the siege. Occasionally a plum pudding or jam pudding was made, and always caused great excitement at the dinner-table. The demand for these delicacies was great. . . . One cup of tea was made for each person at six in the morning. . . . Another cup at the ten o'clock breakfast, and another at night. We enjoyed both sugar and milk in our tea, a luxury which few possessed besides our garrison: and this often attracted friends.

READING REVIEW

1. Why was there a problem getting supplies from the first stores opened during the siege of Lucknow?
2. What, according to the author, was a major cause of desertion by native servants?
3. What, in your opinion, would be the most unpleasant aspect of living in a city under siege? Explain your answer.

The Development of Industrial Society

73 AN ACCIDENT AT THE OPENING OF A RAILROAD LINE

A terrible accident that resulted in the death of William Huskisson, one of Great Britain's leading politicians, marred the official opening of the railroad line between Liverpool and Manchester in 1830. The 21-year-old actress Fanny Kemble was among the guests invited to take the inaugural ride on the line. In the excerpt below from Records of a Girlhood, *she tells of her feelings about traveling by train and of Huskisson's shocking accident. As you read the excerpt, compare Kemble's impressions of travel by train to those of her mother.*

We started [from Liverpool] on Wednesday last, to the number of about eight hundred people, in carriages. . . . The most intense curiosity and excitement prevailed, and, though the weather was uncertain, enormous masses of densely packed people lined the road, shouting and waving hats and handkerchiefs as we flew by them. What with the sight and sound of these cheering multitudes and the tremendous velocity with which we were borne past them, my spirits rose to the true champagne height, and I never enjoyed anything so much as the first hour of our progress. I had been unluckily separated from my mother in the first distribution of places, but by an exchange of seats which she was enabled to make she rejoined me when I was at the height of my ecstasy, which was considerably dampened by finding that she was frightened to death, and intent upon nothing but devising means of escaping from a situation which appeared to her to threaten with instant annihilation herself and all her travelling companions. While I was chewing the cud of this disappointment, which was rather bitter, as I had expected her to be as delighted as myself with our excursion, a man flew by us, calling out through a speaking-trumpet to stop the engine, for that somebody in the directors' carriage had sustained an injury. We were all stopped accordingly, and presently a hundred voices were heard exclaiming that Mr Huskisson was killed; the confusion that ensued is indescribable; the calling out from carriage to carriage to ascertain the truth, the contrary reports which were sent back to us, the hundred questions eagerly uttered at once, and the repeated and urgent demands for surgical assistance, created a sudden turmoil that was quite sickening. At last we distinctly ascertained that the unfortunate man's thigh was broken. From Lady [Wilton] . . . I had the following details. . . . The engine had

Early railroads

stopped to take in a supply of water, and several of the gentlemen in the directors' carriage had jumped out to look about them. Lord [Wilton], Count Batthyany, Count Matuscenitz, and Mr Huskisson among the rest were standing talking in the middle of the road, when an engine on the other line, which was parading up and down merely to show its speed, was seen coming down upon them like lightning. The most active of those in peril sprang back into their seats . . . while poor Mr Huskisson, less active from the effects of age and ill-health, bewildered, too, by the frantic cries of "Stop the engine! Clear the track!" that resounded on all sides, completely lost his head, looked helplessly to the right and left, and was instantaneously prostrated by the fatal machine, which dashed down like a thunderbolt upon him, and passed over his leg, smashing and mangling it in the most horrible way. . . . So terrible was the effect of the appalling accident that . . . not a sound was heard or a word uttered among the immediate spectators of the catastrophe. Lord [Wilton] was the first to raise the poor sufferer, and calling to aid his surgical skill, which is considerable, he tied up the severed artery, and, for a time at least, prevented death by loss of blood. Mr Huskisson was then placed in a carriage with his wife and Lord [Wilton], and the engine . . . conveyed them to Manchester. So great was the shock produced upon the whole party by this event, that the Duke of Wellington declared his intention not to proceed, but to return immediately to Liverpool. However, upon its being represented to him that the whole population of Manchester had turned out to witness the procession, and that a disappointment might give rise to riots and disturbances, he consented to go on, and gloomily enough the rest of the journey was accomplished.

READING REVIEW

1. What was the reaction of the crowd to the train as it traveled between Liverpool and Manchester?
2. Why was Mr. Huskisson unable to avoid the oncoming train?
3. How did Fanny Kemble feel about traveling by train? How did her mother feel? What would be your reaction to being among the first people to travel on a new form of transportation?

74 A WORKING DAY IN A MANCHESTER COTTON MILL

The living and working conditions of the poor became a topic of discussion in newspapers throughout Great Britain after the Sadler Committee of Parliament released its findings in 1832. One newspaper— The Morning Chronicle*—wishing to discover more about the lives of the working classes, sent correspondents to the major industrial areas. In the excerpt below, a correspondent details the daily life of cotton-mill workers in the northern industrial town of Manchester. As you read the excerpt, compare the life of the Manchester mill workers to that of factory workers in the United States today.*

In the majority of mills labour begins at six o'clock A.M. throughout the year. In a certain number, the engine during the dead winter months does not start until a half an hour later. As a general thing, however, operative Manchester is up and stirring before six. The streets in the neighborhood of the mills are thronged with men and women and children flocking to their labour. They talk and laugh cheerily together. The girls generally keep in groups with the shawls twisted round their heads, and every few steps, in the immediate vicinity of the mills, parties are formed round the peripatetic establishments of hot coffee and cocoa venders. The factory bell rings from five minutes before six until the hour strikes. Then—to the moment—the engine starts and the day's work begins. Those who are behind six, be it but a moment, are fined twopence; and in many mills, after the expiration of a very short time of grace, the doors are locked, and the laggard, besides the fine, loses his morning work.

Workers in an early British textile factory

Breakfast hour comes round at half after eight o'clock. The engine stops to the minute, and the streets are again crowded with those of the operatives who live close by the mills. A great many, however, take their breakfasts in the factory, which, as a general rule, supplies them with hot water. The practice of the people taking their meals in the mill, though I believe contrary to the letter of the law, is quite necessary, owing to the distance which many of the workpeople live from their place of labour, and to the short time—only half an hour—allowed for the meal. Its constituents are generally tea and coffee, with plenty of bread and butter, and in many cases a slice or so of bacon. At five minutes to nine the factory bell sounds again, and at nine the engine starts again. The work goes on with the most perfect method and order. There is little if any talking, and little disposition to talk. Everybody sets steadily and tranquilly about his or her duties, in that calm methodical style which betokens perfect acquaintance with the work to be done, and perfect skill wherewith to do it. There is no hurrying or panting or toiling after the machinery. Everything appears—in ordinary phrase—to be "taken easy"; yet everything goes rapidly and continuously on.

The men wear blue striped shirts, trousers and slippers; the women generally envelop themselves in coarse pinafores and loose jackets tying round the throat. Spinners and piecers go about their work generally barefoot, or with such an apology for *chaussure* as forcibly reminds you of the old story of the sedan chair with the bottom out. Were it not for the honor of the thing, they might as well go entirely unshod. I fear that I cannot say much for the cleanliness of the workpeople. They have an essentially greasy look, which makes me sometimes think that water would run off their skins, as it does off a duck's back. In this respect the women are just as bad as the men. The spinners and piecers I have mentioned fling shoes and stockings aside, but I fear it is very seldom that their feet see the interior of a tub, with plenty of hot water and soap.... Efforts have been made for the establishment of baths for the working classes in Manchester, and several mill-owners have actually erected conveniences of the sort, but the operatives in too many cases absolutely declined making use of them, and as a general rule can with very great difficulty, if at all, be made to appreciate the advantages of clean skin and free pores....

In Manchester everybody, master and man, dines at one o'clock. As the chimes sound, all the engines pause together, and from every workshop, from every industrial establishment... the hungry crowd swarms out, and streets and lanes, five minutes before lonely and deserted, are echoing the trampling of hundreds of busy feet. The Manchester operative in prosperous times needs never want, and seldom does want, a dinner of what he calls "flesh meat". This he sometimes partakes of at home, sometimes at a neighbouring cook-shop; occasionally he has it brought to him at the mill. A favourite dish with the operatives is what they call potato pie—a savoury pasty made of meat and potatoes, well seasoned with pepper and salt, and roofed in with a substantial paste.

Many of the men after despatching their dinner, which they do comfortably in half an hour, spend... their leisure in smoking or lounging about, until the never-failing bell proclaims that time is up, and that the engine and its attendant mechanism are ready to resume their labours. The work then proceeds to half after five o'clock, at which all labour finally ceases; the periods of toil having been from six o'clock until half past eight o'clock, from nine o'clock till one o'clock, and from two o'clock until half past five o'clock, making an aggregate of ten hours.

READING REVIEW

1. How were workers punished for being late?
2. What did the correspondent think of the workers' personal hygiene habits?
3. What similarities and differences are there between the life of the Manchester mill workers and the life of workers in a modern factory in the United States?

75 THE TRIAL OF THE TOLPUDDLE MARTYRS

Even after the repeal of the Combination Acts in 1824, British workers continued to have difficulty forming trade unions, for they still could be convicted of conspiracy. In 1834, for example, six farm laborers in Tolpuddle, Dorset, were charged with violating the Mutiny Act of 1749. They were found guilty and banished to Australia for seven years. After prolonged protests, however, they were returned to Britain after serving only two years of their sentences. In the excerpt below from English Popular Literature 1819–1851, *edited by Louis James, George Loveless, the leader of the "Tolpuddle Martyrs," describes their trial. As you read the excerpt, consider why the British government opposed the formation of trade unions.*

Directly after we were put back, a Mr. Young, an attorney employed on our behalf, called me into the conversation room, and, among other things, inquired if I would promise the magistrates to have no more to do with the Union if they would let me go home to my wife and family? I said, "I do not understand you." —"Why," said he, "give them information concerning the Union, who else belongs to it, and promise you will have no more to do with it." —"Do you mean to say I am to betray my companions?" —"That is just it," said he. "No; I would rather undergo any punishment."

The same day we were sent to the high jail, where we continued until the assizes. I had never seen the inside of a jail before, but now I began to feel it—disagreeable company, close confinement, bad bread, and what was worse, hard and cold lodging—a small straw bed on the flags, or else an iron bedstead—"and this," said I to my companions, "is our fare for striving to live honest."...

On the 15th of March, we were taken to the County-hall to await our trial. As soon as we arrived we were ushered down some steps into a miserable dungeon, opened but twice a year, with only a glimmering light; and to make it more disagreeable, some wet and green brushwood was served for firing. The smoke of this place, together with its natural dampness, amounted to nearly suffocation; and in this most dreadful situation we passed three whole days. As to the trial, I need mention but little; the whole proceedings were characterized by a shameful disregard of justice and decency; the most unfair means were resorted to in order to frame an indictment against us; the grand jury appeared to ransack heaven and earth to get some clue against us, but in vain; our characters were investigated from our infancy to the then present moment; our masters were inquired of to know if we were not idle, or attended public-houses, or some other fault in us; and much as they were opposed to us, they had common honesty enough to declare that we were good labouring servants, and that they never heard of any complaint against us; and when nothing whatever could be raked together, the unjust and cruel judge, John Williams, ordered us to be tried for mutiny and conspiracy, under an act... for the suppression of mutiny amongst the marines and seamen, several years ago, at the Nore. The greater part of the evidence against us, on our trial, was put into the mouths of the witnesses by the judge; and when he evidently wished them to say any particular thing, and the witness would say "I cannot remember," he would say, "Now think; I will give you another minute to consider"; and then he would repeat over the words, and ask, "Cannot you remember?" Sometimes, by charging them to be careful what they said, by way of intimidation, they would merely answer, "yes"; and the judge would set the words down as proceeding from the witness. I shall not soon forget his address to the jury, in summing up the evidence: among other things, he told them, that if such Societies [unions] were allowed to exist, it would ruin masters, cause a stagnation in trade, destroy property,—and if *they should not find us guilty, he was certain they would forfeit the opinion of the grand jury.* I thought to myself, there is no danger but we shall be found guilty, as we have a special jury for the purpose, selected from among those who are most unfriendly towards us—the grand jury, landowners, the petty jury, land-renters. Under such a charge, from such a quarter, self-interest alone would induce them to say, "Guilty." The judge then inquired if we had anything to say. I instantly forwarded the following short defence, in writing, to him:—"My Lord, if we have violated any law, it was not done intentionally: we have injured no man's reputation, character, person, or property: we were uniting together to preserve ourselves, our wives, and our children, from utter degradation and starvation. We challenge any man, any number of men, to prove that we have acted, or intend to act, different from the above statement." The judge asked if I wished it to be read in Court. I answered, "Yes." It was

"My Lord, if we have violated any law, it was not done intentionally."

then mumbled over to a part of the jury, in such an inaudible manner, that although I knew what was there, I could not comprehend it. And here one of the counsel prevented sentence being passed, by declaring not one charge brought against any of the prisoners at the bar was proved, and that if we were found guilty a great number of persons would be dissatisfied; "and I shall for one," said he.

Two days after this we were again placed at the bar to receive sentence, when the judge . . . told us, "that not for any thing that we had done, or as he could prove, we intended to do, but for example to others, he considered it his duty to pass the sentence of seven years' transportation across his Majesty's high seas upon each and every one of us."

READING REVIEW

1. Why did George Loveless think "there is no danger but we shall be found guilty"?
2. Why did the judge give such stiff sentences to the Tolpuddle Martyrs?
3. Why do you think eighteenth-century governments, landowners, and industrialists were so opposed to trade unions?

---

76 A VISIT TO NEW LANARK

The Welshman Robert Owen (1771–1858) first put his utopian socialist ideas into action at a group of cotton mills in the Scottish town of New Lanark. He paid his workers wages well above the going rate, cut their work hours, offered them decent housing, and provided free education for their children. In 1819 English poet Robert Southey, who, in his younger years, held views as radical and socialist as Owen's, visited New Lanark. In the excerpt below from Pandaemonium *by Humphey Jennings, Southey reacts to Owen's utopian world. As you read the excerpt, note the contradictions Southey observed in Owen's system of social organization.*

He [Robert Owen] led us through the works with great courtesy, and made as full an exhibition as the time allowed. It is needless to say anything more of the Mills than that they are perfect of their kind, according to the present state of mechanical science, and that they appeared to be under admirable management; they are thoroughly clean, and so carefully ventilated, that there was no unpleasant smell in any of the apartments. Everything required for the machinery is made upon the spot, and the expense of wear and tear is estimated at 8000£ annually. There are stores also from which the people are supplied with all the necessaries of life. They have a credit there to the amount of sixteen shillings a week each, but may deal elsewhere if they choose. The expenses of what he calls the moral part of the establishment, he stated at 700£ a year. But a large building is just completed, with ball and concert and lecture rooms, all for "the formation of character"; and this must surely be set down to Owen's private account, rather than to the cost of the concern.

In the course of going through these buildings, he took us into an apartment where one of his plans . . . was spread upon the floor. And with a long wand in his hand he explained the plan. . . . Meantime the word had been given: we were conducted into one of the dancing rooms; half a dozen fine boys, about nine or ten years old, led the way, playing on fifes, and some 200 children, from four years of age till ten, entered the room and arranged themselves on three sides of it. A man . . . gave the word, . . . and they turned to right or left, faced about, fell forwards and backwards, and stamped at command, performing maneuvers the object of which was not very clear, with perfect regularity. I remembered what T. Vardon had told me of the cows in Holland. When the cattle are housed, the Dutch in their spirit of cleanliness, prevent them from dirtying their tails by tying them up . . . at a certain elevation, to a cross string which extends the whole length of the stalls: and the consequence is that when any one cow wags her tail, all the others must wag theirs also. So I could not but think that these puppet-like motions might, with a little ingenuity, have been produced by the great water-wheel, which is the *primum mobile* [prime source of motion] of the whole Cotton-Mills. A certain number of the children were drawn out, and sung to the pipe of six little pipers. There was too much of all this, but the children seemed to like it. When the exhibition was over, they filed into the adjoining school room.

I was far better pleased with a large room in which all the children of the establishment who are old enough not to require the constant care of their mothers, and too young for instruction of any kind, were brought together while their parents were at work, and left to amuse themselves. They made a glorious noise, worth all the concerts of New Lanark, and of London to boot. It was really delightful to see how the little creatures crowded about Owen to make their bows and their curtsies, looking up and smiling in his face; and the genuine benignity and pleasure with which he noticed them, laying his hand on the head of one, shaking hands with another, and bestowing kind looks and kind words upon all.

"Owen in reality deceives himself."

Owen in reality deceives himself. He is part-owner and sole Director of a large establishment, differing more in accidents than in essence from a plantation: the persons under him happen to be white, and are at liberty by law to quit his service, but while they remain in it they are as much under his absolute management as so many negro-slaves. His humour, his vanity, his kindliness of nature . . . lead him to make these *human machines* as he calls them (and literally believes them to be) as happy as he can, and to make a display of their happiness. And he jumps at once to the monstrous conclusion that because he can do this with 2210 persons, who are totally dependent upon him—all mankind might be governed with the same facility. *Et in Utopia ego.* [I too know about Utopia.] But I never regarded man as a machine; I never believed him to be merely a material being; I never for one moment could . . . suppose, as Owen does, that men may be cast in a mould (like other parts of his mill) and take the impression with perfect certainty. Nor did I ever disguise from myself the difficulties of a system which took for its foundation the community of goods. On the contrary I met them fairly, acknowledged them, and rested satisfied with the belief (whether erroneous or not) that the evils incident in such a system would be infinitely less than those which stare us in the face under the existing order. But Owen reasons from Cotton Mills to the whole empire. He keeps out of sight from others, and perhaps from himself, that his system, instead of aiming at perfect freedom, can only be kept in power by absolute power. Indeed, he never looks beyond one of his own ideal square villages, to the rules and proportions of which he would square the whole human race. *The formation of character!* Why the end of his institutions would be, as far as possible, the destruction of all character. They tend directly to destroy individuality of character and domesticity—in the one of which the strength of men consists, and in the other his happiness. The power of human society, and the grace, would both be annihilated.

Yet I admire the man, and like him too. And the Yahoos who are bred in our manufacturing towns, and under the administration of our Poor Laws are so much worse than the . . . breed which he proposes to raise, that I should be glad to see his regulations adopted, as the Leeds people have proposed, for a colony of paupers.

READING REVIEW

1. What did Southey think of the New Lanark children's precision drilling?
2. According to Southey, why was New Lanark like a plantation?
3. What contradictions did Southey note in Owen's system of social organization? Do you agree with Southey? Why or why not?

---

77 THE FIRST FLIGHT ACROSS THE ENGLISH CHANNEL

In 1909 a London newspaper, the Daily Mail, *offered a prize to the first person who could fly across the English Channel. A French mechanic and aviator, Louis Bleriot took up this challenge. Leaving Calais, France, early in the morning of July 25, he completed the 23.5-mile journey in a little over 36 minutes. In the excerpt below from* The First to Fly: Aviation's Pioneer Days *by Sherwood Harris, Bleriot describes his adventure for the* Mail's *readers. As you read the excerpt, consider the impact that Bleriot's flight had on people's ideas about distance.*

A pilot during the early days of aviation

At 4:30 [on the morning of Sunday, 25 July 1909] we could see all around. Daylight had come. M. Le Blanc endeavored to see the coast of England, but could not. A light breeze was blowing. The air was clear.

Everything was prepared. I was dressed . . . [in] a khaki jacket lined with wool for warmth over my tweed clothes and beneath engineer's suit of blue cotton overalls. My close-fitting cap was fastened over my head and ears. I had neither eaten nor drunk anything since I rose. My thoughts were only upon the flight, and my determination to accomplish it this morning.

4:35! *Tout est pret!* [Everything's ready!] Le Blanc gives the signal and in an instant I am in the air, my engine making 1,200 revolutions—almost its highest speed—in order that I may get quickly over the telegraph wires along the edge of the cliff. As soon as I am over the cliff I reduce my speed. There is now no need to force my engine.

I begin my flight, steady and sure, towards the coast of England. I have no apprehensions, no sensations, *pas du tout.* [not at all.]

The *Escopette* [the escort destroyer] has seen me. She is driving ahead at full speed. She makes perhaps 42 kilometers (about 26 miles per hour). What matters? I am making at least 68 kilometers (42 miles per hour).

Rapidly I overtake her, travelling at a height of 80 meters (about 260 feet).

The moment is supreme, yet I surprised myself by feeling no exultation. Below me is the sea, the surface disturbed by the wind, which is now freshening. The motion of the waves beneath me is not pleasant. I drive on.

Ten minutes have gone. I have passed the destroyer, and I turn my head to see whether I am proceeding in the right direction. I am amazed. There is nothing to be seen—neither the . . . destroyer, nor France, nor England. I am alone. I can see nothing at all—*rien du tout!* [nothing at all!]

Beryl Markham, the first person to fly solo across the Atlantic from west to east

For ten minutes I am lost. It is a strange position, to be alone, unguided, without compass, in the air over the middle of the Channel.

I touch nothing. My hands and feet rest lightly on the levers. I let the airplane take its own course. I care not whither it goes.

For ten minutes I continue, neither rising nor falling, nor turning. And then, twenty minutes after I have left the French coast, I see the green cliffs of Dover, the castle, and away to the west the spot where I intended to land.

What can I do? It is evident that the wind has taken me out of my course. I am almost at St. Margaret's Bay and going in the direction of the Goodwin Sands.

Now it is time to attend to the steering. I press the lever with my foot and turn easily towards the west, reversing the direction in which I am travelling. Now, indeed, I am in difficulties, for the wind here by the cliffs is much stronger, and my speed is reduced as I fight against it. Yet my beautiful aeroplane responds. Still I fly westwards, hoping to cross the harbor and reach the Shakespeare Cliff. Again the wind blows. I see an opening in the cliff.

Although I am confident that I can continue for an hour and a half, that I might indeed return to Calais, I cannot resist the opportunity to make a landing upon this green spot.

Once more I turn my aeroplane, and, describing a half-circle, I enter the opening and find myself again over dry land. Avoiding the red buildings on my right, I attempt a landing; but the wind catches me and whirls me round two or three times.

At once I stop my motor, and instantly my machine falls straight upon the land from a height of 20 meters (65 feet). In two or three seconds I am safe.

Soldiers in khaki run up, and a policeman. Two of my compatriots are on the spot. They kiss my cheeks. The conclusion of my flight overwhelms me. I have nothing to say.

READING REVIEW

1. Why did Bleriot need to force his airplane's engine to its highest speed at the beginning of the flight?
2. What natural force helped Bleriot to fly?
3. After Bleriot's flight one newspaper carried the headline, "There are no islands anymore." What do you think is meant by this headline?

78 TWO TESTIMONIALS FOR ALBERT EINSTEIN

Albert Einstein (1879–1955) did not hold a university position when he published the papers that revolutionized physics in 1905. Rather, he was employed as a clerk in the Swiss patent office. Six years later, even though the vast majority of people in the world of science had accepted Einstein as a great and original thinker, university administrators still had to be convinced that he was worthy of a teaching post. In the excerpt below from Albert Einstein: Creator and Rebel *by Banesh Hoffmann, two leading scientists—physicist Marie Curie and mathematician Jules-Henri Poincaré—offer testimonials on Einstein's behalf. As you read the excerpts, compare the two scientists' estimations of Einstein's qualities.*

Marie Curie

I have greatly admired the works that were published by M. Einstein on questions concerning modern theoretical physics. Moreover, I believe that the mathematical physicists all agree in considering these works as being of the highest order. In Brussels, where I attended a scientific conference in which M. Einstein took part, I was able to appreciate the clarity of his mind, the breadth of his documentation, and the profundity of his knowledge. If one considers that M. Einstein is still very young, one has every right to build the greatest hopes on him and to see in him one of the leading theoreticians of the future. I think that a scientific institution that would give M. Einstein the opportunity to work that he desires by appointing him to a professorship in the conditions he merits, could only be greatly honored by such a decision and would certainly render a great service to science.

Jules-Henri Poincaré

M. Einstein is one of the most original thinkers I have ever met. Despite his youth he has already achieved a most honorable place among the leading scientists of his time. What we must particularly admire in him is the facility with which he adapts himself to new concepts and knows how to draw from them every conclusion. He does not remain attached to classical principles, and when presented with a problem in physics he quickly envisages all its possibilities. This leads immediately in his mind to the prediction of new phenomena which may one day be verified by experiment. I do not mean to say that all these predictions will meet the test of experiment when such tests become possible. Since he seeks in all directions, one must, on the contrary, expect the majority of the paths on which he embarks to be blind alleys. But one must hope at the same time that one of these directions he has indicated may be the right one, and that is enough. This is exactly how one should proceed.

The role of mathematical physics is to ask questions and only experiment can answer them.

READING REVIEW

1. According to Marie Curie, how would a scientific institution benefit by offering Einstein a professorship?
2. According to Poincaré, what is the role of mathematical physics?
3. How are the two estimations of Einstein the same? How do they differ?

---

79 EDWARD JENNER'S CASE STUDIES

In eighteenth-century Britain, the only protection against smallpox was inoculation with fluid from smallpox sores. Because these inoculations had unpleasant—and often deadly side effects, physicians began to look for some safer method of inoculation. As a country doctor in the English county of Gloucestershire, Edward Jenner (1749–1823) was well aware of the popular belief that people who had suffered cowpox did not develop smallpox. In the 1790s, Jenner decided to test this belief by inoculating people who had had cowpox with variolous matter. Some of Jenner's case studies are included in the excerpt below from An Inquiry into the Causes and Effects of the Variole Vaccine, a Disease. *As you read the excerpts, note the similarities among the case studies.*

Edward Jenner vaccinating a patient

Case I

Joseph Merret, now an Under Gardener to the Earl of Berkeley, lived as a Servant with a Farmer near this place in the year 1770, and occasionally assisted in milking his master's cows. Several horses belonging to the farm began to have sore heels, which Merret frequently attended. The cows soon became affected with the Cow Pox, and soon after several sores appeared on his hands. Swellings and stiffness in each axilla [armpit] followed, and he was so much indisposed for several days as to be incapable of pursuing his ordinary employment. Previously to the appearance of the distemper among the cows there was no fresh cow brought into the farm, nor any servant employed who was affected with the Cow Pox.

In April, 1795, a general inoculation taking place here, Merret was inoculated with his family; so that a period of twenty-five years had elapsed from his having the Cow Pox to this time. However, though the variolous matter was repeatedly inserted into his arm, I found it impracticable to infect him with it; an efflorescence only, taking on an [inflamed] look about the centre, appearing on the skin near the punctured parts. During the whole time that his family had the Small Pox, one of whom had it very full, he remained in the house with them, but received no injury from exposure to the contagion.

Case II

Sarah Portlock, of this place, was infected with the Cow Pox, when a Servant at a Farmer's in the neighbourhood, twenty-seven years ago.

In the year 1792, conceiving herself, from this circumstance, secure from the infection of the Small Pox, she nursed one of her own children who had accidentally caught the disease, but no indisposition ensued.—During the time she remained in the infected room, variolous matter was inserted into both her arms, but without any further effect than in the preceding case.

Case IV

Mary Barge, of Woodford, in this parish, was inoculated with variolous matter in the year 1791. An efflorescence of a palish red colour soon appeared about the parts where the matter was inserted, and spread itself rather extensively, but died away in a few days without producing any variolous symptoms*. She has since been repeatedly employed as a nurse to Small-pox patients, without experiencing any ill consequences. This woman had the Cow Pox when she lived in the service of a Farmer in this parish thirty-one years before.

---

*It is remarkable that variolous matter, when the system is disposed to reject it, should excite inflammation on the part to which it is applied more speedily than when it produces Small Pox. Indeed it becomes almost a criterion by which we can determine whether the infection will be received or not. It seems as if a change, which endures through life, had been produced in the action, or disposition to action, in the vessels of the skin; and it is remarkable too, that whether this change has been effected by the Small Pox or the Cow Pox, that the disposition to sudden cuticular inflammation is the same on the application of variolous matter.

Case V

Mrs. H-----, a respectable Gentlewoman of this town, had the Cow Pox when very young. She received the infection in rather than an uncommon manner: it was given by means of her handling some of the same utensils* which were in use among the servants of the family, who had the disease from milking infected cows. Her hands had many of the Cow-pox sores upon them, and they were communicated to her nose, which became inflamed and very much swollen. Soon after this event Mrs. H----- was exposed to the contagion of the Small Pox, where it was scarcely possible for her to have escaped, had she been susceptible of it, as she regularly attended a relative who had the disease in so violent a degree that it proved fatal to him.

In the year 1778 the Small Pox prevailed very much at Berkeley, and Mrs. H----- not feeling perfectly satisfied respecting her safety (no indisposition having followed her exposure to the Small Pox) I inoculated her with active variolous matter. The same appearance followed as in the preceding cases—an efflorescence on the arm without any effect on the constitution.

*When the Cow Pox has prevailed in the dairy, it has often been communicated to those who have not milked the cows, by the handle of the milk pail.

Case IX

Although the Cow Pox shields the constitution from the Small Pox, and the Small Pox proves a protection against its own future poison, yet it appears that the human body is again and again susceptible of the infectious matter of the Cow Pox, as the following history will demonstrate:

William Smith, of Pyrton in this parish, contracted this disease when he lived with a neighbouring Farmer in the year 1780. One of the horses belonging to the farm had sore heels, and it fell to his lot to attend him. By these means the infection was carried to the cows, and from the cows it was communicated to Smith. On one of his hands were several ulcerated sores, and he was affected with such symptoms as have been described.

In the year 1791 the Cow Pox broke out at another farm where he then lived as a Servant, and he became affected with it a second time; and in the year 1794 he was so unfortunate as to catch it again. The disease was equally as severe the second and third time as it was on the first*.

In the spring of the year 1795 he was twice inoculated, but no affection of the system could be produced from the variolous matter; and he has since associated with those who had the Small Pox in its most contagious state without feeling any effect from it.

*This is not the case in general—a second attack is commonly very slight, and so, I am informed, it is among the cows.

READING REVIEW

1. What criterion did Jenner use to determine whether smallpox would develop in his case-study patients?
2. According to Jenner what was unusual about cowpox?
3. What generalizations do you think Jenner might have drawn from his case studies?

---

80 BEETHOVEN'S HEILIGENSTADT TESTAMENT

In 1799 Ludwig van Beethoven (1770–1827) first developed the ailment that eventually left him deaf. Three years later, certain that he soon would die, Beethoven wrote a tortured letter to his brothers. However, Beethoven never delivered the letter, and, as he hoped, his art sustained him through his devastating affliction. Even though completely deaf, he went on to compose some of the most powerful music of his—or any other—time. The text of the letter, which was discovered six months after Beethoven's death, is included in the excerpt below from Beethoven's Letters, *edited by A. Eaglefield-Hull. As you read the excerpt, consider how the tone of the Heiligenstadt Testament is similar to Beethoven's music.*

For My Brothers Carl and [Johann] Beethoven

O ye men who regard or declare me to be malevolent, stubborn or cynical, how unjust are ye towards me. You do not know the secret cause of my seeming so. From childhood onward, my heart and mind prompted me to be kind and tender, and I was ever inclined to accomplish great deeds. But only think that during the last six years, I have been in a wretched condition, rendered worse by unintelligent physicians. Deceived from year to year with hopes of improvement, and then finally forced to the prospect of a *lasting infirmity* (which may last for years, or even be totally incurable). Born with a fiery, active temperament, even susceptive to the diversions of society, I had soon to retire from the world, to live a solitary life. At times, even, I endeavoured to forget all this, but how harshly was I driven back by the redoubled experience of my bad hearing. Yet it was not possible for me to say to men: Speak louder, shout, for I am deaf. Alas! how could I declare the weakness of a *sense* which in me *ought to be* more acute than in others—a sense which *formerly* I possessed in highest perfection, a perfection such as few in my profession enjoy, or ever have enjoyed; no I cannot do it. Forgive, therefore, if you see me withdraw, when I would willingly mix with you. My misfortune pains me doubly, in that I am certain to be

Ludwig van Beethoven

misunderstood. For me there can be no recreation in the society of my fellow creatures, no refined conversations, no interchange of thought. Almost alone, and only mixing in society when absolutely necessary, I am compelled to live like an exile. If I approach near to people, a feeling of hot anxiety comes over me lest my condition should be noticed—for so it has been during these past six months which I spent in the country. Ordered by my intelligent physician to spare my hearing as much as possible, he almost fell in with my present frame of mind, although many a time I was carried away by my sociable inclinations. But how humiliating was it, when some one standing close to me heard a distant flute, and I heard *nothing*, or a *shepherd singing*, and again I heard nothing. Such incidents almost drove me to despair; at times I was on the point of putting an end to my life—*art* alone restrained my hand. Oh! it seemed as if I could not quit this earth until I had produced all I felt within me, and so I continued this wretched life—wretched, indeed, with so sensitive a body that a somewhat sudden change can throw me from the best into the worst state. *Patience,* I am told, I must choose as my guide. I have done so—lasting, I hope, will be my resolution to bear up until it pleases the inexorable [fates] to break the thread. Forced already in my 28th year to become a philosopher, it is not easy; for an artist more difficult than for anyone else. O Divine Being, Thou who lookest down into my inmost soul, Thou understandest; Thou knowest that love for mankind and a desire to do good live therein. Oh, my fellow men, when one day you read this, remember that you were unjust to me, and let the unfortunate one console himself if he can find one like himself, who in spite of all obstacles which nature has thrown in his way, has still done everything in his power to be received into the ranks of worthy artists and men. You, my brothers Carl and [Johann], as soon as I am dead, beg Professor Schmidt, if he be still living, to describe my malady; and annex this written account to that of my illness, so that at least the world, so far as possible, may become reconciled to me after my death. And now I declare you both heirs to my small fortune (if such it may be called). Divide it honourably and dwell in peace, and help each other. What you have done against me, has, as you know, long been forgiven. And you, brother Carl, I especially thank you for the attachment you have shown towards me of late. My prayer is that your life may be better, less troubled by cares, than mine. Recommend to your children *virtue;* it alone can bring happiness, not money. I speak from experience. It was virtue which bore me up in time of trouble; to her, next to my art, I owe thanks for my not having laid violent hands on myself. Farewell, and love one another. My thanks to all friends, especially *Prince Lichnowski and Professor Schmidt.* I should much like one of you to keep as an heirloom the instruments given to me by Prince L., but let no strife arise between you concerning them; if money should be of more service to you, just sell them. How happy I feel that even when lying in my grave, I may be useful to you.

So let it be. I joyfully hasten to meet my death. If it come before I have had opportunity to develop all my artistic faculties, it will come, my hard fate notwithstanding, too soon, and I should probably wish it later—yet even then I shall be happy, for will it not deliver me from a state of endless suffering? Come when thou wilt, I shall face thee courageously—farewell, and when I am dead do not entirely forget me. This I deserve from you, for during my lifetime I often thought of you, and how to make you happy. Be ye so.

LUDWIG VAN BEETHOVEN

Heiligenstadt, the 6th of October, 1802

READING REVIEW

1. Why was his deafness such a blow to Beethoven?
2. What kept Beethoven from committing suicide?
3. How is the tone of this letter a reflection of Beethoven's music? Explain your answer.

81 A SUFFRAGETTE GOES TO PRISON

Although the drive for woman suffrage in Great Britain began during the 1800s, it did not become organized until the formation of the Women's Social and Political Union in 1903. The W.S.P.U.'s initial strategy was to use demonstrations and acts of civil disobedience to make its case. After Parliament rejected a franchise bill in 1910, however, the W.S.P.U.'s activities became more and more militant. In 1913 two suffragettes blew up the house of David Lloyd George, the chancellor of the exchequer. Emmeline Pankhurst, the leader of the W.S.P.U., was soon arrested for inciting this act. In the excerpt below from My Own Story, *Pankhurst describes her trial. As you read the excerpt, consider whether using militant acts to promote freedom and democracy is ever justified.*

When I entered Old Bailey on that memorable Wednesday, April 2nd, 1913, to be tried for inciting to commit a felony, the court was packed with women. A great crowd of women who could not obtain the necessary tickets remained in the streets below for hours waiting news of the trial. A large number of detectives from Scotland Yard, and a still larger number of uniformed police were on duty both inside and outside the court. I could not imagine why it was considered necessary to have such a regiment of police on hand, for I had not, at that time, realised the state of terror into which the militant movement, in its new development, had thrown the authorities.

Mr. Bodkin and Mr. Travers Humphreys appeared to prosecute on behalf of the Crown, and I conducted my own case, in consultation with my solicitor, Mr. Marshall. The Judge, Mr. Justice Lush, having taken his seat I entered the dock and listened to the reading of the indictment. I pled "not guilty," not because I wished to evade responsibility for the explosion,—I had already assumed that responsibility—but because the indictment accused me of having wickedly and maliciously incited women to crime. What I had done was not wicked of purpose, but quite the opposite of wicked. I could not therefore truthfully plead guilty. The trial having opened the Judge courteously asked me if I would like to sit down. I thanked him, and asked if I might also have a small table on which to place my papers. By orders of the Judge a table was brought me.

Mr. Bodkin opened the case by explaining the "Malicious Damages to Property Act" of 1861, under which I was charged, and after describing the explosion which had damaged the Lloyd-George house at Walton, said that I was accused of being in the affair an accessory before the fact. It was not suggested, he said, that I was present when the crime was committed, but it was charged that I had moved and incited, counselled and procured women whose names were unknown to carry out that crime. It would be for the jury to decide, after the evidence had been presented, whether the facts did not point most clearly to the conclusion that women, probably two in number, who committed the crime were members of the Women's Social and Political Union, which had its office at Kingsway in London, and of which the defendant was the head, moving spirit and recognised leader. . . .

[In response, I said]: "Over one thousand women have gone to prison in the course of this agitation, have suffered their imprisonment, have come out of prison injured in health, weakened in body, but not in spirit. I come to stand my trial from the bedside of one of my daughters, who has come out of Holloway Prison, sent there for two months' hard labour for participating with four other people in breaking a small pane of glass. She has hunger-struck in prison. She submitted herself for more than five weeks to the horrible ordeal of feeding by force, and she has come out of prison having lost nearly two stone [28 pounds] in weight. She is so weak that she cannot get out of her bed. And I say to you, gentlemen, that is the kind of punishment you are inflicting upon me or any other woman who may be brought before you. I ask you if you are prepared to send an incalculable number of women to prison—I speak to you as representing others in the same position—if you are prepared to go on doing that kind of thing indefinitely, because that is what is going to happen. There is absolutely no doubt about it. I think you have seen enough even in this present case to convince you that we are not women who are notoriety hunters. We could do that, heaven knows, much more cheaply if we sought it. We are women, rightly or wrongly, convinced that this is the only way in which we can win power to alter what for us are intolerable conditions, absolutely intolerable conditions. . . .

Suffragettes in New York

And if you convict me, gentlemen, if you find me guilty, I tell you quite honestly and quite frankly, that whether the sentence is a long sentence, whether the sentence is a short sentence, I shall not submit to it. I shall, the moment I leave this court, if I am sent to prison, whether to penal servitude or to the lighter form of imprisonment . . . whatever my sentence is, from the moment I leave this court I shall quite deliberately refuse to eat food—I shall join the women who are already in Holloway on the hunger strike. I shall come out of prison, dead or alive, at the earliest possible moment; and once out again, as soon as I am physically fit I shall enter into this fight again. Life is very dear to us all. I am not seeking . . . to commit suicide. I do not want to commit suicide. I want to see the women of this country enfranchised, and I want to live until that is done. . . .

There is only one way to put a stop to this agitation; there is only one way to break down this agitation. It is not by deporting us, it is not by locking us up in gaol; it is by doing us justice. And so I appeal to you gentlemen, in this case of mine, to give a verdict, not only on my case, but upon the whole of this agitation. I ask you to find me not guilty of malicious incitement to a breach of the law. . . ."

The jury retired, and soon after the afternoon session of the court opened they filed in, and in reply to the usual question asked by the clerk of arraigns, said that they had agreed upon a verdict. Said the clerk:

"Do you find Mrs. Pankhurst guilty or not guilty?"

"Guilty," said the foreman, "with a strong recommendation to mercy.". . .

Mr. Justice Lush, in passing sentence, said: ". . . I cannot, and I will not, regard your crime as a merely trivial one. It is not. It is a most serious one, and, whatever you may think, it is a wicked one. I have paid regard to the recommendation of the jury. . . . The least sentence I can pass upon you is a sentence of three years' penal servitude."

As soon as the sentence was pronounced the intense silence which had reigned throughout the trial was broken, and an absolute pandemonium broke out among the spectators. At first it was merely a confused and angry murmur of "Shame!" "Shame!" The murmurs quickly swelled into loud and indignant cries, and then from the gallery of the court there arose a great chorus uttered with the utmost intensity and passion. "Shame!" "Shame!" The women sprang to their feet, in many instances stood on their seats, shouting "Shame!" "Shame!" as I was conducted out of the dock. . . . "Keep the flag flying!" shouted a woman's voice, and the response came in a chorus: "We will!" "Bravo!" "Three cheers for Mrs. Pankhurst!" That was the last I heard of the courtroom protest.

Afterwards I heard that the noise and confusion was kept up for several minutes longer, the Judge and the police being quite powerless to obtain order. Then the women filed out singing the Women's Marseillaise—

"March on, march on,
Face to the dawn,
The dawn of liberty.". . .

At three o'clock, when I left the court by a side entrance in Newgate Street, I found a crowd of women waiting to cheer me. . . . I entered a four wheeler and was driven to Holloway to begin my hunger strike. Scores of women followed in taxicabs, and when I arrived at the prison gates there was another protest of cheers for the cause and boos for the law. In the midst of all this intense excitement I passed through the grim gates into the twilight of prison, now become a battleground.

READING REVIEW

1. Why did Mrs. Pankhurst plead not guilty to the charge of inciting to commit a felony?
2. What did Mrs. Pankhurst say she would do if she was found guilty and sent to prison?
3. (a) Do you think the statement "The end justifies the means" is true with reference to the militant suffragettes' actions? (b) Are violent actions justified if they are committed in the name of a good cause? Why or why not?

---

82 THE DEATH OF PRESIDENT LINCOLN

On April 14, 1865, just a few days after Robert E. Lee surrendered to Ulysses S. Grant at Appomattox, the actor John Wilkes Booth, a fanatic supporter of the Confederacy assassinated President Abraham Lincoln. Booth escaped the scene of the assassination but was hunted down and killed in a barn in Virginia a few days later. In the excerpt below from The Works of Walt Whitman, *Whitman relates the circumstances of President Lincoln's death. As you read the excerpt, ask yourself how Whitman felt about President Lincoln.*

The President came betimes, and, with his wife, witness'd the play from the large stage-boxes of the second tier, two thrown into one, and profusely draped with the national flag. The acts and scenes of the piece—one of those singularly written compositions which have at least the merit of giving entire relief to an audience engaged in mental action or business excitements and cares during the day, as it makes not the slightest call on either the moral, emotional, esthetic, or spiritual nature—a piece ("Our American Cousin,") in which, among other characters, so call'd, a Yankee, certainly such a one as was never seen, or the least like it ever seen, in North America, is introduced in England, with a fol-de-rol of talk, plot, scenery, and such phantasmagoria as goes to make up popular drama—had progress'd through perhaps a couple of its acts, when in the midst of this comedy, or non-such, or whatever it is to be call'd, and to offset it, or finish it out, as if in Nature's and the great Muse's mockery of these poor mimes, came interpolated that scene, not really or exactly to be described at all, (for on the many hundreds who were there it seems to this hour to have left a passing blur, a dream, a blotch)—and yet partially to be described as I now proceed to give it. There is a scene in the play representing a modern parlor, in which two unprecedented English ladies are inform'd by the impossible Yankee that he is not a man of fortune, and therefore undesirable for marriage-catching purposes; after which, the comments being finish'd, the dramatic trio make exit, leaving the stage clear for a moment. At this period came the murder of Abraham Lincoln. . . . Through the general hum following the stage pause . . . came the muffled sound of a pistol-shot, which not one-hundredth part of the audience heard at the time—and yet a moment's hush—somehow, surely, a vague startled thrill—and then, through the ornamented, draperied, starr'd and striped space-way of the President's box, a sudden figure, a man, raises himself with hands and feet, stands a moment on the railing, leaps below to the stage, (a distance of perhaps fourteen or fifteen feet,) falls out of position, catching his boot-heel in the copious drapery, (the American Flag,) falls on one knee, quickly recovers himself, rises as if nothing had happen'd, (he really sprains his ankle, but unfelt then)—and so the figure, Booth, the murderer, dress'd in plain black broadcloth, bare-headed, with full, glossy, raven hair, and his eyes like some mad animal's flashing with light and resolution, yet with a certain strange calmness, holds aloft in one hand a large knife . . . turns fully toward the audience his face of statuesque beauty, lit by those basilisk eyes, flashing with desperation, perhaps insanity—launches out in a firm and steady voice the words *Sic semper tyrannis* [Thus always to tyrants]—and then walks with neither slow nor very rapid pace diagonally across to the back of the stage, and disappears. (Had not all this terrible scene—making the mimic ones preposterous—had it not all been rehears'd, in blank, by Booth, beforehand?)

A moment's hush—a scream—the cry of *murder*—Mrs. Lincoln leaning out of the box, with ashy cheeks and lips, with involuntary cry, pointing to the retreating figure, *He has kill'd the President.* And still a moment's strange, incredulous suspense—and then the deluge!—then that mixture of horror, noises, uncertainty—(the sound, somewhere back, of a horse's hoofs clattering with speed)—the people burst through the chairs and railings, and break them up—there is inextricable confusion and terror—women faint—quite feeble persons fall, and are trampled on—many cries of agony are heard—the broad stage suddenly fills to suffocation with a dense and motley crowd, like some horrible carnival—the audience rush generally upon it, at least the strong men do—the actors and actresses are all there in their play-costumes and painted faces, with mortal fright showing through the rouge—the screams and calls, confused talk—redoubled, trebled—two or three manage to pass up water from the stage to the President's box—others try to clamber up. . . .

"And still a moment's strange, incredulous suspense—and then the deluge!"

In the midst of all this, the soldiers of the President's guard, with others, suddenly drawn to the scene, burst in—(some two hundred altogether)—they storm the house, through all the tiers, especially the upper ones, inflamed with fury, literally charging the audience with fix'd bayonets, muskets and pistols, shouting *Clear out! clear out!*. . . . Such a wild scene, or a suggestion of it rather, inside the play-house that night.

Outside, too, in the atmosphere of shock and craze, crowds of people, fill'd with frenzy, ready to seize any outlet for it, come near committing murder several times on innocent individuals. . . .

And in the midst of that pandemonium, infuriated soldiers, the audience and the crowd, the stage, and all its actors and actresses, its paint-pots, spangles, and gas-lights—the life blood from those veins, the best and sweetest of the land, drips slowly down, and death's ooze already begins its little bubbles on the lips.

READING REVIEW

1. What ironic incident led to Booth spraining his ankle?
2. What was the audience's reaction after Booth shot Lincoln?
3. How do you think Whitman viewed Lincoln? Support your answer with evidence from the excerpt.

---

83 THE LAST DAY OF THE PARIS COMMUNE

In March 1871, shocked that the French government had surrendered to the Prussians, the people of Paris set up their own government, the Commune. Some six weeks later, on May 21, 1871, about 70,000 French government troops, under the command of Marshal MacMahon, stormed into Paris. The forces of the Commune, known as the Federalists, fought a ferocious battle of retreat through the city and made their last stand among the gravestones of Père-Lachaise cemetery on May 27. In the excerpt below from Eyewitness to History, *edited by John Carey, a British journalist describes the fate of the few Federalists who lived through the battle. As you read the excerpt, ask yourself how the journalist felt about the government troops' actions in Père-Lachaise.*

Travelling to England, and writing hard all the way in train and boat, I reached London on the early morning of Thursday, May 25th, and was back in Paris the following day. All was then virtually over. The hostages in La Roquette had been shot, and the Hotel de Ville [City Hall] had fallen on the afternoon of the day I had left. When I returned the Communists were at their last gasp in Château d'Eau, the Buttes de Chaumont, and Père-Lachaise. On the afternoon of the 28th, after just one week of fighting, Marshal MacMahon announced, "I am absolute master of Paris." On the following morning I visited Père-Lachaise, where the very last shots had been fired. Bivouac fires had been fed with the souvenirs of pious sorrow, and the trappings of woe had been torn down to be used as bedclothes. But there had been no great amount of fighting in the cemetery itself. An infallible token of close and heavy firing are the dents of many bullets, and of those there were comparatively few in Père-Lachaise. Shells, however, had fallen freely, and the results were occasionally very ghastly. But the ghastliest sight in Père-Lachaise was in the south-eastern corner, where, close to the boundary wall, there had been a natural hollow. The hollow was now filled up by dead. One could measure the dead by the rood. There they lay, tier above tier, each successive tier powdered over with a coating of chloride of lime—two hundred of them patent to the eye, besides those underneath hidden by the earth covering layer after layer. Among the dead were many women. There, thrown up in the sunlight, was a well-rounded arm with a ring on one of the fingers. . . . And yonder were faces which to look upon made one shudder—faces distorted out of humanity with ferocity and agony combined. The ghastly effect of the dusty white powder on the dulled eyes, the gnashed teeth, and the jagged beards cannot be described. How died these men and women? Were they carted hither and laid out in this dead-hole of Père-Lachaise? Not so: the hole had been replenished from close by. Just yonder was where they were posted up against that section of pock-pitted wall—there was no difficulty in reading the open book—and were shot to death as they stood or crouched.

READING REVIEW

1. How did the journalist know that there had not been much fighting in Père-Lachaise cemetery?
2. Why did the journalist think the Federalists in the common grave had been executed?
3. How do you think the journalist felt about the scenes in Père-Lachaise? Explain your answer.

---

84 THE GREAT LIBERATOR

Simón Bolívar (1783–1830), the son of a wealthy Venezuelan family, was educated in Europe. There he became familiar with the ideas of the Enlightenment, and on his return to South America he vowed to free his country from Spanish rule. In the fight for freedom, Bolívar soon gained a reputation as a courageous and brilliant military leader, and his triumphs on the battlefield won him the title of "Great Liberator." In the excerpt below from Volume 1 of Latin American Civilization: The Colonial Origins, *edited by Benjamin Keen, the Frenchman Louis Peru de Lacroix, a member of Bolívar's staff, describes his commander. As you read the excerpt, consider how Bolívar's character contributed to his abilities as a leader.*

The General-in-Chief, Simón José Antonio Bolívar, will be forty-five years old on July 24 of this year [1828], but he appears older, and many judge him to be fifty. He is slim and of medium height; his arms, thighs, and legs are lean. He has a long head, wide between the temples, and a sharply pointed chin. A large, round, prominent forehead is furrowed with wrinkles that are very noticeable when his face is in repose, or in moments of bad humor and anger. His hair is crisp, bristly, quite abundant, and partly gray. His eyes have lost the brightness of youth but preserve the luster of genius. They are deep-set, neither small nor large; the eyebrows are thick, separated, slightly arched, and are grayer than the hair on his head. The nose is aquiline and well formed. He has prominent cheekbones, with hollows beneath. His mouth is large, and the lowly lip protrudes; he has white teeth and an agreeable smile. . . . His tanned complexion darkens when he is in a bad humor, and his whole appearance changes; the wrinkles on his forehead and temples stand out much more prominently; the eyes become smaller and narrower; the lower lip protrudes considerably, and the mouth turns ugly. In fine, one sees a completely different countenance: a frowning face that reveals sorrows, sad reflections, and sombre ideas. But when he is happy all this disappears; his face lights up, his mouth smiles, and the spirit of the Liberator shines over his countenance. His Excellency is clean-shaven at present. . . .

"His eyes have lost the brightness of youth but preserve the luster of genius."

The Liberator has energy; he is capable of making a firm decision and sticking to it. His ideas are never commonplace—always large, lofty, and original. His manners are affable, having the tone of Europeans of high society. He displays a republican simplicity and modesty, but he has the pride of a noble and elevated soul, the dignity of his rank, and the *amour-propre* [self-esteem] that comes from consciousness of worth and leads men to great actions. Glory is his ambition, and his glory consists in having liberated ten million persons and founded three republics. He has an enterprising spirit, combined with great activity, quickness of speech, an infinite fertility in ideas, and the constancy necessary for the realization of his projects. He is superior to misfortunes and reverses; his philosophy consoles him and his intelligence finds ways of righting what has gone wrong. . . .

He loves a discussion, and dominates it through his superior intelligence; but he sometimes appears too dogmatic, and is not always tolerant enough with those who contradict him. He scorns servile flattery and base adulators. He is sensitive to criticism of his actions; calumny against him cuts him to the quick, for none is more touchy about his reputation than the Liberator. . . .

His heart is better than his head. His bad temper never lasts; when it appears, it takes possession of his head, never his heart, and as soon as the latter recovers its dominance it immediately makes amends for the harm that the former may have done. . . .

In all the actions of the Liberator, and in his conversation, . . . one observes an extreme quickness. His questions are short and concise; he likes to be answered in the same way, and when someone wanders away from the question he impatiently says that that is not what he asked; he has no liking for a diffuse answer. He sustains his opinions with force and logic, and generally with tenacity. When he has occasion to contradict some assertion, he says: "No, sir, it is not so, but thus. . . ." He is very observant, noting even the least trifles; he dislikes the poorly educated, the bold, the windbag, the indiscreet, and the discourteous. Since nothing escapes him, he takes pleasure in criticizing such people, always making a little commentary on their defects. . . .

The ideas of the Liberator are like his imagination: full of fire, original, and new. They lend considerable sparkle to his conversation, and make it extremely varied. When His Excellency praises, defends, or approves something, it is always with a little exaggeration. The same is true when he criticizes, condemns, or disapproves of something. In his conversation he frequently quotes, but his citations are always well

Simón Bolívar

chosen and pertinent. Voltaire is his favorite author, and he has memorized many passages from his works, both prose and poetry. He knows all the good French writers and evaluates them competently. He has some general knowledge of Italian and English literature and is very well versed in that of Spain.

The Liberator takes great pleasure in telling of his first years, his voyages, and his campaigns, and of his relations and old friends. His character and spirit dispose him more to criticize than to eulogize, but his criticisms or eulogies are never baseless; he could be charged only with an occasional slight exaggeration. I have never heard his Excellency utter a calumny. He is a lover of truth, heroism, and honor and of the public interest and morality. He detests and scorns all that is opposed to these lofty and noble sentiments.

READING REVIEW

1. According to Lacroix, how did anger affect Bolívar's appearance?
2. What faults did Lacroix notice in Bolívar's character?
3. Which of Bolívar's personal characteristics helped him as a leader? Explain your answer.

---

85 A VOLUNTEER'S VIEW OF GARIBALDI AT THE BATTLE OF THE VOLTURNO

Giuseppe Garibaldi's personal warmth, incredible courage, and fiery devotion to his cause drew many non-Italians into the fight for Italian freedom. Volunteers from the Americas and from every country in Europe joined his army of Red Shirts. In the excerpt below from Garibaldi, *edited by Denis Mack Smith, one of these volunteers—Englishman W. B. Brooke—describes the Battle of the Volturno in 1860, one of the last actions in Garibaldi's southern Italian campaign. As you read the excerpt, note the impact that Garibaldi's presence had on his troops.*

Garibaldi, while intending to keep the defensive, was perfectly ready to take the offensive at the first opportunity.

At six o'clock, 16,000 [of the enemy] had left Capua; 5,000 of these were cavalry. At the same time 5,000 men marched on to Maddaloni to cut off the retreat of the Garibaldians by taking them in the rear. As soon as Egerton and myself heard the firing, we rushed off up the street, where we were met by an old man, who said the Neapolitans had driven the Garibaldians over the fifteen arches of the railway, and that he apprehended the worst. Thinking, right or not, that St. Angelo would give us the best chance of service, Egerton and I, in spite of the balls and grape-shot now hotly whistling about on every side, started off for St. Angelo, along the dusty high road from Santa Maria.

That morning, profiting by the thick mists which rise from the low ground near the river, I had seen them so thick indeed—and they were at that time—that you could hardly see with any certainty at the least distance—[the enemy] had advanced nearly up to a barricade constructed to guard a position at a point where a by-road from Capua to St. Angelo cuts the road from Santa Maria, where the road turns up to St. Angelo.

They had affected this advance under cover of the dry beds of mountain torrents, steep and well screened with brushwood. With the nature of the ground, and the thick white mist likewise in their favor, they rushed at the barricade with terrible impetuosity, and drove the Garibaldini at first across the main road, right away towards St. Angelo. Along the road are open fields, where I have many a time since then sat and boiled my coffee in my canteen over a wood fire, or with a writing-case on my knee indited letters to my friends at home, with the scene vividly before me. Taking up position there, they formed well.

They had, it seems, been equally successful on the left; for they had driven the Garibaldians also away from a trench near the river. Moreover, a column of theirs had actually got up the hill which commands St. Angelo.

Nothing but the genius of Garibaldi in that terrible hour could have turned his fortunes so far. He arrived in the very nick of time. He came along rapidly with his staff in carriages from Santa Maria, and was rattling along the main road with grape-shot and bullets flying over him. Very soon he was in sight of the enemy, when luckily the carriages, except one, had time to turn into a covered way. The last carriage was smashed by a cannon-ball.

On through the covered way then went the General with his "six-shooter" in his hand towards St. Angelo. When he arrived his men gave a shout. His presence now as ever was their best stimulant.

The enemy had a column in the rear on the hills to the left. But some skirmishers were thrown out on the heights above them. Then on came thundering the Neapolitan cavalry; but this time they met no cravens [cowards]. The fierce Calabrese emptied their saddles, bayonetted them, and in one or two instances slew them with their stilettoes. And yet, glorious as it is to see brave men in a good cause dying for freedom with Spartan fortitude, it seemed to me something like a desecration of the loveliness of the scene, on which the sun shone brightly, all this carnage and slaughter. What struck me at the time more than anything else, was the stern, silent determination with which every man fought. This time there were no rallying cries, no encouraging shouts—not a word—but grim, deadly conflict. Foeman standing before foemen with bent brows and compressed lips in stern hate, asking no quarter and giving none.

Then a red cloud came before my eyes, and I seemed to feel no more, save that I was one in a *melée,* shooting away, or bayonetting, or using a revolver as opportunity offered. And the calm sun all this while, and the green olive trees looked down on us at out work of death, as so many

Giuseppe Garibaldi

stern and silent foemen drove their reeking bayonets into the hearts of their adversaries, and riflemen sent their deadly bullets crashing through some hussar's brain. Then were steeds screaming harshly in their agony, and running riderless among us. Then were seen fierce death-struggles in several places, Calabrese locked in conflict with Neapolitans till the pistol or the dagger settled the matter. There were not really . . . more than 3,000 men there of ours that day. The Neapolitans had actually three times that number.

Our main object was to take care of the main road to Santa Maria and the pontoons, etc., prepared towards the river. Bloody work it was for all. We had to push our line of defense further than the actual main road itself, and come down well into the open. As for defensive works, we there had none, save a barricade of sandbags with four guns on the road leading from Capua to St. Angelo. All day long there was terrific fighting going on for possession of the barricade. I saw John Egerton that day doing his duty like an Englishman who is in earnest. What better description can I give than that to Englishmen? I saw Garibaldi, with his red shirt wringing wet with perspiration, his eye sternly gleaming, his face flushed with the heat of conflict, and blackened by the smoke and dust. I heard his voice commanding—but it was no longer now the calm, clear voice of quieter times. It was hoarse and guttural, and choked with emotion. For the good general saw his gallant band unfalteringly pouring out their life-blood.

READING REVIEW

1. Why did Brooke think the fighting at the Volturno was a "desecration"?
2. Why was Garibaldi's victory at the Volturno so remarkable?
3. Many of Garibaldi's Red Shirts said they were ready to follow him into battle, no matter what the odds against them were. Why do you think the Red Shirts were so loyal to Garibaldi?

---

86 BISMARCK "EDITS" THE EMS DISPATCH

To complete the unification of Germany, Bismarck needed to persuade the independent states in southern Germany to join his North German Confederation. Since these states feared attack by France, Bismarck realized that if he could draw France into a war the southern states would rush to join. When Bismarck received a telegram from King William I of Prussia who was staying at the resort town of Ems, the Iron Chancellor saw his opportunity. He edited the telegram so that it sounded as though the king had insulted the French ambassador. When the telegram was published, it so infuriated the French that they declared war. In the excerpt below from Bismarck, *edited by Frederic B. M. Hollyday, Bismarck relates the circumstances surrounding the editing of the Ems dispatch. As you read the excerpt, consider how Bismarck's action fit in with his efforts to make Germany the leading nation in Europe.*

I conversed with the Minister of War, von Roon: we had got our slap in the face from France, and had been reduced, by our complaisance, to look like seekers of a quarrel if we entered upon war, the only way we could wipe away the stain. My position was now untenable, solely because, during his course at the baths [at Ems], the King under pressure of threats, had given audience to the French ambassador for four consecutive days, and had exposed his royal person to insolent treatment from this foreign agent. . . .

Having decided to resign, in spite of the remonstrances which Roon made against it, I invited him and [Military Chief of Staff] Moltke to dine with me . . . and communicated to them at table my views and prospects for doing so. Both were greatly depressed, and reproached me indirectly with selfishly availing myself of my greater facility for withdrawing from service. I maintained the position that I could not offer up my sense of honor to politics, that both of them, being professional soldiers and consequently without freedom of choice, need not take the same point of view as a responsible Foreign Minister. During our conversation, I was informed that a telegram from Ems . . . was being deciphered. When the copy was handed to me . . . I read it to my guests, whose dejection was so great that they turned away from food and drink. On a repeated examination of the document I lingered upon the authorization of his Majesty, which included a command, immediately to communicate . . . [the telegram] both to our ambassadors and to the press. I put a few questions to Moltke as to the extent of his confidence in the state of our preparations, especially as to the time they would still require in order to meet this sudden risk of war. He answered that if there was to be war he expected no advantage to us by deferring its outbreak; and even if we should not be strong enough at first to protect all the territories on the left bank of the Rhine against French invasion, our preparations would nevertheless soon overtake those of the French, while at a later period this advantage would be diminished; he regarded a rapid outbreak as, on the whole, more favorable to us than delay.

In view of the attitude of France, our national sense of honor compelled us, in my opinion, to go to war; and if we did not act according to the demands of this feeling, we should lose, when on the way to its completion, the entire impetus towards our national development won in 1866, while the German national feeling south of the Main, aroused by our military successes in 1866, and shown by the readiness of the southern states to enter the alliances, would have to grow cold again. . . .

I [also felt] convinced that the gulf, which diverse dynastic and family-influences and different habits of life had in the course of history created between the south and the north of the Fatherland, could not be more effectually bridged over than by a joint national war against the neighbor who had been aggressive for many centuries. . . .

All these considerations, conscious and unconscious, strengthened my opinion that war could be avoided only at the cost of the honor of Prussia and of the national confidence in it. Under this conviction I made use of the royal authorization communicated to me . . . to publish the contents of the telegram; and in the presence of my two guests I reduced the telegram by striking out words, but without adding or altering . . . The difference in the effect of the abbreviated text of the Ems telegram as compared with that produced by the original was not the result of stronger words but of the form, which made this announcement appear decisive, while [the original] version would only have been regarded as a fragment of a negotiation still pending, and to be continued at Berlin.

After I had read out the concentrated edition to my two guests, Moltke remarked: "Now it has a different ring; it sounded before like a parley; now it is like a flourish in answer to a challenge." I went on to explain: "If in execution of his Majesty's order I at once communicate this text, which contains no alteration in, or addition to, the telegram, not only to the newspapers, but also by telegraph to all our embassies, it will be known in Paris before midnight, and not only on account of its contents, but also on account of the manner of its distribution, it will have the effect of a red flag upon the Gallic bull. Fight we must if we do not want to act the part of the vanquished without a battle. Success, however, essentially depends upon the impression which the origination of the war makes upon us and others; it is important that we should be the party attacked, and this Gallic overweening and touchiness will [play into our hands] if we announce in the face of Europe . . . that we fearlessly meet the public threats of France."

This explanation brought about in the two generals . . . a more joyous mood, the liveliness of which surprised me. They had suddenly recovered their pleasure in eating and drinking and spoke in a more cheerful vein. Roon said: "Our God of old lives still and will not let us perish in disgrace." Moltke so far relinquished his passive equanimity that, glancing up joyously toward the ceiling and abandoning his usual punctiliousness [carefulness] of speech, he smote his hand upon his breast and said: "If I may but live to lead our armies in such a war, then the devil may come directly afterward and fetch away [my] 'old carcass'. . . ."

READING REVIEW

1. Why did Roon and Moltke reproach Bismarck for threatening to resign?
2. What, according to Bismarck, would be the difference in effect of the edited and original versions of the Ems dispatch?
3. How did Bismarck's editing of the Ems dispatch fit in with the other methods he used to achieve his grand design for Germany?

---

87 CZAR NICHOLAS I'S APPROACH TO GOVERNMENT—ORTHODOXY, AUTOCRACY, NATIONALITY

Worried by the unrest stirred up among the Russian people by nationalist and liberal ideas from western Europe, Czar Nicholas I attempted to shut the door to Western influence. In a memorandum to Nicholas in 1834, the Russian Minister of Public Education, S.S. Uvarov, outlined this new policy. In the excerpt below from Russia and the West from Peter to Khrushchev, *edited by L. Jay Oliva, Uvarov describes the three main themes of the policy—orthodoxy, autocracy, and nationality. As you read the excerpt, ask yourself why Nicholas feared the influence of western ideas.*

Amid the rapid decay of religious and civilian institutions in Europe and the universal spread of destructive notions, in view of the sad occurrences that surround us on all sides, it was necessary to fortify our Fatherland on the firm foundations which are the basis for the prosperity, the strength, and the life of the people; to find the principles that constitute the distinguishing character of Russia and belong to her exclusively; to gather into one whole the sacred remains of her native essence and cast on these the anchor of our salvation. Fortunately, Russia has kept a warm faith in the saving principles without which she cannot prosper, gain strength, or live.

Sincerely and deeply attached to the Church of his fathers, the Russian has, from the earliest times, looked upon it as the pledge of social and family happiness.

Without love for the faith of its ancestors, a people, just as an individual, is bound to perish. A Russian devoted to his country will no more consent to the loss of one of the tenets of our *Orthodoxy* than to the theft of one pearl from the crown. . . .

"Without love for the faith of its ancestors, a people, just as an individual, is bound to perish."

Autocracy constitutes the chief condition of the political experience of Russia. The Russian colossus stands on it as on the cornerstone of its greatness. This truth is felt by the overwhelming majority of Your Majesty's subjects: they feel it fully, though they are placed in various walks of life and differ in their education and in their relations to the government. The saving conviction that Russia lives and is preserved by the spirit of a strong, humane, enlightened autocracy must permeate public education and develop with it.

Beside these two national principles, there is a third, no less important, no less powerful: *nationality.* The question of nationality does not have the unity of the preceding one; but both take their origin from the same source and are linked on every page of the history of the Russian Empire. All the difficulty concerning nationality consists in harmonizing old and new conceptions; but nationality does not compel us to go back or stand still; it does not require immobility in ideas. The government system, as the human body, must change its aspect with time; features alter with years, but their character must not alter.

READING REVIEW

1. What do you think Uvarov meant by orthodoxy?
2. According to Uvarov what constituted the chief condition of the Russian political experience?
3. Why do you think Nicholas I felt the need to adopt the policy of "orthodoxy, autocracy, nationality"? Explain your answer.

---

88 AN OFFICIAL REPORT ON "BLOODY SUNDAY" IN ST. PETERSBURG

On Sunday, January 22, 1905, a group of St. Petersburg workers—under the leadership of Father Gapon, an Orthodox priest—went to the Palace to petition the Czar on their grievances. Army units, however, blocked their way, and when the workers refused to disperse, the troops opened fire, killing and wounding hundreds. This violent clash on "Bloody Sunday" sparked the Revolution of 1905. The excerpt below from Octobrists to Bolshviks: Imperial Russia 1905–1917 *by Martin McCauley contains the official report of the incident by the chief of the St. Petersburg secret police. As you read the excerpt, consider whether the action of the troops was justified.*

Today, at about 10 A.M., workers began to gather at the Narva Gates, in the Vyborg and Petersburg districts, and also on Vasilievsky Island at the premises of the Assembly of Factory Workers, with the aim, as announced by Father Georgy Gapon, of marching to Palace Square to present a petition to the Emperor. When a crowd of several thousand had assembled in the Narva district, Father Gapon said prayers and then together with the crowd, which had at its head banners and icons stolen from the Narva chapel as well as portraits of Their Majesties, moved off towards the Narva Gates where they were confronted by troops. Despite pleas by local police officers and cavalry charges, the crowd did not disperse but continued to advance. . . . Two companies then opened fire, killing ten and wounding twenty. . . .

A little later about 4,000 workers who had come from the Petersburg and Vyborg districts approached the Trinity Bridge: Father Gapon was also with them. A volley was fired into the crowd, killing five and seriously injuring ten. . . .

Towards 1 P.M. people began to gather in the Alexander Garden, overflowing out of the garden itself into the adjoining part of Palace Square. The cavalry made a series of charges to disperse the crowd, but as this had no effect a number of volleys were fired into the crowd. The numbers of dead and wounded from these volleys is not known as the crowd carried off the victims.

The crowd then engulfed Nevsky Prospect and refused to disperse: a number of shots were fired, killing sixteen people, including one woman. . . .

In the evening a large crowd assembled on Vasilievsky Island and began to build barricades in the streets. . . . It was fired on . . . and two people were killed. . . .

In all some seventy-five people were killed and 200 wounded. It appears that among the dead are numbered women and children.

READING REVIEW

1. How did the workers indicate that they were not challenging the authority of the church and the czar?
2. Who do you think the head of the St. Petersburg secret police held responsible for the bloodshed? Explain your answer.
3. Do you think the troops were justified in opening fire on the crowd? Why or why not?

89 A JUSTIFICATION OF BRITISH COLONIALISM IN AFRICA

In the early 1900s, when their activities in Africa and the Far East came under attack, a number of European powers defended their colonial policies. In his book The Dual Mandate in British Tropical Africa, *Lord Frederick Lugard, a veteran colonial administrator and the first British governor-general of Nigeria, summed up major arguments of the imperial powers. In the excerpt below, Lugard explains the nature of the "dual mandate." As you read the excerpt, ask yourself whether you agree with Lugard's point of view.*

These products [food supplies and raw materials] lay wasted and ungarnered in Africa because the natives did not know their value. Millions of tons of oil-nuts, for instance, grew wild without the labour of man, and lay rotting in the forests. Who can deny the right of the hungry people of Europe to utilise the wasted bounties of nature, or that the task of developing these resources was, as Mr. [Joseph] Chamberlain expressed it, a "trust for civilisation" and for the benefit of mankind? Europe benefited by the wonderful increase in the amenities of life for the mass of her people which followed the opening up of Africa at the end of the nineteenth century. Africa benefited by the influx of manufactured goods, and the substitution of law and order for the methods of barbarism.

Thus Europe was impelled to the development of Africa primarily by the necessities of her people, and not by the greed of the capitalist. Keen competition assured the maximum prices to the producer. It is only when monopolies are granted that it can be argued that profits are restricted to the few, and British policy has long been averse to monopolies in every form. The brains, the research, the capital, and the enterprise of the merchant, the miner, and the planter have discovered and utilised the surplus products of Africa. The profits have been divided among the shareholders representing all classes of the people, and no small share of them has gone to the native African merchant and the middleman as well as the producer. It is true to say that "a vast area of activity has been opened up to the British workman, in which he shares with the capitalist the profits of the development of tropical resources."

In accepting responsibility for the control of these new lands, England obeyed the tradition of her race. British Africa was acquired not by groups of financiers, nor yet . . . by the efforts of her statesmen, but in spite of them. It was the instinct of the British democracy which compelled us to take our share. . . . Even if it were true . . . that we could do as lucrative a trade in the tropical possessions of other nations, there can be no doubt that the verdict of the British people has been emphatic that we will not ask the foreigner to open markets for our use, or leave him the responsibility and its reward. . . .

Let it be admitted at the outset that European brains, capital, and energy have not been, and never will be, expended in developing the resources of Africa from motives of pure philanthropy; that Europe is in Africa for the mutual benefit of her own industrial classes, and of the native races in their progress to a higher plane; that the benefit can be made reciprocal, and that it is the aim and desire of civilised administration to fulfill this dual mandate.

By railways and roads, by reclamation of swamps and irrigation of deserts, and by a system of fair trade and competition, we have added to the prosperity and wealth of these lands, and checked famine and disease. We have put an end to the awful misery of the slave-trade and inter-tribal war, to human sacrifice and the ordeals of the witch-doctor. Where these things survive they are severely suppressed. We are endeavouring to teach the native races to conduct their own affairs with justice and humanity, and to educate them alike in letters and in industry. . . .

As Roman imperialism laid the foundations of modern civilisation, and led the wild barbarians of these islands [Great Britain] along the path of progress, so in Africa to-day we are repaying the debt, and bringing to the dark places of earth, the abode of barbarism and cruelty, the torch of culture and progress, while ministering to the material needs of our own civilisation. In this task the nations of Europe have pledged themselves to co-operation by a solemn covenant. Towards the common goal each will advance by the methods most consonant with its national genius. British methods have not perhaps in all cases produced ideal results, but I am profoundly convinced that there can be no question but that British rule has promoted the happiness and welfare of the primitive races. Let those who question it examine the results impartially. If there is unrest, and a desire for independence, as in India and Egypt, it is because we have taught the value of liberty and freedom, which for centuries these peoples had not known. Their very discontent is a measure of their progress.

We hold these countries because it is the genius of our race to colonise, to trade, and to govern. The task in which England is engaged in the tropics . . . has become part of her tradition, and she has ever given of her best in the cause of liberty and civilisation. There will always be those who cry aloud that the task is being badly done, that it does not need doing, that we can get more profit by leaving others to do it, that it brings evil to subject races and breeds profiteers at home. These were not the principles which prompted our forefathers, and secured for us the place we hold in the world to-day in trust for those who shall come after us.

READING REVIEW

1. Why, according to Lugard, was Europe "impelled to the development of Africa"?
2. What was Europe's dual mandate in Africa?
3. Do you agree or disagree with Lugard's justification of colonialism? Why or why not?

90 THE DOCTRINE OF PASSIVE RESISTANCE

One of the most interesting figures of the Indian nationalist movement of the early 1900s was Aurobindo Ghose (1872–1950). Educated in England until he was 20 years old, Ghose returned to India a stranger in his own land. Seeking knowledge of his cultural heritage, Ghose made friends with a group of fanatic nationalists. He soon became a spokesperson for this group, and his articles in nationalist journals made him famous throughout India. At the height of his fame, however, he withdrew from politics and became a religious mystic. In the excerpt below from Sources of Indian Tradition, *compiled by William Theodore de Bary, Ghose explains his program for winning independence. As you read the excerpt, compare Ghose's ideas on passive resistance with those of Mahatma Gandhi.*

We desire to put an end to petitioning until such a strength is created in the country that a petition will only be a courteous form of demand. We wish to kill utterly the pernicious delusion that a foreign and adverse interest can be trusted to develop us to its own detriment, and entirely to do away with the foolish and ignoble hankering after help from our natural adversaries. Our attitude to bureaucratic concession is that of Laocoon [the priest who warned the Trojans against the wooden horse]: "We fear the Greeks even when they bring us gifts." Our policy is self-development and defensive resistance. But we would extend the policy of self development to every department of national life; not only Swadeshi [the policy of boycotting foreign goods to encourage the development of Indian industry] and National Education, but national defense, national arbitration courts, sanitation, insurance against famine or relief of famine—whatever our hands find to do or urgently needs doing, we must attempt ourselves and no longer look to the alien to do it for us. And we would universalize and extend the policy of defensive resistance until it ran parallel on every line with our self-development. We would not only buy our own goods, but boycott British goods; not only have our own schools, but boycott government institutions; not only organize our league of defense, but have nothing to do with the bureaucratic executive except when we cannot avoid it. At present even in Bengal where boycott is universally accepted, it is confined to the boycott of British goods and is aimed at the British merchant and only indirectly at the British bureaucrat. We would aim it directly both at the British merchant and at the British bureaucrat who stands behind and makes possible exploitation by the merchant. . . .

"We fear the Greeks even when they bring us gifts."

The double policy of self-development and defensive resistance is the common standing-ground of the new spirit all over India. Some may not wish to go beyond its limits, others may look outside it; but so far all are agreed. For ourselves we avow that we advocate passive resistance without wishing to make a dogma of it. In a subject nationality, to win liberty for one's country is the first duty of all, by whatever means, at whatever sacrifice; and this duty must override all other considerations. The work of national emancipation is a great and holy yajna [ritual sacrifice] of which boycott, Swadeshi, national education, and every other activity, great and small, are only major or minor parts. Liberty is the fruit we seek from the sacrifice and the Motherland the goddess to whom we offer it; into the seven leaping tongues of the fire of the yajna we must offer all that we are and all that we have, feeding the fire even with our blood and lives and happiness of our nearest and dearest; for the Motherland is a goddess who loves not a maimed and imperfect sacrifice, and freedom was never won from the gods by a grudging giver. But every great yajna has its Rakshasas [demons] who strive to baffle the sacrifice, to bespatter it with their own dirt, or by guile or violence put out the flame. Passive resistance is an attempt to meet such disturbers by peaceful and self-contained *Brahmatej* [divine power]; but even the greatest Rishis

The Reverend Martin Luther King, Jr. and his wife Coretta (third and fourth from left) applying the principles of passive resistance in an American civil rights march

[teachers] of old could not, when the Rakshasas were fierce and determined, keep up the sacrifice without calling in the bow of the Kshatriya [warrior]. We should have the bow of the Kshatriya ready for use, though in the background. Politics is especially the business of the Kshatriya, and without Kshatriya strength at its back, all political struggle is unavailing.

Vedantism accepts no distinction of true or false religions, but considers only what will lead more or less surely, more or less quickly to moksha [liberation from worldly life], spiritual emancipation and the realization of the Divinity within. Our attitude is a political Vedantism. India, free, one and indivisible, is the divine realization to which we move, emancipation our aim; to that end each nation must practice the political creed which is the most suited to its temperament and circumstances; for that is the best for it which leads most surely and completely to national liberty and national self-realization. But whatever leads only to continued subjection must be spewed out as mere vileness and impurity. Passive resistance may be the final method of salvation in our case or it may be only the preparation for the final sadhana [spiritual discipline]. In either case, the sooner we put it into full and perfect practice, the nearer we shall be to national liberty.

READING REVIEW

1. According to Ghose what is the first duty of people of a subject nationality?
2. Ghose became a religious mystic in later life. What in this excerpt suggests that religious mysticism occupied his mind even during his years in politics?
3. Read the paragraphs on India's most famous nationalist leader Mahatma Gandhi on page 694 in your textbook. How do Gandhi's ideas on passive resistance differ from those of Ghose?

---

91 THE LIVING CONDITIONS OF JAPANESE INDUSTRIAL WORKERS DURING THE MEIJI PERIOD

As happened earlier in Europe and the United States, industrialization in Japan drew many people from the countryside to work in factories, foundries, and mills in cities and towns. In the excerpt below from Imperial Japan 1800–1945, *edited by Jon Livingston, a Japanese social historian discusses the living and working conditions these people faced. As you read the excerpt, compare the living and working conditions in early industrial Japan to those in early industrial America.*

After the beginning of the Meiji period daughters and younger sons of farmers were forced to seek work in textile factories, foundries, glass or cement works, and so on. When a new factory was set up in a provincial town, it solicited labor from the nearby villages, and the metropolitan factories sent representatives to the rural districts for the same purpose. We might note incidentally that many city enterprises showed a preference for workers of one particular [district].

The revision of the tax system affected many landowners adversely, but often they recouped their losses by speculating on rice or simply passed on the taxes to their tenant farmers. The economic gap between landowner and tenant widened, and, when the impoverished tenants heard the bright promises of the labor scouts, they did not long hesitate to send their younger brothers and offspring off to the factories. Those who went boarded the train with high hopes, but they rarely found factory life up to their expectations.

In those days the laborer had no contract with the management. He might be forced to work at any time of day or night, and he had to manage to live on a pittance. The average worker wanted nothing so much as to pack his bags and go home, and in the early years of the period the resulting labor turnover was exceedingly high, especially in the textile mills. Those who forced themselves to put up with working conditions sooner or later lost their health and returned to their homes to spread the tuberculosis virus. Even if they managed to get out of the factory while they were still healthy enough to wield a spade, however, they were likely to find that there was no land in which to sink it. Consequently, more and more stayed in the towns. In this connection, we cannot of course overlook that, despite grueling working conditions, many who had had a taste of city life found it difficult to go back to the farm and take up where they had left off.

The textile companies who employed mostly women seem to have had to compete to secure an adequate labor supply. Wily farmers sometimes made contracts for their daughters with labor recruiters from two or three different companies in order to collect the money that was given upon the signing of the agreement, and it is said that the factories thus defrauded had little recourse. In some cases the recruiter, having discovered that a girl had made an arrangement with another company as well as his own, either carried her away virtually by force or used sweet blandishments to coax her into coming to his company. Under the circumstances, once the girls had started working, the company kept a close watch on them, even when they were off duty, for fear they would run away. Wages were low everywhere, but since the girls were governed by a complicated system of efficiency merits and demerits, they rarely complained even when they were exploited and deceived.

The women textile workers were crowded into dormitories, to which they were unaccustomed, and there they were so jealously supervised that they had no chance to organize themselves into a self respecting social group. Some reacted to these conditions by becoming wanton and offending against what are called public morals.

Japanese workers producing silk

As a rule, even when the girls returned home to their parents they became the targets of much criticism. Actually, they had by no means grown accustomed to luxury in the cities, as the country people often said, but they had indeed often grown so unaccustomed to the rhythm of village life that they found it difficult to readjust. Too, they had often missed out on much of the training in housework that a young woman was expected to have received, and it was consequently difficult to find husbands for them.

READING REVIEW

1. Why did the early years of industrialization in Japan have a high labor turnover?
2. Why were Japanese textile companies forced to compete to ensure an adequate supply of female labor?
3. How did the living and working conditions faced by Japanese female textile workers compare to those faced by their counterparts in the United States?

92 A CHANGE IN UNITED STATES POLICY TOWARD NICARAGUA

In 1909 the United States supported a revolt that forced the anti-American dictator of Nicaragua, Jose Santos Zelaya, to resign. Three years later, with Nicaragua on the verge of civil war, President William Howard Taft sent in the marines, ostensibly to protect American economic interests there. In the excerpt below from The Central American *Crisis Reader, edited by Robert S. Leiken, a modern historian discusses how Taft's move was viewed in Central America. As you read the excerpt, consider how Taft's action was different from the United States' Latin American policy at the time.*

The intervention in Nicaragua in 1912 marked a turning point in American policy in the Caribbean. Before 1912, the navy had frequently made a show of force to prevent fighting which would endanger foreigners or to discourage revolutionary activities. Sometimes, as in Nicaragua in 1910, such measures had influenced, or decided, the outcome of a civil war, but there had been no case before 1912 where American forces had actually gone into battle to help suppress a revolution. American public opinion, as reflected in the press, seemed on the whole to approve what was done, but many voices were raised in protest. Senator Bacon, who had criticized previous actions of the State Department in Central America and had presented a resolution denying the right of the President to use the military forces in operations in a foreign country without the express consent of Congress, again spoke out when the marines first began to arrive in Nicaragua, pointing out that the State Department had gone ahead with its financial projects in spite of the Senate's refusal to approve them and that the power of the United States was being used to support private interests in profitable, speculative operations. The Senate unanimously approved his resolution for an inquiry.

The intervention intensified the already prevalent fear and mistrust of the United States in the other Central American countries. On the other hand, for several years after 1912 the recollection of what had happened . . . discouraged potential revolutionists throughout the isthmus. Except for a *coup d'état* staged by the Minister of War of Costa Rica in 1917, there was no case where a government was overturned by force in Central America between 1912 and 1919. When disturbances threatened, the appearance of an American warship was enough to restore tranquility. The belief that the United States would intervene to uphold constituted governments helped the groups in power in each country to remain in power with little regard for the rights of their opponents, but it at least gave Central America an era of much needed peace.

In Nicaragua, the continued presence of the legation guard was interpreted to mean that no revolution would be tolerated. This meant that the conservatives would stay in power, though everyone, including the State Department, knew that they were a minority party. The arguments advanced in defense of this policy: the assertion that the liberals included a large proportion of the "ignorant mob," and most of their leaders represented the evil *zelayista* tradition, were perhaps put forward in all sincerity by officials who had little contact with any except the conservatives, but they made little sense to anyone who had friends in both parties. The support of a minority government was inconsistent with the principles that governed American policy in the Caribbean, but for more than ten years no Secretary of State wanted to assume responsibility for the revolution that would almost certainly follow the legation guard's withdrawal.

READING REVIEW

1. How did the sending of marines to Nicaragua change American policy in the Caribbean?
2. What impact did Taft's action have on people in Central America?
3. What United States foreign policy statement did Taft's action in Nicaragua illustrate? Explain your answer.

World War in the Twentieth Century

93 THE HOME FRONT IN GERMANY

During World War I, also known as the Great War, the soldiers at the front were not the only ones who suffered the hardships of war. The people at home, too, faced great adversity as they attempted to lead normal lives amid the horrors of war. To ensure that the soldiers had all the supplies needed to fight the war, people on the home front had to endure shortages of food, fuel, clothes, and other items. In many areas of Germany people had to give up such items as new clothes and coffee that they had taken for granted before the war. In the excerpt below from The Home Fronts: Britain, France and Germany 1914–1918 *by John Williams, the author describes what life was like on the German home front during World War I. As you read the excerpt, consider what it would be like to live under wartime conditions.*

In October [1916] a Frenchwoman repatriated from Germany reported her impression that Germany lacked nothing, but that everything was meticulously regulated. Total regulation there certainly was, but, despite that, many commodities were now simply not available. By the autumn of 1916 the country was being squeezed and strained for every scrap of usable material. Wastage had virtually disappeared because there was nothing left to waste. Garbage-saving had been in force since 1914. Households had been scoured for copper and brass, and recently an appeal had been launched for people to bring out their gold. Church bells were being smelted, old iron was fetching fancy prices. Used paper was at a premium. Horse-droppings were being collected as fertiliser, while the streets themselves were left unswept and dirty. To save fuel, summertime [daylight savings] had been introduced, public transport drastically reduced and early closing decreed for shops, cafes and restaurants. And to meet the grave coal shortage, villagers had been allowed to lop dead wood in the State forests. The summer had seen a huge berry-gathering drive, followed by a massive harvesting of nuts and mushrooms. The countryside itself presented a dismal picture. Buildings lacked whitewash; their shutters were dilapidated and walls streaked with damp. Gardens were neglected and such [animal] stock as remained looked uncared-for. Clothing was becoming an increasingly serious problem. With textiles desperately scarce and the best materials going to the troops, civilians were put to all kinds of shifts to garb themselves. Every old garment was pressed into use or sold to the rag-man for reworking, and recourse was had to "shoddy" (the waste arising from the manufacture of wool). It was found that, with a little added fibre, one old suit could be converted into two. Profiteers reaped rich rewards by selling 'shoddy' as new and asking steep prices for a suit that might disintegrate in the first rain-shower. If the customer complained, he would be told to blame the war.

This picture of Germany as Christmas 1916 approached is reinforced by an observer's impressions. There was, he notes, an almost total absence of young men from the towns and countryside. Through the streets ran ancient horse-drawn cabs and taxis—four-fifths of the latter electrified and, owing to the rubber shortage, almost none with solid composite rubber tyres. Laughter was rare, there was no applause in theatres, night-life had virtually disappeared and dancing was unheard of. Beer-cellars were doing better business than supper restaurants, but the beer was weak and watery. No spirits [hard liquor] could be sold after 9 P.M. Food and drink were largely ersatz. The great staple of German diet was tuna fish, disguised as roast beef, steak, veal chops and so on. There were substitutes for coffee, sugar, milk, butter, eggs and condiments. But on so-called meatless days meat could be obtained from black-market restaurants. Evening clothes were hardly ever seen, and their wearer would be viewed with suspicion. Despite the enormous casualties, little mourning [clothing] was worn, this being in deference to a wish expressed by the Kaiser early in the war. But fashion-conscious women were still obtaining Paris-styled clothes, called "Viennese" by the couturieres, through neutral Berne. There were collecting stations everywhere, for anything from old bottles to paper, bits of rubber, string and rags. And a feature reminiscent of Britain at the end of this year was the nation-wide cultivation of allotments. In an effort to combat the food shortage, Germans were utilising every spare plot of ground, mostly to grow potatoes.

"The great staple of German diet was tuna fish, disguised as roast beef, steak, veal chops and so on."

The food difficulties were graphically reflected in the crowded poorer quarters of Berlin's East End. The butchers' shops were almost bare of meat, and long queues—some of them for horse-flesh—were common. The number of empty shops was growing, many small provision-sellers being put out of business by the centralised distribution of food. Bakers did little business except at morning and evening. The dwindling supply of cattle and pigs had allowed the conversion of some slaughterhouses into People's Kitchens, to which thousands of Berliners came for stew that could be bought at 5d. a quart for taking away. In another district the huge Alexander Market was regularly serving 30,000 people. The pervading dreariness of the East End was in contrast to the city's West End and central area, where, as one writer put it, "the cafe lights were bright and music made the restricted menu cards easier to bear." Along with the lights, music helped to bolster war-wearied spirits. The strains of military bands were commonly heard, sometimes accompanying columns of lightly wounded soldiers to and from hospital.

READING REVIEW

1. What steps did the Germans take to conserve fuel?
2. How did the Germans compensate for shortages of food and drink?
3. What do you think would be the greatest hardship of living under wartime conditions? Explain your answer.

---

94 SONGS OF A CAMPAIGN

In late April 1915, in a daring attempt to guarantee Russian access to the Mediterranean Sea through the Dardanelles, Allied forces made a landing on the Gallipoli Peninsula. The Anzacs—members of the Australian and New Zealand Army Corps—spearheaded this landing. Leon Gellert was among the first 500 Anzacs ashore, and he managed to survive the terrible bombardment of Gallipoli's beaches unscathed for nearly three months. In July, however, he was wounded and evacuated to North Africa. While recuperating, he wrote a series of poems, titled Songs of a Campaign, *on his experiences at Gallipoli. Three of Gellert's poems are included in the excerpt below. As you read the poems, ask yourself what Gellert's attitude to war was.*

Before Action

We always had to do our work at night.
I wondered why we had to be so sly.
I wondered why we couldn't have our fight
Under the open sky.

I wondered why I always felt so cold.
I wondered why the orders seemed so slow,
So slow to come, so whisperingly told,
So whisperingly low.

I wondered if my packing-straps were tight,
And wondered why I wondered . . . Sound went wild . . .
An order came . . . I ran into the night,
Wondering why I smiled.

A Night Attack

Be still. The bleeding night is in suspense
Of watchful agony and coloured thought,
And every beating vein and trembling sense,
Long-tired with time, is pitched and overwrought.

French troops at Gallipoli

And for the eye, the darkness holds strange forms,
Soft movements in the leaves and wicked glows
That wait and peer. The whole black landscape swarms
With shapes of white and grey that no one knows;
And for the ear, a sound, a pause, a breath,
A distant hurried footstep moving fast.
The hand has touched the slimy face of death.
The mind is raking at the ragged past. . . .
A sound of rifles rattles from the south,
And startled orders move from mouth to mouth.

The Attack at Dawn

'At every cost,' they said, 'it must be done.'
They told us in the afternoon.
We sit and wait the coming of the sun.
We sit in groups,—grey groups that watch the moon.

We stretch our legs and murmur half in sleep,
And touch the tips of bayonets and yawn.
Our hands are cold. They strangely grope and creep,
Tugging at ends of straps. We wait the dawn!

Some men come stumbling past in single file.
And scrape the trench's side and scatter sand.
They trip and curse and go. Perhaps we smile.
We wait the dawn! . . . The dawn is so close at hand!

A gentle rustling runs along the line.
'At every cost,' they said, 'it must be done.'
A hundred eyes are staring for the sign.
It's coming! Look! . . . Our God's own laughing sun!

READING REVIEW

1. How would you describe the feelings Gellert expressed in the first two poems? Explain your answer.
2. In the third poem, how does Gellert show that the soldiers are nervous about the attack?
3. How do you think Gellert felt about war? Give reasons for your answer.

---

95 THE STORMING OF THE WINTER PALACE

After the abdication of Czar Nicholas II, the moderate provisional government, under the leadership of Alexander Kerensky, tried to hold Russia together. But Lenin's political platform of "land, peace, and bread" won many people to the Bolshevik cause. With the masses against it, the provisional government could not last long, and in November 1917 it was overthrown by the Bolsheviks in a relatively bloodless coup. In the excerpt below from Ten Days That Shook the World, *John Reed, a radical American journalist, describes the major action in the coup—the storming of the Winter Palace in St. Petersburg. As you read the excerpt, note the reactions of the soldiers and people on entering the Winter Palace.*

Here [on the way to the Winter Palace] it was absolutely dark, and nothing moved but pickets of soldiers and Red Guards grimly intent. In front of the Kazan Cathedral a three-inch field-gun lay in the middle of the street, slewed sideways from the recoil of its last shot over the roofs. Soldiers were standing in every doorway talking in low tones and peering down toward the Police Bridge. . . . At the corners patrols stopped all passersby. . . . The shooting had ceased.

Just as we came to the Morskaya somebody was shouting: "The *yunkers* [provisional government troops] have sent word they want us to go and get them out!" Voices began to give commands, and in the thick gloom we made out a dark mass moving forward, silent but for the shuffle of feet and the clinking of arms. We fell in with the first ranks.

Like a black river, filling all the street, without song or cheer we poured through the Red Arch, where the man just ahead of me said in a low voice: "Look out, comrades! Don't trust them. They will fire, surely!" In the open we began to run, stooping low and bunching together, and jammed up suddenly behind the pedestal of the Alexander Column. . . .

After a few minutes huddling there, some hundreds of men, the army seemed reassured and, without any orders, suddenly began again to flow forward. By this time, in the light that streamed out of all the Winter Palace windows, I could see that the first two or three hundred men were Red Guards, with only a few scattered soldiers. Over the barricade of firewood we clambered, and leaping down inside gave a triumphant shout as we stumbled on a heap of rifles thrown down by the *yunkers* who had stood there. On both sides of the main gateway the doors stood wide open, light streamed out, and from the huge pile came not the slightest sound.

Carried along by the eager wave of men we were swept into the right hand entrance, opening into a great bare vaulted room, the cellar of the East wing, from which issued a maze of corridors and stair-cases. A number of huge packing cases stood about, and upon these the Red Guards and soldiers fell furiously, battering them open with the butts of their rifles, and pulling out carpets, curtains, linen, porcelain plates, glassware. . . . One man went strutting around with a bronze clock perched on his shoulder; another found a plume of ostrich feathers, which he stuck in his hat. The looting was just beginning when somebody cried, "Comrades! Don't touch anything! Don't take anything! This is the property of the People!" Immediately twenty voices were crying, "Stop! Put everything back! Don't take anything! Property of the People!" Many hands dragged the spoilers down. Damask and tapestry were snatched from the arms of those who had them; two men took away the bronze clock. Roughly and hastily the things were crammed back in their cases, and self-appointed sentinels stood guard. It was all spontaneous. Through corridors and up stair-cases the cry could be heard growing fainter and fainter in the distance, "Revolutionary discipline! Property of the People. . . ."

We crossed back over to the left entrance, in the West wing. There order was also being established. "Clear the Palace!" bawled a Red Guard, sticking his head through an inner door. "Come, comrades, let's show that we're not thieves and bandits. Everybody out of the Palace except the Commissars, until we get sentries posted."

Two Red Guards, a soldier and an officer, stood with revolvers in their hands. Another soldier sat at a table behind them, with pen and paper. Shouts of "All out! All out!" were heard far and near within, and the Army

Nikolai Lenin

began to pour through the door, jostling, expostulating, arguing. As each man appeared he was seized by the self-appointed committee, who went through his pockets and looked under his coat. Everything that was plainly not his property was taken away, the man at the table noted it on his paper, and it was carried into a little room. The most amazing assortment of objects were thus confiscated; statuettes, bottles of ink, bedspreads worked with the Imperial monogram, candles, a small oil-painting, desk blotters, gold-handled swords, cakes of soap, clothes of every description, blankets. One Red Guard carried three rifles, two of which he had taken away from *yunkers;* another had four portfolios bulging with written documents. The culprits either sullenly surrendered or pleaded like children. All talking at once the committee explained that stealing was not worthy of the people's champions; often those who had been caught turned around and began to help go through the rest of the comrades.

Yunkers came out, in bunches of three or four. The committee seized upon them with an excess of zeal, accompanying the search with remarks like, "Ah, Provocators! . . . Counter-revolutionists! Murderers of the People!" But there was no violence done, although the *yunkers* were terrified. They too had their pockets full of small plunder. It was carefully noted down by the scribe, and piled in the little room. . . . The *yunkers* were disarmed. "Now, will you take up arms against the People any more?" demanded clamouring voices.

"No," answered the *yunkers,* one by one. Whereupon they were allowed to go free.

We asked if we might go inside. The committee was doubtful, but the big Red Guard answered firmly that it was forbidden. "Who are you anyway?" he asked. "How do I know that you are not all Kerenskys?". . .

"Way, Comrades!" A soldier and a Red Guard appeared in the door, waving the crowd aside, and other guards with fixed bayonets. After them followed single file half a dozen men in civilian dress—the members of the Provisional Government. First came Kishkin, his face drawn and pale, then Rutenberg, looking sullenly at the floor; Tereshchenko was next, glancing sharply around; he stared at us with cold fixity. . . . They passed in silence; the victorious insurrectionists crowded to see, but there were only a few angry mutterings. It was only later that we learned how the people in the street wanted to lynch them, and shots were fired—but the sailors brought them safely to Peter-Paul. . . .

In the meanwhile unrebuked we walked into the Palace. There was still a great deal of coming and going, of exploring new-found apartments in the vast edifice, of searching for hidden garrisons of *yunkers* which did not exist. We went upstairs and wandered through room after room. This part of the Palace had been entered also by other detachments. . . . The paintings, statues, tapestries and rugs of the great state apartments were unharmed; in the offices, however, every desk and cabinet had been ransacked, the papers scattered over the floor, and in the living rooms beds had been stripped of their coverings and wardrobes wrenched open. The most highly prized loot was clothing, which the working people needed. In a room where furniture was stored we came upon two soldiers ripping the elaborate Spanish leather upholstery from chairs. They explained it was to make boots with. . . .

The old Palace servants in their blue and red and gold uniforms stood nervously about, from force of habit repeating, "You can't go in there. . . . It is forbidden----" We penetrated at length to the gold and malachite chamber with crimson brocade hangings where the Ministers had been in session all that day and night, and where the *shveitzari* had betrayed them to the Red Guards. The long table covered with green baize was just as they had left it, under arrest. Before each empty seat was pen and ink and paper; the papers were scribbled over with beginnings of plans of action, rough drafts of proclamations and manifestos. Most of these were scratched out, as their futility became evident, and the rest of the sheet covered with absent-minded geometrical designs, as the writers sat despondently listening while Minister after Minister proposed chimerical [impossible] schemes. I took one of these scribbled pages, in the hand writing of Konovalov, which read, "The Provisional Government appeals to all classes to support the Provisional Government—"

READING REVIEW

1. Why did the Red Guards order the people to stop looting the Winter Palace?
2. What did the people in the street want to do with the members of the provisional government held by the Red Guards? Why?
3. Why do you think the people acted as they did in the Winter Palace? Explain your answer.

96 THE GERMANS ARE INFORMED OF THE TERMS OF THE TREATY OF VERSAILLES

The Treaty of Versailles, which ended World War I, was largely the work of the leaders of the three major Allied powers, Georges Clemenceau of France, David Lloyd George of Great Britain, and Woodrow Wilson of the United States. The Germans were not told of the terms of the treaty until it had been completed. In the excerpt below from Woodrow Wilson and the Lost Peace, *diplomatic historian Thomas Bailey describes the reaction of the leader of the German delegation to the treaty. As you read the excerpt, consider what impact presenting the peace treaty as an ultimatum had on Germany.*

The Treaty of Versailles was formally presented to the German representatives on May 7, 1919, by coincidence the fourth anniversary of the sinking of the *Lusitania*.

The scene was the Trianon Palace at Versailles. The day was one of surpassing loveliness, and brilliant spring sunlight flooded the room. Dr. Walter Simons, Commissioner-General of the German delegation, noted that "outside of the big window at my right there was a wonderful cherry tree in bloom, and it seemed to me the only reality when compared with the performance in the hall. This cherry tree and its kind will still be blooming when the states whose representatives gathered here exist no longer."

The crowd was small, for the room was small—merely the delegates of both sides, with their assistants, and a few carefully selected press representatives. The grim-visaged Clemenceau sat at the center of the main table: Wilson at his right, Lloyd George at his left.

The air was surcharged with electricity: German and Allied diplomats had not met face to face since the fateful summer of 1914. Would the Germans do something to offend proprieties?

When all were seated, the doors swung open. At the cry, [*"Gentlemen, the German plenipotentiaries!"*] the whole assembly rose and stood in silence while the German delegates filed in before their conquerors and sat at a table facing Clemenceau.

The Tiger [Clemenceau] rose to his feet, and, his voice vibrant with the venom of 1871, almost spat out his speech with staccato precision: "It is neither the time nor the place for superfluous words. . . . The time has come when we must settle our accounts. You have asked for peace. We are ready to give you peace."

Already a secretary had quietly walked over to the table at which the Germans sat, and laid before them the thick, two-hundred-odd-page treaty—"the book."

With Clemenceau still standing, the pale, black-clad Count Brockdorff-Rantzau, head of the German delegation, began reading his reply—*seated*.

An almost perceptible gasp swept the room, for the failure of the German to rise was taken as a studied discourtesy. Some felt that he was too nervous and shaken to stand. Others felt that he wanted to snub his "conquerors." The truth is he planned to sit, not wishing to stand like a culprit before a judge to receive sentence.

Nothing could better reflect the spirit of the Germans. They felt the war had been more or less a stalemate; they had laid down their arms expecting to negotiate with a chivalrous foe. As equals, why should they rise like criminals before the Allied bar?

If Brockdorff-Rantzau's posture was unfortunate, his words and the intonation of his words were doubly so.

The Germans had not yet read the Treaty, but they had every reason to believe that it would be severe. They had not been allowed to participate in its negotiation; they would not be allowed to discuss its provisions *orally* with their conquerors. Brockdorff-Rantzau decided to make the most of this his only opportunity to meet his adversaries face to face and comment on the unread Treaty. Both his manner and his words were sullen, arrogant, unrepentant.

Speaking with great deliberation and without the usual courteous salutation to the presiding officer, he began by saying that the Germans were under "no illusions" as to the extent of their defeat and the degree of the "powerlessness." This was not true, for both he and his people were under great illusions.

Then he referred defiantly but inaccurately to the demand that the Germans acknowledge that "we alone are guilty of having caused the war. Such a confession in my mouth would be a lie." And the word "lie" fairly hissed from between his teeth.

Bitterly he mentioned the "hundreds of thousands" of German noncombatants who had perished since Armistice Day as a result of Allied insistence on continuing the blockade during the peace negotiations. This shaft struck home, especially to the heart of Lloyd George.

When the echo of Brockdorff-Rantzau's last tactless word had died away, Clemenceau spoke. His face had gone red during the harangue, but he had held himself in check with remarkable self-restraint. Harshly and peremptorily he steam-rolled the proceedings to an end: "Has anybody any more observations to offer? Does no one wish to speak? If not, the meeting is closed."

The German delegates marched out, facing a battery of clicking moving picture cameras. Brockdorff-Rantzau lighted a cigarette with trembling fingers.

Lloyd George, who had snapped an ivory paper knife in his hands, remarked angrily: "It is hard to have won the war and have to listen to that." . . .

Brockdorff-Rantzau's ill-timed tirade was followed with intense concentration by President Wilson. Dr. Simons noted that the German argument "obviously made its impression upon him, although not a favorable one."

This was absolutely correct. Wilson might have been deeply moved by a clear, dispassionate reference to concrete cases, but this blanket condemnation left him indignant and stubborn. To Lloyd George he turned and said, "Isn't it just like them!"

The German delegate undoubtedly made a grave error in judgment. A short, tactful speech would have kept the door open to compromise; his long, defiant diatribe forced the victors to defend what they had done.

READING REVIEW

1. What did Bailey mean by saying that Clemenceau was "vibrant with the venom of 1871"?
2. What explanations did the delegates have for Brockdorff-Rantzau reading his reply while remaining seated?
3. In your opinion, how did the presentation of the Treaty of Versailles as an ultimatum have on the German people? Explain your answer.

---

97 ELEANOR ROOSEVELT'S CONTRIBUTION TO THE NEW DEAL

President Franklin Delano Roosevelt's wife, Eleanor, was a tireless supporter of his New Deal programs. In 1933 she traveled alone more than 40,000 miles back and forth across the country promoting the New Deal. Also, she openly championed the causes of those who usually had no voice in government—African Americans, women, the young. In time, she became known as the "conscience of the administration." In the excerpt below from The Making of the New Deal, *edited by Katie Loucheim, Claude Pepper—a stalwart supporter of President Roosevelt—describes Mrs. Roosevelt's contribution to the New Deal. As you read the excerpt, ask yourself why Pepper called Mrs. Roosevelt the co-President.*

All who knew anything about the Roosevelt administration and what it meant to the United States and to the world appreciate the immeasurable contribution that Mrs. Roosevelt made. In the first place, she was absolutely necessary to the President, since he had a physical handicap and limitation. She brought him information that could come only from someone who could go out and *see*. She went into mines, down into coal mines, and the men at the bottom of the mine said, "My God, there's Mrs. Roosevelt!" She went into the schoolrooms, she went into the factories, she went *everywhere*.... Prodding, looking, seeking information, and coming back and disclosing that information to the President, she was his eyes, his ears, and his feet. Through her he got facts that were essential to him and to the proponents of his important program.

Mrs. Roosevelt also had an almost unparalleled compassion for other people. She, who was of patrician birth and upbringing, like President Roosevelt, somehow or other had the spiritual growth within her that made her compassionate and sensitive to the needs of people. There she was out doing more things than anybody ever tried before: to help people in every walk of life where there was a need, a genuine need for assistance. And she was so dedicated to this cause.

In the field of education, of course, she was especially active, for she realized the value of education. Jobs—she just went everywhere to try to help people get jobs, to try to help them grow, to do better work. She tried to help people get homes; she'd go into shacks, into the slums, and see the state of the houses in which people lived. She'd try her best to get decent housing. And medical care was one of her primary concerns. Of course she supported national health insurance, or any kind of plan that would provide better health for the needs of people. She also was trying to help handicapped children. In other words, the scope of her interests was the scope of human need. And her compassion and her

Eleanor Roosevelt presenting an award to singer Marian Anderson

concern were as wide as the breadth of human need. That was what she was dedicated to.

Mrs. Roosevelt told me that she thought all of our people had basic rights—a right to live in decent housing, a right to have a decent diet, a right to wear decent clothes, a right to get decent medical care, and a right to get a decent education that would enable them to do something useful in life. She assumed that these were ordinary rights that the people of the United States had, and she discovered that these needs were not available to the people all over this country. She was aware of the acuteness of these needs and she was a wonderful advocate, a most persuasive advocate of the government's doing something. . . .

Mrs. Roosevelt sort of imposed on the President to do this, do that, or the other, often when he did not want to discuss the matter. But she didn't have too many times to talk to him; she was away a great deal, seeing, doing. I believe she was almost literally the co-President in the sense that she had an active part in a perfectly proper way. I don't think she tried to dominate the President, but rather she tried to urge him, to push to do things. He was like the rest of us; a lot of times he'd let something sort of stay on the back burner. She'd get after him again and again. . . .

"Mrs. Roosevelt, to one degree or another, had a large part in nearly all of the welfare programs."

Mrs. Roosevelt, to one degree or another, had a large part in nearly all of the welfare programs. She would come back and tell the President the need, and sometimes she'd go out to the agencies themselves and press for her programs. Take the NYA. I know she had a lot to do with the initiation of the National Youth Administration program for education. I know she was working very closely with Aubrey Williams and those who ran those programs. She worked very closely with Harry Hopkins when he was in charge of the WPA program, the Works Progress Administration. When he had problems, when he needed her to speak to the President, or to somebody else in Congress, he could go to her, get her help.

Everybody who was head of a big program tried to get Mrs. Roosevelt's help. Bernard Baruch [President Roosevelt's economic adviser] told me many times about how he liked to talk to Mrs. Roosevelt. A lot of times he'd take advantage of an opportunity to talk to her when he didn't get a chance to talk to the President. Maybe he sometimes preferred to talk to Mrs. Roosevelt. A lot of other people talked to Mrs. Roosevelt as a way of getting ideas to the President. She had a lot more ideas even than President Roosevelt did. She was just full of them; she was calling for this and that.

READING REVIEW

1. In what way was Mrs. Roosevelt the President's eyes, ears, and feet?
2. According to Pepper what was the scope of Mrs. Roosevelt's interests?
3. Do you think it is acceptable for the first lady to act as a co-president? Why or why not?

98 THE JARROW CRUSADE

Throughout the 1930s in Great Britain only about 25 percent of the working population was employed. To gain unemployment benefits, the unemployed had to prove they were truly seeking work, even if there was no work available. After six months of receiving benefits, they had to undergo a means test by the Public Assistance Committee (PAC), in which their total wealth was assessed. If the PAC deemed they had the sufficient funds to support themselves and their families, the unemployed workers became ineligible for benefits. Unemployed workers in the northeastern town of Jarrow, where unemployment was about twice the national rate, decided to demonstrate against what they considered demeaning and unfair treatment. On October 5, 1936, about 200 unemployed workers set out to march the 250 miles to London to present a petition to the House of Commons calling for "the right to work and the means to live." In the excerpt below from Jarrow March *by Tom Pickard, a number of people involved in the march talk of their experiences. As you read the excerpt, consider the motives of the Jarrow crusaders.*

The people in Jarrow are so demoralized, unknown to themselves, that they are eating out of the hands of these people [the government and business leaders]. They are now nothing more than what might be called parasites. If we put this case before the public it cannot be denied. We have the highest death rate in the country. Infantile mortality is the second highest and the Public Assistance Committee allowances [welfare] are certainly the highest. . . .

If the appalling conditions that exist in the town are put before the public any decent man can't help feeling for Jarrow. If they could see, as I do as chairman of the PAC, the terrible hardship there is in the town they would feel like bowing their heads in their hands in shame. There have been many times when I have been on the verge of weeping at the depth to which people have been driven. I am not so ready as I was to support an ordinary march to London. I am willing enough to march . . . and there was a time when I would have suggested that we put the women and children on buses while the men of the town marched with the Council at their head. But now I think we should get down to London with a couple of bombs in our pockets. Oh . . . yes, I am perfectly serious. We should go down there with bombs in our pockets. These people of Westminster [the government] have no use for us anyway. These people do not realize that there are people living in Jarrow today under conditions which a respectable farmer would not keep swine. Do not put any limits on your demonstration. Get down there. And I think we should go to the absolute extreme. If it was good to march to London two or three years ago it is good to march now. We must do something so outrageous it will make the country sit up. If people in other distressed areas like Wales would march to London with us we should be such an army that the government could stem the tide by only one way . . . by shooting us down, and they daren't do it.

It was first of all intended to call it the Jarrow Hunger March . . . and I changed it when I was made marshal of the march. I said that, in effect, was not a very nice name to have and I said I'd think a Crusade would be a better title. And of course we adopted the idea. Called it a crusade instead of a march. At the time there was quite a number of marches being held all over the country, and they weren't being too well received in many places. Although the reasons for the marches were no worse than ours.

David Riley
Town Councillor and Crusade Marshal

Well, it was decided that we must do something and the idea of the march . . . not just a collection of men banding themselves together and perhaps going on a hunger march. No, it had to be something different to that. We realized we wanted it to be well organized, something that could be well looked up to . . . and we had such a motive for it, something in effect which was like life itself.

Jean Clark
Council Employee

The time is not too far distant when we shall stand shoulder to shoulder as members of the working class to protect, if needs be to fight for the interests of the working-class movement. You will have certain people coming to you and saying, "Why should you go to London? You can remain here and do just as much." I want to warn you to be very careful of those persons. . . . You can do nothing more in Jarrow. We are going to show this government we are determined not to accept their fascist principles.

The responsibility rests on you. . . .

As we came into London the spirit of the men was such that we were expecting something. We were expecting to prove to the capital at that time that here's men from Jarrow, the spirit they had shown all the way down, here we are, we want work and we are going to put our case that we must have work, for the benefit of our wives and children.

Joe Symonds
Town Councillor and Crusader

Well, the point was that this was a crusade in the real sense of the word. We were more or less missionaries of the distressed areas of the country, let alone Jarrow. We had distressed towns as well as Jarrow . . . and we took the poverty to the people that didn't know poverty existed and didn't know what it meant. The degradation that followed it. And I feel that was something worthwhile doing, because we had a body of people living in Jarrow and we had them living in Merseyside and the Clyde and Merthyr Tydfil, all decent people who were being run down by the Means Test, unemployment benefit and all that sort of thing, Parish Relief . . . and no chance to get out of it. We thought we'd get out of it by showing our protests to the House of Commons and the proper way we [did] it . . . demand the right not for increased unemployment benefits or increased money matters, but for the right to work. . . .

A resolution was moved suggesting that we take the unemployed down [to London], who were the people that really mattered. . . . The people had suffered that long unemployment and those difficulties for many years . . . that some were keen for it. We had no trouble getting the two hundred [marchers] organized. . . .

That was one of the biggest turnouts the town ever had. It was the Monday morning and we lined up at the town hall entrance and there was just one mass of people. I think the whole population turned out for it and they marched to the church on the invitation of the clergy.

The send-off we had I think it raised everyone's spirits. And that we were doing something very important, I think that would be the feeling of all the marchers, who for days before that had been standing at corners wondering what the end was going to be. Despondent as you could find them.

Paddy Scullion
Town Councillor and Crusader

There were two hundred fighting-fit men, they'd been marching down there, they'd been well fed all the way down . . . the fresh air, the exercise. Two hundred fighting-fit men marched into Hyde Park [London] all in the Sunday best.

Sam Rowan
Council Employee

READING REVIEW

1. Why did David Riley suggest that the marchers take bombs to London?
2. Why did Paddy Scullion think the march was truly a crusade?
3. **(a)** What did the Jarrow crusaders hope to achieve by their march? **(b)** Do you think the march had any impact on unemployment in Great Britain? Explain your answer.

---

99 THE BURNING OF THE BOOKS

The Nazis believed that all non-Aryan culture had a corrupting influence on the German people. So when they came to power, they imposed strict censorship and confiscated all the published materials they deemed unacceptable. By May 1933 the political police had seized more than 500 tons of books and magazines in Berlin alone. On May 10 the Nazis symbolically purified the German nation by burning the works of 24 "undesirables"—including Albert Einstein, Sigmund Freud, Karl Marx, and Thomas Mann—in Berlin and other university towns. The excerpt below from The Goebbels Diaries, *edited by Louis P. Lochner, contains an eyewitness account of this act of "purification." As you read the excerpt, note the reaction of foreign journalists to the book-burning.*

The whole civilized world was shocked when on the evening of May 10, 1933, the books of the authors displeasing to the Nazis, including those of our own Helen Keller, were solemnly burned on the immense Franz Joseph Platz between the University of Berlin and the State Opera on Unter den Linden. I was a witness to the scene.

All afternoon Nazi raiding parties had gone into public and private libraries, throwing into the streets such books as Dr. Goebbels in his supreme wisdom had decided were unfit for Nazi Germany. From the streets Nazi columns of beer-hall fighters had picked up these discarded volumes and taken them to the square above referred to.

Here the heap grew higher and higher, and every few minutes another howling mob arrived, adding more books to the impressive pyre. Then, as night fell, students from the university, mobilized by the little doctor [Goebbels], performed veritable Indian dances and incantations as the flames began to soar skyward.

Nazis burning books

When the orgy was at its height, a cavalcade of cars hove into sight. It was the Propaganda Minister [Goebbels] himself, accompanied by his bodyguard and a number of fellow torch bearers of the New Nazi *Kultur*.

"Fellow students, German men and women!" he said as he stepped before a microphone for all Germany to hear him. "The age of extreme Jewish intellectualism has now ended, and the success of the German revolution has again given the right of way to the German spirit. . . .

"You are doing the right thing in committing the evil spirit of the past to the flames at this late hour of the night. It is a strong, great, and symbolic act—an act that is to bear witness before all the world to the fact that the spiritual foundation of the November Republic has disappeared. From these ashes there will rise the phoenix of a new spirit. . . .

The past is lying in flames. The future will rise from the flames within our own hearts. . . . Brightened by these flames our vow shall be: The Reich and the Nation and our Fuehrer Adolf Hitler: *Heil! Heil! Heil!*"

The few foreign correspondents who had taken the trouble to view this "symbolic act" were stunned. What had happened to the "Land of Thinkers and Poets?" they wondered.

READING REVIEW

1. According to Dr. Goebbels, what did the burning of the books symbolize?
2. What do you think Lochner felt about Dr. Goebbels? Support your answer with evidence from the excerpt.
3. What do you think the foreign journalists meant by " 'What had happened to the "Land of the Thinkers and Poets?' "

---

100 THE TRIAL OF NIKOLAI BUKHARIN

During the 1930s the Russian leader Joseph Stalin systematically imprisoned or executed everyone who constituted a challenge to his authority. Most were simply picked up by the secret police and were never seen again. Of these, some were executed, while others were sent to labor camps in Siberia. Stalin reserved special treatment for his rivals within the Communist Party. In show trials, they were forced to admit to trumped-up charges of treason and conspiracy with capitalist countries. Among Stalin's most notable rivals was Nikolai Bukharin, whom Lenin had called "the most valuable and greatest theoretician" of the Communist Party. In the excerpt below from Russia and the West from Peter to Khrushchev, *edited by L. Jay Oliva, state prosecutor Andrei Vyshinsky interrogates Bukharin on his involvement in a conspiracy against the Soviet Union. As you read the excerpt, consider why Stalin wanted the show trials held.*

VYSHINSKY: Allow me to begin the interrogation of the accused Bukharin. Formulate briefly what exactly it is you plead guilty to.

BUKHARIN: Firstly, to belonging to the counter-revolutionary "bloc of Rights and Trotskyites."

VYSHINSKY: Since what year?

BUKHARIN: From the moment the bloc was formed. Even before that, I plead guilty to belonging to the counter-revolutionary organization of the Rights.

VYSHINSKY: Since what year?

BUKHARIN: Roughly since 1928. I plead guilty to being one of the outstanding leaders of this "bloc of Rights and Trotskyites." Consequently, I plead guilty to what follows directly from this, the sum total of crimes committed by this counter-revolutionary organization, irrespective of whether or not I knew of, whether or not I took a direct part, in any particular act. Because I am responsible as one of the leaders and not as a cog of this counter-revolutionary organization.

VYSHINSKY: What aims were pursued by this counter-revolutionary organization?

BUKHARIN: This counter-revolutionary organization, to formulate it briefly . . .

VYSHINSKY: Yes, briefly for the present.

BUKHARIN: The principal aim it pursued although, so to speak, it did not fully realize it, and did not dot all the "i's"—was essentially the aim of restoring capitalist relations in the U.S.S.R.

VYSHINSKY: The overthrow of the Soviet power?

BUKHARIN: The overthrow of the Soviet power was a means to this end.

VYSHINSKY: By means of?

BUKHARIN: As is known . . .

VYSHINSKY: By means of a forcible overthrow?

BUKHARIN: Yes, by means of the forcible overthrow of this power.

VYSHINSKY: With the help of?

BUKHARIN: With the help of all the difficulties encountered by the Soviet power; in particular, with the help of a war which prognostically was in prospect.

VYSHINSKY: Which was prognostically in prospect, with whose help?

BUKHARIN: With the help of foreign states.

VYSHINSKY: On condition?

BUKHARIN: On condition, to put it concretely, of a number of concessions.

VYSHINSKY: To the extent of . . .

BUKHARIN: To the extent of the cession of territory.

VYSHINSKY: That is?

BUKHARIN: If all the "i's" are dotted—on condition of the dismemberment of the U.S.S.R.

VYSHINSKY: The severance of whole regions and republics from the U.S.S.R.?

BUKHARIN: Yes.

VYSHINSKY: For example?

BUKHARIN: The Ukraine, the Maritime Region, Byelorussia.

VYSHINSKY: In whose favour?

BUKHARIN: In favour of the corresponding states, whose geographical and political . . .

VYSHINSKY: Which exactly?

BUKHARIN: In favour of Germany, in favour of Japan, and partly in favour of England.

VYSHINSKY: So, that was the agreement with the circles concerned? I know of one agreement which the bloc had.

BUKHARIN: Yes, the bloc had an agreement.

VYSHINSKY: And also by means of weakening the [Soviet] defensive power?

BUKHARIN: You see, this question was not discussed, at least not in my presence.

VYSHINSKY: And what was the position with regard to wrecking?

BUKHARIN: The position with regard to wrecking was that in the end, especially under pressure of the Trotskyite part of the so-called contact centre, which arose roughly in 1933, despite a number of internal differences and manipulatory political mechanics, which are of no interest to the investigation, after various vicissitudes, disputes and so on, the orientation on wrecking was adopted.

VYSHINSKY: Did it tend to weaken the defensive power of the country?

BUKHARIN: Naturally.

VYSHINSKY: Consequently, there was an orientation on the weakening, the undermining of defensive power?

BUKHARIN: Not formally, but essentially it was so.

VYSHINSKY: But the actions and activity in this direction were clear?

BUKHARIN: Yes.

READING REVIEW

1. Why were the Trotskyites so reviled by Stalin and his supporters?
2. According to Bukharin's testimony, how did he and the other counterrevolutionaries intend to return the Soviet Union to capitalism?
3. Why do you think Stalin staged the show trials?

101 GANDHI EMERGES AS INDIA'S NEW LEADER

Jawaharlal Nehru (1889–1964), the son of a well-to-do Brahman family, was educated in England. On returning to India, he expected to follow his father's example and practice law. He became deeply involved, however, in the independence movement. His activities for the cause often landed him in prison, and during the 1920s and 1930s he served sentences totalling about 10 years. While in prison Nehru wrote long, rambling letters to his daughter, Indira. In these letters he provided his daughter with an outline of world history and a discussion of India's drive for independence. In the excerpt below from Glimpses of World History, *Nehru tells his daughter how Mahatma Gandhi came to lead the freedom movement. As you read this excerpt, ask yourself how Nehru felt about Gandhi.*

Within a few months [of World War I], the first fruits of the new British policy, so eagerly waited for, appeared in the shape of a proposal to pass special laws to control the [independence] movement. Instead of more freedom, there was to be more repression. These Bills were based on the report of a committee and were known as the Rowlatt Bills. But very soon they were called the "Black Bills" all over the country, and were denounced everywhere and by every Indian, including even the most moderate. They gave great powers to the government and the police to arrest, keep in prison without trial, or to have a secret trial of, any person they disapproved of or suspected. . . . As the outcry against the Bills gained volume, a new factor appeared, a little cloud on the political horizon which grew and spread rapidly till it covered the Indian sky.

This new factor was Mohandas Karamchand Gandhi. He had returned to India from South Africa during war-time and settled down with his colony in an *ashram* in Sabarmati. He had kept away from politics. He had even helped the government in recruiting men for the war. He was, of course, very well known in India since his *satyagraha* [passive resistance] struggle in South Africa. In 1917 he had championed with success the miserable down-trodden tenants of the European planters in the Champaran District of Bihar. Later he stood up for the peasantry of Kaira in Gujarat. Early in 1919 he was very ill. He had barely recovered from it when the Rowlatt Bill agitation filled the country. He also joined his voice to the universal outcry.

But this voice was somehow different from the others. It was quiet and low, and yet it could be heard above the shouting of the multitude; it was soft and gentle, and yet there seemed to be steel hidden away somewhere in it; it was courteous and full of appeal, and yet there was something grim and frightening in it; every word used was full of meaning and seemed to carry a deadly earnestness. Behind the language of peace and friendship there was power and the quivering shadow of action and a determination not to submit to a wrong. We are familiar with that voice now... but it was new to us in February and March 1919; we did not quite know what to make of it, but we were thrilled. This was something very different from our noisy politics of condemnation and nothing else, long speeches always ending in the same futile and ineffective resolutions of protest which nobody took very seriously. This was the politics of action, not of talk.

Mahatma Gandhi organized a *Satyagraha Sabha* of those who were prepared to break chosen laws and thus court imprisonment. This was quite a novel idea then, and many of us were excited but many shrank back. To-day it is the most commonplace of occurrences, and for most of us it has become a fixed and regular part of our lives!

As usual with him, Gandhi sent a courteous appeal and warning to the Viceroy. When he saw that the British Government were determined to pass the law in spite of the opposition of a united India, he called for an all-India day of mourning, a *hartal,* a stoppage of business, and meetings on the first Sunday after the Bills became law. This was to inaugurate the *Satyagraha* movement, and so Sunday, April 6, 1919, was observed as the Satyagraha Day all over the country, in town and village. It was the first all-India demonstration of the kind, and it was a wonderfully impressive one, in which all kinds of people and communities joined. Those of us who had worked for this *hartal* were amazed at its success. It had been possible for us to approach only a limited number of people in the cities. But a new spirit was in the air, and somehow the message managed to reach the remotest villages of our huge country. For the first time the villager as well as the town worker took part in a political demonstration on a mass scale.

Gandhi (sixth from left) leading a march

READING REVIEW

1. What powers did the Rowlatt Bills give to the British government? Why were the Indians so upset by the passage of these bills?
2. What is the difference between *satyagraha* and *hartal?*
3. How do you think Nehru felt about Gandhi? Give reasons for your answer.

---

102 THE NEW AFRICA

Nnamdi Azikiwe, like other African nationalist leaders, attended Christian mission schools in Africa and then went to a university in the West. Educated in the Western ideals of freedom, equality, and democracy, Azikiwe returned to his native land, Nigeria, only to find that the colonial government regarded him as a second-class citizen. He soon began to work to free Nigeria from the chains of British colonial rule. His actions drew the attention of the authorities, and in 1937 he was convicted of seditious libel and sent to prison. The excerpt below from Zik: A Selection from the Speeches of Nnamdi Azikiwe *is a speech Azikiwe made just after his conviction. In it declares his readiness to make any sacrifice for the "New Africa." As you read the excerpt, ask yourself how Azikiwe's mission background comes through in the speech.*

I am becoming convinced day by day that the New Africa is destined to become a reality. No force under heaven can stem it. Even my death cannot postpone its crystallization. If because I am an instrument of destiny through which imperialism in West Africa is to be challenged and liquidated, and if in this mission I am compelled to pay the supreme penalty, then there is no need for me to quake or to quiver.

Gethsemane was there to be conquered. Golgotha was there to be trodden under the feet of man. Calvary was to be overcome. And when a son of the New Africa is faced with the [agonies] and tribulations of Gethsemane, and Golgotha and Calvary, there is no need for the spirit to weaken. At this stage of my life I cannot be mere flesh. I cannot be part of the corruptible phase of man's organism. I am a living spirit of an idea—the idea of a New Africa. I am a living spirit of an ideal—the ideal of man's humanity to man. I am a living spirit of an ideology—the ideology of the effacement of man's inhumanity to man.

Happily for the gospel according to the New Africa, there exist today on this continent Renascent Africans: literate and illiterate, poor and wealthy, high and low; and they have expressed to me, by their words and their deeds, during the last few days of the crucial moments of the existence of my flesh on this earth, that the New Africa is born to me.

Conceived in the indestructible nature of the spirit, and born of a selfless desire to utilize culture for the service of humanity, it is destined that Renascent Africans must carry the torch of this gospel of a new awakening from West to East, and from North to South, Africa.

READING REVIEW

1. Why did Azikiwe think that the New Africa would become a reality?
2. What do you think Azikiwe meant by the term *Renascent Africans?*
3. How does Azikiwe's Christian-mission-school background come through in his speech? Cite examples from the excerpt to support your answer.

---

103 A PORTRAIT OF MAO ZEDONG

When the Chinese Communists arrived in the mountain town of Yan'an after the Long March, they chose Mao Zedong as their leader. During 1936 and 1937, Helen Foster Snow—the wife of Mao's biographer, Edgar Snow—spent some time in Yan'an and conducted a number of interviews with Mao. In the excerpt below from My China Years, *she writes of her impressions of Mao after these early meetings. As you read the excerpt, consider whether or not you agree with her comparison of Mao to Abraham Lincoln.*

Mao [Zedong] . . . took off his limp red-starred cap, letting a shock of plentiful black hair fall around his ears. He crossed his remarkably beautiful, powerful, and aristocratic hands over each other, and looked up at me quizzically. . . . These hands showed real power. They were not at all like the usual hands of an intellectual in China, nor were they like those of the working class. Mao was unusually tall and well-built for a Chinese, and his hands were appropriate to his physique.

There was nothing harmless about Mao. . . . He was well-bred, but inside he was made of steel, of hard resistance, of tough tissue—the kind of tissue the Boxers thought they had by magic, and bared their solar plexuses to foreign bullets. Agnes Smedley told me she thought Mao sinister and feminine, and hated him on first sight. She had a hard time overcoming this feeling and . . . she told me she was afraid of him. But I liked him and felt a rapport with him. . . .

Neither Agnes Smedley nor Evans Carlson had the least understanding of Mao [Zedong] for some reason. Evans wrote of him as "a humble, kindly, lonely genius, striving here in the darkness of the night to find a peaceful . . . way of life for the people."

Of all the things Mao [Zedong] was *not,* Evans had the list—except that he *was* a genius. That was obvious to everyone, and probably had been clear to Mao and his friends since his boyhood. Evans judged people by the Christian yardstick, which got in the way of his clarity of vision. To him, humility was a beautiful thing, especially in a commander in chief. . . .

During the summer I had a special relationship with Mao. . . . I sent him a long list of questions and we had several interviews. He was much interested in my questions, many of which asked for explanations of what seemed to be contradictions. He would chuckle audibly and say, "Some things in China are very strange, you see." He would sometimes turn in his chair and ask: "And what is your opinion?" This made me uneasy. I realized later that he genuinely wanted to know what such a foreigner thought. . . .

Mao was never a dogmatist. If he had been, much in China would have been different. He was flexible, willing to change and learn, and most of all, patient—up to [a] breaking point. He waited for a nadir, then took action on the upturn of the wheel, not too soon, not too late. He led history by following it. . . .

Mao [Zedong] became deified in his old age for various reasons. He came to personify the "New China," with both its aspirations and its limitations. He was a complicated person with a dialectical mind, and Western categories do not describe him and his career, except at the risk of beclouding more than clarifying. He was the most optimistic person of his entire era, yet he was also cynical and did not trust fools gladly, if at all. He was more open to outside influences than any man of his age in China—and yet he sifted out the chaff from the grain with marvelous dexterity and an instinct for true value.

Mao [Zedong] was a folk figure, writ large. He was China, writ small. He personified the 80 percent of his country that was the village Chinese. The other 20 percent feared him, but in the end recognized his authority and more or less went along with the deification as long as Mao was alive. Mao more resembled Abraham Lincoln than he did any other Westerner, even to being of tall, large presence, grand in natural simplicity. He had the same insatiable desire for learning; even in the 1970s he was studying English to set an example for the people.

READING REVIEW

1. Why do you think Snow said that there was "nothing harmless about Mao"?
2. How does Snow suggest that people in the West may have misunderstood Mao?
3. Do you agree with Snow's comparison of Mao with Abraham Lincoln? Why or why not?

104 A JUSTIFICATION OF JAPANESE EXPANSIONISM

During the 1920s and 1930s, the Western powers began to strongly criticize Japan for its expansionist policies. This criticism reached its height in 1931, after Japan's unprovoked attack on Manchuria. Stung by what they considered Western interference in their internal affairs, the Japanese immediately issued a defense of their policies. In the excerpt below from Sources of the Japanese Tradition, *compiled by Ryusaku Tsunoda, a Japanese government official offers the standard justification of expansionism. As you read the excerpt, note how the official defends his government's policies.*

We have already said that there are only three ways left to Japan to escape from the pressure of surplus population. We are like a great crowd of people packed into a small and narrow room, and there are only three doors through which we might escape, namely emigration, advance into world markets, and expansion of territory. The first door, emigration, has been barred to us by the anti-Japanese immigration policies of other countries. The second door, advance into world markets, is being pushed shut by tariff barriers and the abrogation of commercial treaties. What should Japan do when two of the three doors have been closed against her?

It is quite natural that Japan should rush upon the last remaining door.

It may sound dangerous when we speak of territorial expansion, but the territorial expansion of which we speak does not in any sense of the word involve the occupation of the possessions of other countries, the planting of the Japanese flag thereon, and the declaration of their annexation to Japan. It is just that since the Powers [Western governments] have suppressed the circulation of Japanese materials and merchandise abroad, we are looking for some place overseas where Japanese capital, Japanese skills and Japanese labor can have free play, free from the oppression of the white race.

We would be satisfied with just this much. What moral right do the world powers who have themselves closed to us the two doors of emigration and advance into world markets have to criticize Japan's attempt to rush out of the third and last door?

If they do not approve of this, they should open the doors which they have closed against us and permit the free movement overseas of Japanese emigrants and merchandise. . . .

At the time of the Manchurian incident, the entire world joined in criticism of Japan. They said that Japan was an untrustworthy nation.

They said that she had recklessly brought cannon and machine guns into Manchuria, which was the territory of another country, flown air-

A cartoonist's view of Japanese aggressions

planes over it, and finally occupied it. But the military action taken by Japan was not in the least a selfish one. Moreover, we do not recall ever having taken so much as an inch of territory belonging to another nation. The result of this incident was the establishment of the splendid new nation of Manchuria. The Powers are still discussing whether or not to recognize this new nation, but regardless of whether or not other nations recognize her, the Manchurian empire has already been established, and now, seven years after its creation, the empire is further consolidating its foundations with the aid of its friend, Japan.

And if it is still protested that our actions in Manchuria were excessively violent, we may wish to ask the white race just which country it was that sent warships and troops to India, South Africa, and Australia and slaughtered innocent natives, bound their hands and feet with iron chains, lashed their backs with iron whips, proclaimed these territories as their own, and still continues to hold them to this very day?

They will invariably reply, these were all lands inhabited by untamed savages. These people did not know how to develop the abundant resources of their land for the benefit of mankind. Therefore it was the wish of God, who created heaven and earth for mankind, for us to develop these underdeveloped lands and to promote the happiness of mankind in their stead. God wills it.

This is quite a convenient argument for them. Let us take it at face value. Then there is another question that we must ask them.

Suppose that there is still on this earth land endowed with abundant natural resources that have not been developed at all by the white race. Would it not then be God's will and the will of Providence that Japan go there and develop those resources for the benefit of mankind?

And there still remain many such lands on this earth.

READING REVIEW

1. What three "doors" were open to Japan to solve the problem of a surplus population?
2. How did the government official answer the charges that Japanese actions in Manchuria were too violent?
3. How did the government official turn the expansionist arguments of the West to support his country's case?

---

105 TWO POEMS OF THE SPANISH CIVIL WAR

Many writers and artists served in the International Brigade in Spain during the Spanish Civil War. Among these were English poets Laurie Lee and John Cornford. Lee survived the war and went on to become a widely-respected author, writing what many people consider to be one of the finest books on childhood, Cider With Rosie. *Cornford, the youngest unit commander in the International Brigade, was killed in action in 1936, just one day after his twenty-first birthday. The excerpt below from* Poetry of the Thirties, *edited by Robin Skelton, contains poems by Lee and Cornford on their experiences in Spain. As you read the excerpt, compare the two poets' attitudes to war.*

A Letter from Aragon

This is a quiet sector of a quiet front.
We buried Ruiz in a new pine coffin,
But the shroud was too small and his washed feet stuck out.
The stink of his corpse came through the clean pine boards
And some of the bearers wrapped handkerchiefs round their faces.
Death was not dignified.
We hacked a ragged grave in the unfriendly earth
And fired a ragged volley over the grave.
You could tell from our listlessness, no one much missed him.

This is a quiet sector of a quiet front.
There is no poison gas and no H.E.

But when they shelled the other end of the village
And the streets were choked with dust
Women came screaming out of the crumbling houses,
Clutched under one arm the naked rump of an infant.
I thought: how ugly fear is.

This is a quiet sector of a quiet front.
Our nerves are steady; we all sleep soundly.

In the clean hospital bed my eyes were so heavy
Sleep easily blotted out one ugly picture,
A wounded militiaman moaning on a stretcher,
Now out of danger, but still crying for water,
Strong against death, but unprepared for such pain.
This on a quiet front.

But when I shook hands to leave, an Anarchist worker
Said: 'Tell the workers of England
This was a war not of our making,
We did not seek it.
But if ever the Fascists again rule Barcelona
It will be as a heap of ruins with us workers beneath it.'

John Cornford, 1936

Music in a Spanish Town

In the street I take my stand
with my fiddle like a gun against my shoulder,
and the hot strings under my trigger hand
shooting an old dance at the evening walls.

Each salt-white house is a numbered tomb
its silent window crossed with blood;
my notes explode everywhere like bombs
when I should whisper in fear of the dead.

So my fingers falter, and run in the sun
like the limbs of a bird that is slain,
as my music searches the street in vain.

Suddenly there is a quick flutter of feet
and children crowd about me,
listening with sores and infected ears,
watching with lovely eyes and vacant lips.

Laurie Lee, 1936

READING REVIEW

1. Some people have described Cornford's poem as ironic. What do you think they meant by this?
2. Why did Lee think his music was out of place in the Spanish town?
3. How do the two poets' views of war compare? Explain your answer.

---

106 THE EVACUATION OF DUNKIRK

In late May of 1940, it appeared that the war was practically over. Some 400,000 Allied troops were trapped on the beaches of Dunkirk in northern France, the sea behind them, in front of them the advancing German army. But an armada of close to 900 ships—minesweepers, tugs, paddle steamers, lifeboats, fishing vessels, yachts, practically anything that would float—embarked on a rescue mission and brought 335,000 of the trapped soldiers back to Britain. In the excerpt below from Masterpieces of War Reporting, *edited by Louis L. Snyder, Douglas Williams, a reporter with the London* Daily Telegraph, *describes the evacuation of Dunkirk. As you read the excerpt, consider the great impact the rescue mission had on Allied morale.*

AT A SOUTHEAST COAST PORT, JUNE 1, 1940. Undeterred by heavy German gunfire and constant bombing, which increased as the day wore on, the Navy today continued the stupendous task of ferrying the B.E.F. [British Expeditionary Forces] home to England across the Channel under the very noses of the encircling German army.

As the German forces thrust impatiently against the British rear-guard a number of boats of all sizes and descriptions shuttled to and fro across the 45 miles of water in an intensive effort to evacuate the large body of soldiers still remaining on the beaches around Dunkirk.

From dawn this morning I stood for hours on the dock and watched a succession of vessels, British, French, Dutch, and Belgian, unloading endless columns of tired, hungry, dirty but cheerful British and French soldiers, rescued as by a miracle at the eleventh hour from what had a couple of days ago appeared to them inevitable elimination.

To-day I saw one tiny craft measuring less than 25 feet long arriving loaded to the gunwales with 25 men having taken 12 hours to make the crossing.

The men so fortunately snatched from enemy hands had most of them been lying for hours—some for days—on beaches around Dunkirk, hungry and thirsty, constantly bombed and machine-gunned by low-flying aircraft, yet maintaining perfect discipline, raising no murmur of complaint and patiently awaiting the orders of their officers to embark.

The vessels waiting to transport them to safety were compelled owing to the shallowness of the water to lie at least half a mile off the beach, and to reach the small boats in which to cross this gap many of the men had to wade waist or even neck deep though water covered with a thick scum of oil from the petrol tanks destroyed by the Royal Air Force at Dunkirk. . . .

All day long and during the night evacuation continued. Rescue vessels raced across the Channel loaded with men to the fullest capacity as fast as conditions would permit, steamed back at full speed across the narrow strip of water to return again with undiminished enthusiasm for fresh batches. . . .

Their [the troops] position at Dunkirk becomes hourly more dangerous as German batteries begin to receive a full allotment of ammunition from their supply columns. Shelling of the town directed at the moles to destroy the landing jetties becomes more and more intense.

Parts of the town are in flames, and entire quarters in ruins. Outside, the main roads present scenes of confusion and destruction. Innumerable abandoned motor-cars and lorries lie ditched in every field, while others set alight blaze fiercely.

Bodies of refugees killed by German machine-gun bullets are seen at frequent intervals, and everywhere long lines of soldiers hurry down to the sea and safety.

Yet the work of evacuation continues uninterruptedly with calm efficiency, while a powerful rear-guard fights magnificently to delay the constantly increasing masses of German troops that are being thrown into the fight in one last desperate attempt to capture the remainder of our force before it can be embarked. . . .

Arrangements for receiving the thousands of men as they land are excellent. From the quayside, where each receives an apple and a piece of chocolate to stay their hunger, they are marshaled into waiting trains and proceed to a point where they find ready for them a hot meal. . . .

They are then reloaded into their trains and taken to a certain depot where they are routed to barracks in various Commands to be reclothed and relaxed by a bath and rest.

I was enormously impressed by their wonderful condition and good spirits. Many sang "Roll out the Barrel" as they waited to disembark or gave three cheers for the ships' companies.

All showed the strain of the past few days of hunger, sleeplessness and constant attack printed on their faces in heavy lines of fatigue.

Most of them had their equipment and rifles, and while their uniforms were soiled, very few showed any hint of untidiness or neglect. None showed the slightest sign of demoralization or discouragement. . . .

As I left the dock two young RMAC [Royal Medical Auxiliary Corps] doctors rushed up to me. "Which destroyer," they asked, "is the next to go back to Dunkirk? We have urgent orders to proceed there to reinforce the medical staff."

"I stared at them in amazed admiration of their courage."

I stared at them in amazed admiration of their courage.

That the town was in flames, that every hour German occupation became more and more inevitable had apparently not entered their minds. They had their orders, they would carry them out.

READING REVIEW

1. Why did many of the rescue ships have to lie at least half a mile off Dunkirk's beaches?
2. Why did the Germans throw more and more troops into the fight at Dunkirk?
3. In an editorial on the rescue mission, an American reporter wrote: "So long as the English tongue survives, the word Dunkirk will be spoken with reverence." What do you think the reporter meant by this?

---

107 THE DISCOVERY OF ANNE FRANK'S HIDING PLACE

When Otto Frank and his family, Jews living in Amsterdam, decided to escape Nazi persecution by going into hiding in an attic above a warehouse, a number of Gentile friends came to their aid. Among them was Miep Gies, an Austrian immigrant who worked at Frank's import business. Miep's husband, Henk, obtained forged ration cards for the Franks and the other people hiding with them, and Miep persuaded local grocers and butchers to sell her extra food. She even managed to find books, paper, and other gifts for Frank's daughters, Margot and Anne. And after the Franks had been discovered and shipped off to concentration camps, it was Miep who rescued Anne's diary from the attic. In the excerpt below from Anne Frank Remembered, *Miep describes the discovery of the hiding place. As you read the excerpt, consider how Miep and the Austrian officer felt about each other.*

It was just an ordinary Friday morning, August 4, 1944. First thing in the morning, I'd gone into the hiding place to get the shopping list. Lonely after the long night locked together, my friends were hungry for a good visit. Anne, as usual, had many questions to ask and urged me to talk a little. I promised that I'd come back and sit and we could have a real talk in the afternoon when I returned with the groceries. But conversation would have to wait until then. I went back to the office and got started with my work.

Elli Vossen and Jo Koophuis were working across from me in the office. Sometime between eleven and twelve o'clock, I looked up. There in the doorway stood a man in civilian clothes. I hadn't heard the door. He was holding a revolver, pointing it at us. He came in. "Stay put," he said in Dutch. "Don't move."

Then he walked toward the back office where Mr. Kraler was working, leaving us alone. We were petrified.

Jo Koophuis said to me, "Miep, I think the time has come."

Elli began to tremble and shake. Meanwhile, Mr. Koophuis' eyes darted toward the doorway. No one but the man with the gun seemed to be about.

As soon as the man with the gun left our office, I quickly took the illegal ration cards, the money, and Henk's lunch out of my bag. Then I waited. It was about the time that Henk would come for lunch. After a very short time I heard the familiar sound of Henk's footsteps on the stairs. Before he could come inside, I jumped up, ran to the door, opened it, grabbed him by the arm, and said, "Henk, it's wrong here."

I shoved everything into his hands and gave him a little push. Henk understood me immediately and disappeared.

My breath caught in my chest, I went back to my desk, where the man with the gun had told me to stay.

After Henk left, Mr. Koophuis saw that Elli was very upset and was crying. He reached into his pocket and took out his wallet, handed it to Elli, and said to her, "Take this. Go to the drugstore on the Leliegracht. The owner is a friend of mine. He'll let you use the telephone. Telephone my wife and tell her what has happened and then disappear."

Elli gave me a frightened look. I nodded my agreement with Koophuis. She took the wallet and dashed out the door.

Mr. Koophuis locked eyes with me and said, "Miep, you can also leave."

The staircase leading to Anne Frank's hiding place

"I can't," I responded. It was true. I couldn't.

Jo Koophuis and I remained seated as we'd been ordered for perhaps three-quarters of an hour. Then another man came through the door into our room and called to Koophuis to come inside with him, and they went into Mr. Kraler's office. I continued to sit there, not knowing what was going on anywhere else in the building, too afraid to imagine what might be happening.

I heard a door open. The door to the storeroom was also open. Koophuis came back out, leaving the door open, so that I could see through the storeroom between Kraler's office and the front office. At that moment, a German man followed Koophuis, and I heard him say in German, "Turn the keys over to the young lady." Then the man returned to Kraler's office.

Koophuis came to me, handed me the keys, and said, "Miep, see to it that you stay out of this."

I shook my head.

Jo Koophuis' eyes burned into mine. "No. See to it that you stay out of this. It's up to you to save what can be saved here. It's in your hands."

Then, before I could do anything but absorb his words, he squeezed my hand, then returned to Kraler's office, shutting the door behind him.

During this interlude, I thought two things. First, there was something familiar about the German's accent; and second, it struck me that they might have thought I did not know anything about the people in hiding.

The bookcase concealing the staircase to Anne Frank's hiding place

A few minutes later, the Dutchman who had first entered our office, the man with the gun, came back into my room. Ignoring me, he sat down at Elli's desk across from me and dialed the telephone. I heard him asking that a car be sent.

He had left the door to the hallway open. I heard the German speaking sharply, then I heard Kraler's voice, and then the German's voice again. Suddenly, what had been familiar about this man's voice clicked in my mind. He was speaking German with a distinct Viennese accent. He spoke exactly like all my relatives, the ones I had left so many years ago.

This man came back into my office, but his tone was changing, and I could see he no longer regarded me as an innocent. Obviously, he had figured out that I was also part of what had been secret. He came in and stood over me, saying, in a harsh voice, "Now it's your turn." He reached down and took the keys Koophuis had given me.

I stood up, coming face to face with this man. I could feel his hot breath, we were standing so close. I looked him right in the eye and said in German, "You are Viennese. I am from Vienna too."

He stopped, frozen. I could tell I'd surprised him; he'd not expected this. He suddenly looked dazed, almost as if he were mixed up, and exploded, "Your papers. Identification."

I got out my identity card, which said "Born in Vienna. Married to a Dutchman." He studied my card. Then he noticed the man sitting across from me, making the phone call. He shouted at the man, who was in the middle of his call, "Get out of here."

The man hung up and slunk out like a little puppy. Then the Austrian went and closed the door to the hallway, shutting us together.

In a fury, he flung my identification card at my head and approached me almost in a bent-over position, as though bent with rage. "Aren't you ashamed that you are helping Jewish garbage?" he snarled at me. He then began to curse me, shouting terrible words and saying that I was a traitor, that I would get a terrible punishment. He kept on cursing uncontrollably. I remained standing as tall as I could, not reacting at all to his words. The more he shouted, the more nervous he became. He began to pace from wall to wall. Suddenly, he spun on his heel and said, "What shall I do with you?"

At that moment, I began to feel that I was getting a little more control of the situation. I felt as though I'd grown a little in height. He studied me. I could hear him thinking, Here are two people standing across from each other who are from one country, from one city. One hunts Jews and the other protects them. He quieted down a bit; his face became more human. He kept studying me, and finally he said, "From personal sympathy . . . from me personally, you can stay. But God help you if you run away. Then we take your husband."

I thought, This isn't wise, but I couldn't help bursting out, "You will keep your hands off my husband. This is my business. He doesn't know anything about it."

He sneered at me and tossed his head back. "Don't be so dumb. He's involved in this too."

He went to the door, opened it, then turned around and said to me, "I'll come back to make sure you're still here."

I said to myself, You can do what you like, even drink poison, but I will stay here.

Then he said again, "I'll be back to check on you. One wrong move and off you go to prison too." He turned and shut me into the room alone.

I had no idea where he'd gone. I had no idea what was going on in the rest of the house. I was in a terrible mental state. I felt as though I were falling into a bottomless hole. What could I do? I sat down again. I was in shock.

Then, along the corridor past Mr. Kraler's office and our office, down the old wooden stairway, I could hear the sound of our friends' feet. I could tell from their footsteps that they were coming down like beaten dogs.

READING REVIEW

1. How does Miep indicate that life in the attic was difficult?
2. How did Miep dispose of the Franks' illegal ration cards?
3. What feelings did Miep have for the Austrian officer? How do you think he felt about her?

---

108 THE MORNING OF THE 500-TON BOMB

On the morning of August 6, 1945, an American B-29 bomber dropped a single atomic bomb on the Japanese city of Hiroshima. Much of the city was leveled, and 80,000 people—about a quarter of the city's total population—were killed instantly. Michihiko Hachiya was a doctor at a Hiroshima hospital during World War II, and on that fateful morning he was resting after a long night of duty as an air warden. In the excerpt below from Hiroshima Diary, *he describes the first few minutes after the dropping of the bomb. As you read the excerpt, consider whether the use of such weapons as the atomic bomb is ever justified.*

The hour was early; the morning still, warm, and beautiful. Shimmering leaves, reflecting sunlight from a cloudless sky, made a pleasant contrast with shadows in my garden as I gazed absently through wide-flung doors open to the south.

Clad in drawers and undershirt, I was sprawled on the living room floor exhausted because I had just spent a sleepless night on duty as an air warden in my hospital.

Suddenly, a strong flash of light startled me—and then another. So well does one recall little things that I remember vividly how a stone

Bustling Hiroshima before the atomic bomb

lantern in the garden became brilliantly lit and I debated whether this light was caused by a magnesium flare or sparks from a passing trolley.

Garden shadows disappeared. The view where a moment before all had been so bright and sunny was now dark and hazy. Through swirling dust I could barely discern a wooden column that had supported one corner of my house. It was leaning crazily and the roof sagged dangerously.

Moving instinctively, I tried to escape, but rubble and fallen timbers barred the way. By picking my way cautiously I managed to reach the *roka* and stepped down into my garden. A profound weakness overcame me, so I stopped to regain my strength. To my surprise I discovered that I was completely naked. How odd! Where were my drawers and undershirt?

What had happened?

All over the right side of my body I was cut and bleeding. A large splinter was protruding from a mangled wound in my thigh, and something warm trickled into my mouth. My cheek was torn, I discovered as I felt gingerly, with the lower lip laid wide open. Embedded in my neck

Hiroshima after the atomic bomb

was a sizable fragment of glass which I matter-of-factly dislodged, and with the detachment of one stunned and shocked I studied it and my blood-stained hand.

Where was my wife?

Suddenly thoroughly alarmed, I began to yell for her: "Yaeko-san! Yaeko-san! Where are you?"

Blood began to spurt. Had my carotid artery been cut? Would I bleed to death? Frightened and irrational, I called out again: "It's a five-hundred-ton bomb! Yaeko-san, where are you? A five-hundred-ton bomb has fallen!"

Yaeko-san, pale and frightened, her clothes torn and blood-stained, emerged from the ruins of our house holding her elbow. Seeing her, I was reassured. My own panic assuaged, I tried to reassure her.

"We'll be all right," I exclaimed. "Only let's get out of here as fast as we can."

She nodded, and I motioned for her to follow me. . . .

We stood in the street, uncertain and afraid, until a house across from us began to sway and then with a rending motion fell almost at our feet.

Our own house began to sway, and in a minute it, too, collapsed in a cloud of dust. Other buildings caved in or toppled. Fires sprang up and whipped by a vicious wind began to spread.

It finally dawned on us that we could not stay there in the street, so we turned our steps towards the hospital. Our home was gone; we were wounded and needed treatment; and after all, it was my duty to be with my staff. This latter was an irrational thought—what good could I be to anyone, hurt as I was.

We started out, but after twenty or thirty steps I had to stop. My breath became short, my heart pounded, and my legs gave way under me. An overpowering thirst seized me and I begged Yaeko-san to find me some water. But there was no water to be found. After a little my strength somewhat returned and we were able to go on. . . .

Our progress towards the hospital was interminably slow, until finally, my legs, stiff from drying blood, refused to carry me farther. The strength, even the will, to go on deserted me, so I told my wife, who was almost as badly hurt as I, to go on alone. . . .

All who could were moving in the direction of the hospital. I joined in the dismal parade when my strength was somewhat recovered, and at last reached the gates of the Communications Bureau.

Familiar surroundings, familiar faces. There was Mr. Iguchi and Mr. Yoshihiro and my old friend, Mr. Sera, the head of the business office. They hastened to give me a hand, their expressions of pleasure changing to alarm when they saw that I was hurt. I was too happy to see them to share their concern.

No time was lost over greetings. They eased me onto a stretcher and carried me into the Communications Building, ignoring my protests that I could walk. Later, I learned that the hospital was so overrun that the Communications Bureau had to be used as an emergency hospital. The rooms and corridors were crowded with people, many of whom I recognized as neighbors. To me it seemed that the whole community was there.

My friends passed me through an open window into a janitor's room recently converted to an emergency first-aid station. The room was a shambles; fallen plaster, broken furniture, and debris littered the floor; the walls were cracked; and a heavy steel window casement was twisted and almost wrenched from its seating. What a place to dress the wounds of the injured.

To my great surprise who should appear but my private nurse, Miss Kado. . . . [She] set about examining my wounds without speaking a word. No one spoke. . . . Why was everyone so quiet?

Miss Kado finished the examination, and in a moment it felt as if my chest was on fire. She had begun to paint my wounds with iodine and no amount of entreaty would make her stop. With no alternative but to endure the iodine, I tried to divert myself by looking out the window.

The hospital lay directly opposite with part of the roof and the third floor sunroom in plain view, and as I looked up, I witnessed a sight which made me forget my smarting wounds. Smoke was pouring out of the sunroom windows. The hospital was afire! . . .

Fires sprang up on every side as violent winds fanned flames from one building to another. Soon, we were surrounded.... As the flames came closer the heat became more intense, and if someone in our group had not had the presence of mind to drench us with water from a fire hose, I doubt if anyone could have survived.

Hot as it was. I began to shiver. The drenching was too much. My heart pounded; things began to whirl until all before me blurred.

"*Kurushii*," I murmured weakly. "I am done."

READING REVIEW

1. What surprised Hachiya when he stopped to regain his strength in the garden?
2. What in the excerpt suggests that casualties from the bomb were very heavy?
3. Do you think the Allies were justified in dropping the bomb on Hiroshima? Why or why not?

The World Since 1945

109 THE UNIVERSAL DECLARATION OF HUMAN RIGHTS

The United Nations Charter encouraged respect for human rights as one of the major purposes of the organization. In 1948 the UN General Assembly took a step toward fulfilling this purpose by adopting the Universal Declaration of Human Rights, a document that outlined the basic rights and freedoms of citizens of member nations and territories under UN jurisdiction. The major articles of the Universal Declaration are included in the excerpt below. As you read the excerpt, consider whether respect for human rights should be a factor in international relations.

United Nations headquarters

The General Assembly

Proclaims this Universal Declaration of Human Rights as a common standard of achievement for all peoples and all nations, to the end that every individual and every organ of society, keeping this Declaration constantly in mind, shall strive by teaching and education to promote respect for these rights and freedoms and by progressive measures, national and international to secure their universal and effective recognition and observance, both among the people of Member States themselves and among the peoples of territories under their jurisdiction.

Article 1

All human beings are born free and equal in dignity and rights. They are endowed with reason and conscience and should act towards one another in the spirit of brotherhood.

Article 2

Everyone is entitled to all the rights and freedoms set forth in this Declaration, without distinction of any kind, such as race, colour, sex, language, religion, political or other opinion, national or social origin, property, birth or other status.

Furthermore, no distinction shall be made on the basis of the political, jurisdictional or international status of the country or territory to which a person belongs. . . .

Article 3

Everyone has the right to life, liberty and the security of person.

Article 4

No one shall be held in slavery or servitude; slavery and the slave trade shall be prohibited in all their forms.

Article 5

No one shall be subjected to torture or to cruel, inhuman or degrading treatment or punishment.

Article 6

Everyone has the right to recognition everywhere as a person before the law.

Article 7

All are equal before the law and are entitled without any discrimination to equal protection of the law. All are entitled to equal protection against any discrimination in violation of this Declaration and against any incitement to such discrimination.

Article 8

Everyone has the right to an effective remedy by the competent national tribunals for acts violating the fundamental rights granted him by the constitution or by law.

Article 9

No one shall be subjected to arbitrary arrest, detention or exile.

Article 10

Everyone is entitled in full equality to a fair and public hearing by an independent and impartial tribunal, in the determination of his rights and obligations and of any criminal charge against him.

Article 11

1. Everyone charged with a penal offence has the right to be presumed innocent until proved guilty according to law in a public trial at which he has had all the guarantees necessary for his defence. . . .

Article 12

No one shall be subjected to arbitrary interference with his privacy, family, home or correspondence, nor to attacks upon his honour and reputation. Everyone has the right to the protection of the law against such interference and attacks.

Article 13

1. Everyone has the right to freedom of movement and residence within the borders of each State.
2. Everyone has the right to leave any country, including his own, and to return to his country.

Article 14

1. Everyone has the right to seek and to enjoy in other countries asylum from persecution.
2. This right may not be invoked in the case of prosecutions genuinely arising from non-political crimes or from acts contrary to the purposes and principles of the United Nations.

Article 15

1. Everyone has the right to a nationality.
2. No one shall be arbitrarily deprived of his nationality nor denied the right to change his nationality.

Article 16

1. Men and women of full age, without any limitation due to race, nationality or religion, have the right to marry and to found a family. They are entitled to equal rights as to marriage, during marriage and at its dissolution.
2. Marriage shall be entered into only with the free and full consent of the intending spouses.
3. The family is the natural and fundamental group unit of society and is entitled to protection by society and the State.

Article 17

1. Everyone has the right to own property alone as well as in association with others.
2. No one shall be arbitrarily deprived of his property.

Article 18

Everyone has the right to freedom of thought, conscience and religion; this right includes freedom to change his religion or belief, and freedom, either alone or in community with others and in public or private, to manifest his religion or belief in teaching, practice, worship and observance.

Article 19

Everyone has the right to freedom of opinion and expression; this right includes freedom to hold opinions without interference and to seek, receive and impart information and ideas through any media and regardless of frontiers.

Article 20

1. Everyone has the right to freedom of peaceful assembly and association.
2. No one may be compelled to belong to an association.

Article 21

1. Everyone has the right to take part in the government of his country, directly or through freely chosen representatives.
2. Everyone has the right of equal access to public service in his country.
3. The will of the people shall be the basis of the authority of government; this will shall be expressed in periodic and genuine elections which shall be by universal and equal suffrage and shall be held by secret vote or by equivalent free voting procedures.

Article 22

Everyone, as a member of society, has the right to social security and is entitled to realization, through national effort and international co-operation and in accordance with the organization and resources of each State, of the economic, social and cultural rights indispensable for his dignity and the free development of his personality.

Article 23

1. Everyone has the right to work, to free choice of employment, to just and favourable conditions of work and to protection against unemployment.
2. Everyone, without any discrimination, has the right to equal pay for equal work.

3. Everyone who works has the right to just and favourable remuneration ensuring for himself and his family an existence worthy of human dignity, and supplemented, if necessary, by other means of social protection.

4. Everyone has the right to form and to join trade unions for the protection of his interests.

Article 24

Everyone has the right to rest and leisure, including reasonable limitation of working hours and periodic holidays with pay.

Article 25

1. Everyone has the right to a standard of living adequate for the health and well-being of himself and his family, including food, clothing, housing and medical care and necessary social services, and the right to security in the event of unemployment, sickness, disability, widowhood, old age or other lack of livelihood in circumstances beyond his control.

2. Motherhood and childhood are entitled to special care and assistance. All children, whether born in or out of wedlock, shall enjoy the same social protection.

Article 26

1. Everyone has the right to education. Education shall be free, at least in the elementary and fundamental stages. Elementary education shall be compulsory. Technical and professional education shall be made generally available and higher education shall be equally accessible to all on the basis of merit.

2. Education shall be directed to the full development of the human personality and to the strengthening of respect for human rights and fundamental freedoms. It shall promote understanding, tolerance and friendship among all nations, racial or religious groups, and shall further the activities of the United Nations for the maintenance of peace.

3. Parents have a prior right to choose the kind of education that shall be given to their children.

Article 27

1. Everyone has the right to freely participate in the cultural life of the community, to enjoy the arts and to share in scientific advancement and its benefits.

2. Everyone has the right to the protection of the moral and material interests resulting from any scientific, literary or artistic production of which he is the author.

Article 28

Everyone is entitled to a social and international order in which the rights and freedoms set forth in this Declaration can be fully realized.

Article 29

1. Everyone has duties to the community in which alone the free and full development of his personality is possible.

2. In the exercise of his rights and freedoms, everyone shall be subject only to such limitations as are determined by law solely for the purpose of securing due recognition and respect for the rights and freedoms of others and of meeting the just requirements of morality, public order and the general welfare in a democratic society.

3. These rights and freedoms may in no case be exercised contrary to the purposes and principles of the United Nations.

Article 30

Nothing in this declaration may be interpreted as implying for any State, group or person any right to engage in any activity or to perform any act aimed at the destruction of any of the rights and freedoms set forth herein.

READING REVIEW

1. According to the Universal Declaration, how should respect for human rights be promoted?
2. Which article of the Universal Declaration do you think is the most important? Give reasons for your answer.
3. Should a nation's record on human rights be the major factor in determining the United States' relationship with that nation? Explain your answer.

---

110 GEORGE MARSHALL OUTLINES THE NEED FOR A EUROPEAN REHABILITATION PROGRAM

The devastation of Europe after World War II presented special problems for President Truman and his advisers. Fearing that the Soviet Union would take advantage of the discontent and chaos to establish Communist governments throughout the continent, Truman looked for a way to aid economic recovery in Europe. He settled on the European Recovery Plan, often known as the Marshall Plan after its chief architect, Secretary of State George C. Marshall. In the excerpt below from Volume II of Great Issues in Western Civilization, *edited by Brian Tierney, Marshall outlines the need for such a program before the Senate Foreign Relations Committee. As you read the excerpt, consider what might have happened in Europe if the Marshall Plan had not been put into effect.*

I need not tell you gentlemen that the world situation is very serious. That must be apparent to all intelligent people. I think one difficulty is that the problem is one of such enormous complexity that the very mass of facts presented to the public by press and radio make it exceedingly difficult for the man in the street to reach a clear appraisement of the situation. Furthermore, the people of this country are distant from the troubled areas of the earth and it is hard for them to comprehend the plight and consequent reactions of the long-suffering peoples, and the effect of those reactions on their governments in connection with our efforts to promote peace in the world.

In considering the requirements for the rehabilitation of Europe, the physical loss of life, the visible destruction of cities, factories, mines, and railroads was correctly estimated, but it has become obvious during recent months that this visible destruction was probably less serious than the dislocation of the entire fabric of European economy. For the past 10 years conditions have been highly abnormal. The feverish preparation for war and the more feverish maintenance of the war effort engulfed all aspects of national economies. Machinery has fallen into disrepair or is entirely obsolete. Under the arbitrary and destructive Nazi rule, virtually every possible enterprise was geared into the German war machine. Long-standing commercial ties, private institutions, banks, insurance companies, and shipping companies disappeared, through loss of capital, absorption through nationalization, or by simple destruction. In many countries, confidence in the local currency has been so severely shaken. The breakdown of the business structure of Europe during the war was complete. Recovery has been seriously retarded by the fact that two years after the close of hostilities a peace settlement with Germany and Austria has not been agreed upon. But even given a more prompt solution of these difficult problems, the rehabilitation of the economic structure of Europe quite evidently will require a much longer time and greater effort than had been foreseen.

There is a phase of this matter which is both interesting and serious. The farmer has always produced the foodstuffs to exchange with the city dweller for the other necessities of life. This division of labor is the basis of modern civilization. At the present time it is threatened with breakdown. The town and city industries are not producing adequate goods to exchange with the food-producing farmer. Raw materials and fuel are in short supply. Machinery is lacking or worn out. The farmer or the peasant cannot find the goods for sale which he desires to purchase. So the sale of his farm produce for money which he cannot use seems to him an unprofitable transaction. He, therefore, has withdrawn many fields from crop cultivation and is using them for grazing. He feeds more grain to stock and finds for himself and his family an ample supply of food, however short he may be on clothing and the other ordinary gadgets of civilization. Meanwhile people in the cities are short of food and fuel. So the governments are forced to use their foreign money and credits to procure these necessities abroad. This process exhausts funds which are urgently needed for reconstruction. Thus a very serious situation is rapidly developing which bodes no good for the world. The modern system of the division of labor upon which the exchange of products is based is in danger of breaking down.

The truth of the matter is that Europe's requirements for the next three or four years of foreign food and other essential products—principally from America—are so much greater than her present ability to pay that she must have substantial additional help or face economic, social, and political deterioration of a very grave character.

The remedy lies in breaking the vicious circle and restoring the confidence of the European people in the economic future of their own countries and of Europe as a whole. The manufacturer and the farmer throughout wide areas must be able and willing to exchange their products for currencies the continuing value of which is not open to question.

Aside from the demoralizing effect on the world at large and the possibilities of disturbances arising as a result of the desperation of the people concerned, the consequences to the economy of the United States should be apparent to all. It is logical that the United States should do whatever it is able to do to assist in the return of normal economic health in the world, without which there can be no political stability and no assured peace. Our policy is directed not against any country or doctrine but against hunger, poverty, desperation, and chaos. Its purpose should be the revival of a working economy in the world so as to permit the emergence of political and social conditions in which free institutions can exist. Such assistance, I am convinced, must not be on a piecemeal basis as various crises develop. Any assistance that this Government may render in the future should provide a cure rather than a palliative. Any government that is willing to assist in the task of recovery will find full cooperation, I am sure, on the part of the United States Government. Any government which maneuvers to block the recovery of other countries cannot expect help from us. Furthermore, governments, political parties, or groups which seek to perpetuate human misery in order to profit therefrom politically or otherwise will encounter the opposition of the United States.

"Our policy is directed not against any country or doctrine but against hunger, poverty, desperation, and chaos."

It is already evident that, before the United States Government can proceed much further in its efforts to alleviate the situation and help start the European world on its way to recovery, there must be some agreement among the countries of Europe as to the requirements of the situation and the part those countries themselves will take in order to give proper effect to whatever action might be undertaken by this Government. It would be neither fitting nor efficacious for this Government to undertake to draw up unilaterally a program designed to place Europe on its feet economically. This is the business of the Europeans. The initiative, I think, must come from Europe. The role of this country should consist of friendly aid in drafting of a European program and of later support of such a program so far as it may be practical for us to do so. The program should be a joint one, agreed to by a number, if not all, European nations.

An essential part of any successful action on the part of the United States is an understanding on the part of the people of America of the character of the problem and the remedies to be applied. Political passion and prejudice should have no part. With foresight, and a willingness on the part of our people to face up to the vast responsibility which history has clearly placed upon our country, the difficulties I have outlined can and will be overcome.

READING REVIEW

1. Why did Marshall think it would be difficult for ordinary Americans to see the need for a European recovery program?
2. What, according to Marshall, was to be the role of the United States in this European recovery program?
3. What do you think would have taken place in Europe if the Marshall Plan had not been instituted? Explain your answer.

---

111 THE BATTLE OF THE SORBONNE

In March 1968 radical students at the Nanterre division of the University of Paris issued a statement demanding reforms in the French educational system. Strikes and sit-ins held in support of these demands led to the closure of Nanterre in May. Trouble soon spread to the university's largest campus—the Sorbonne—in Paris's Latin Quarter. When the police attempted to clear the Sorbonne, a riot developed. For the next few nights, violence rocked the Latin Quarter as the police and students battled for control of the streets. The first week's incidents are described in the excerpt below from Time *magazine. As you read the excerpt, ask yourself why there was so much turmoil on university campuses throughout the world in 1968.*

"This is real guerrilla action," said Paris Police Chief Maurice Grimaud. Indeed it was. In a year that has been marked almost everywhere by student upheaval, Paris last week captured the record for the largest student riots so far in 1968. While the city prepared for the opening of Vietnamese peace talks, students staged the sharpest street fighting since the end of World War II. By week's end, the gulf between the government and the students—who were joined by France's major unions—had widened into a serious anarchical challenge to Charles de Gaulle's government.

The trouble began two weeks ago, when authorities abruptly closed the Nanterre College of Letters, a suburban branch of the 150,000-student University of Paris, because a small band of Maoist, Marxist, Trotskyite and Guevarist militants had thrown the campus into a turmoil with strikes and threats of gang war. Next day the Nanterre leftists streamed into Paris' Latin Quarter, began demonstrating in the Sorbonne campus quadrangle. After the university called in police to eject them, bloody clashes brought 600 arrests and forced the Sorbonne, France's oldest university, to close.

A confrontation between students and police, Paris 1968

Burning Cars. That served only to rally broad support for the trouble-makers. Massing by the thousands along Boulevard St. Germain and cross streets, students ripped up paving stones and steel posts, bombarded steel-helmeted police from behind barricades of overturned and burning cars. The police fought back with nightsticks and tear-gas grenades in a battle lasting some seven hours.

Obviously embarrassed by such disorder on the eve of Viet Nam peace talks, Charles de Gaulle warned that further violence would not be tolerated. Yet the clashes continued: 30,000 students marched up the Champs Elysees to the Arc de Triomphe, singing the Communist *Internationale* on the way. By mid-week, student strikes and demonstrations had spread to a dozen provincial cities, and even high school pupils picketed in large numbers to demand the release of 100 jailed rioters. Nanterre reopened, but students and nearly half the faculty struck in sympathy with the still-shuttered Sorbonne.

To insulate the Right-Bank peace-talk site (and the U.S. delegation) from violence, police cordoned off all major bridges across the Seine. On the other side, students chanting *"De Gaulle assassin!"* massed and marched. Then, after flickering hopes for a compromise with the government faded, they rebuilt their paving-stone-and-auto barricades. Late at night, the gendarme phalanxes charged—and nearly a square mile of Paris turned into a battlefield. As retreating students hurled Molotov cocktails and set fire to many autos, the explosion of their gasoline tanks mixed with the pop of police tear-gas grenades. In a belated weekend effort to restore calm, Premier Georges Pompidou proclaimed on radio and television that reform of the university system was "indispensable," and promised to reopen the Sorbonne this week. He even hinted that appeal courts would deal lightly with already convicted student leaders.

Smoldering Hostility. The seeds of the student revolt have long existed in France's archaic system of higher education. Overcrowded to a point that stifles learning, lamentably short of professors, and managed by a mammoth but mediocre bureaucracy that resists change, French universities annually flunk some 20% of their 550,000 students while another 50% give up and quit. Resentment against the system erupted in the rioting.

Astonishingly, no lives were lost, but before the week's carnage ended, 1,158 combatants were hurt (596 of them police) and 1,081 arrested. In support of the rioters, Communist, Socialist, Christian Socialist and teachers' labor unions ordered an illegal 24-hour general strike, a move that could leave France without railroads, buses, subways, electricity, schools and other public services.

READING REVIEW

1. According to the excerpt, who started the troubles in Paris in 1968?
2. Why was the outbreak of violence at the Sorbonne an embarrassment for the French government?
3. Why do you think that 1968 was such a violent year on the world's university campuses? Explain your answer.

---

112 SOVIET DISSIDENTS DECRY THE INVASION OF CZECHOSLOVAKIA

To protest the Soviet invasion of their country, a number of Czech students publicly burned themselves to death. Shocked by this terrible waste of young lives, dissidents in the Soviet Union called for the immediate withdrawal of their troops. In the excerpt below from Samizdat, *edited by George Saunders, two leading dissidents—Pyotr Grigorenko, a former Red Army general, and Ivan Yakhimovich, at one time a collective farm manager in Latvia—outline why Soviet troops should leave Czechoslovakia. As you read the excerpt, consider the value of dissident activities in a totalitarian society.*

The campaign of self-immolation initiated on January 16, 1969, by the Prague student Jan Palach as a protest against the intervention in the international affairs of the Czechoslovakian Socialist Republic has not ended. Another human torch [the student Jan Zajic], the latest, flared up in Prague's Wenceslas Square on February 21.

This protest, which took such a frightful form, was intended above all for us, Soviet citizens. It is the unsolicited and unjustified presence of our troops that arouse such anger and despair among the Czechoslovak people. For good reason the death of Jan V. Palach stirred the whole of working Czechoslovakia into action.

We all share a part of the guilt for his death, as well as for the death of other Czechoslovak brothers who have committed suicide. By our approving the venture of our troops, justifying it, or simply keeping silent, we contribute to the continued burning of human torches in the squares of Prague and other cities. The Czechs and the Slovaks always considered us their brothers. Will we let the word "Soviet" become synonymous in their eyes with the word "foe"?

"We all share a part of the guilt for his death, as well as for the death of other Czechoslovak brothers who have committed suicide."

Citizens of our great country! The greatness of a country is not shown by the power of its armies being brought down upon a small, freedom-loving people, but by its moral power. Shall we really continue to look on in silence while our brothers perish? By now it is clear to everyone that the presence of our troops on the territory of the Czechoslovakian Socialist Republic is not called for by the defense needs of our country nor the needs of the socialist community. Do we not have enough courage to admit that a tragic mistake has been made and to do everything in our power to correct it? That is our right and our duty!

We call upon all Soviet people, without doing anything rash or hasty and by all legal methods, to bring about the withdrawal of Soviet troops from Czechoslovakia and the renunciation of interference in its internal affairs. Only by these means can the friendship between our peoples be restored.

Long live the heroic Czechoslovak people!
Long live Soviet-Czechoslovak friendship!

READING REVIEW

1. According to Grigorenko and Yakhimovich, why did the Soviet people share the guilt for Jan Palach's suicide?
2. What methods did Grigorenko and Yakhimovich suggest the Soviet people should use to bring about the withdrawal of their troops from Czechoslovakia?
3. What purpose do you think dissidents serve in totalitarian societies? Explain your answer.

113 REWRITING HISTORY IN CHINA

Throughout the first half of 1989, students across China demonstrated for greater intellectual and political freedoms. The largest of these demonstrations was held in Tiananmen Square in the center of Beijing. At times, more than 100,000 students and workers crammed into the square, calling on the country's ageing leaders to hand the reigns of government over to younger, more liberal politicians. However, when the government imposed martial law, the crowds began to dwindle and by early June only about 1,000 students remained camped out in Tiananmen. Then in the early morning of June 3, army units moved in to clear these people from the square. In the clashes that ensued, untold numbers were killed and wounded. In the excerpt below from The New York Times, *a reporter describes how the Chinese government tried to deny that the crackdown in Tiananmen Square took place. As you read the excerpt, consider why the Chinese government thought it necessary to hide the truth from its people.*

SHANGHAI, June 11, [1989]—In the week since the bloody crackdown on the democracy movement in Beijing, the Chinese propaganda machinery has been put into full swing, seeking to transform the event into a heroic operation that saved the country from "a counterrevolutionary plot."

. . . In every . . . city in China, the newspapers and television stations have mounted a barrage of film clips, interviews and statements from leaders portraying accounts of the crackdown by diplomats, foreign journalists and witnesses as "rumors."

The bloody massacre described in the foreign press—and in foreign radio broadcasts beamed at China—never took place, Chinese news reports say. According to the official television stations and newspapers, what actually occurred was a largely peaceful operation, vigorously supported by public opinion, aimed at "quelling the turmoil" brought about by "a small number of bad elements."

The campaign is reminiscent of past efforts in this country to rewrite history. The difference this time is that the rewriting is taking place within days of the historic event itself.

An extraordinary series of broadcasts over several nights on national television illustrates the tone of the propaganda effort. For two nights, both the early and late evening news programs broadcast segments of a street interview done by ABC News in Beijing shortly after the army's assaults. A man is shown being interviewed, his voice rising with anger and his arms imitating the motion of a machine gun, as he describes a scene of terrible carnage committed, he says, by the army. . . .

A caption on the bottom of the screen during the interview identifies the man as "somebody spreading rumors about the cleanup of Tiananmen Square." After the man speaks, the news announcer warns the public to beware of believing such rumors, then says that the man is wanted by the police and he appeals to the public to turn him in.

Tonight the national news showed the same man, looking haggard and terrified, in police custody, retracting in front of the cameras what he had said to ABC News. The news announcer says that the man, whose name he gives as Xiao Bin, identifying him as an unemployed 42-year-old factory worker, was turned in one hour after the appeal to the public by two shop assistants who recognized him from his picture. They said they caught him in the act of telling someone that 20,000 people had been killed in the crackdown.

"I never saw anything," Mr. Xiao says of the Beijing crackdown. He goes on, his head bowed, "I apologize for bringing great harm to the party and the country." He also admitted that he was a counterrevolutionary....

A Chinese soldier threatening a protestor in Tiananmen Square

In essence, the official version of the events is this: The troops arrived in Tiananmen Square about 4 A.M. on Sunday morning, June 4. The protesting students who were camped out on the square withdrew quickly, so that after only about half an hour the operation was complete. Television footage accompanying this account showed soldiers in the early morning peacefully beginning to clean up the debris from the long occupation of the square.

In a televised interview, Yuan Mu, the official government spokesman, said that at most 300 people were killed in the operation, many of them soldiers. An army commander standing nearby then said that "not a single student was killed" in Tiananmen Square, although the government acknowledged that 23 were killed that day.

Neither man explained how the dissidents, if they were only "a very small group," nonetheless managed to kill up to 300 heavily armed soldiers and to disable or destroy dozens of tanks, armored personnel carriers and trucks.

Early in the propaganda campaign, television reports showed pictures of the mutilated and burned bodies of soldiers. For the last few days, there have been segments on the news programs showing local Beijing leaders visiting wounded soldiers in the hospital.

A heavily bandaged soldier interviewed on television tonight described in detail how his unit was attacked by "hooligans" with clubs and metal rods. All during the week, individuals described as witnesses have testified on television that the army's behavior was disciplined and orderly and that they were attacked by hooligans.

Chinese television has not shown scenes of families grieving over the deaths of loved ones in the crackdown or images of hospitals full of civilian dead and wounded. Both were frequently shown in foreign reporting of the army crackdown.

Instead, people arrested since the crackdown, often looking bruised and exhausted, have been shown on television admitting that they instigated the violence by attacking troops. Chinese journalists have conducted interviews in the streets of many cities and inside factories in which citizens express their "anger" at the "foreign rumors" concerning the Beijing operation. . . .

"Visitors flying into Shanghai in recent days have said that airlines ask passengers to throw all newspapers into a garbage bag before they disembark."

It remains unclear whether the government's propaganda is effectively countering contrary versions of events that are available through a large number of other sources. These include efforts by students to disperse to other cities and give their own accounts of the Beijing crackdown, which stress indiscriminate firing by the army at unarmed civilians and heavy loss of life among students and others.

Walls and shop windows . . . have been full of reproductions of Hong Kong Chinese newspapers containing full accounts and numerous photographs of the Tiananmen incident. In the last couple of days, virtually all of them have been torn down and the Chinese authorities have tried to stop the dissemination of information from outside the country. Visitors flying into Shanghai in recent days have said that airlines ask passengers to throw all newspapers into a garbage bag before they disembark.

Another major source of unofficial information is the radio. Transcripts of Chinese-language broadcasts by the Voice of America and the BBC were tacked onto walls in many places here for several days. Consequently, one subtheme of the official propaganda campaign has been to attack the credibility of the Voice of America.

"Every thoughtful Chinese is reflecting on what the Voice of America is really trying to accomplish," a newscaster said on tonight's broadcast. "Researchers have carefully compared the Voice of America reports with our own reports and they have concluded that our own reports are better."

In Shanghai during the last week, many Chinese have told reporters that they do not believe the official version of the events in Beijing. But people expressing this point of view to foreign reporters may not represent a majority view. Foreign analysts here are undecided over which version, the official or the foreign, is most believed.

"On the one hand," said one foreign observer, "the Chinese are not badly informed. Many of them over the years have become highly cynical about most of what they read or see in the official media."

"But, it is also possible," he went on, "that many people might prefer the official version of things because, in this instance, the truth is so unpalatable. People might just have a hard time believing that their own Government could have done such a thing."

READING REVIEW

1. According to the reporter, what question was not answered by the official version of events in Tiananmen Square?
2. Why did some analysts feel that many Chinese would eventually accept the official version of the Tiananmen crackdown?
3. Why do you think the Chinese government wanted to cover up the truth about the Tiananmen crackdown? Explain your answer.

---

114 THE JAPANESE PASSION FOR COMICS

Reading comics is among the most popular pastimes in Japan. The most popular comic books, called manga, *have circulations equal to the leading American news magazines, yet the population of Japan is less than half that of the United States. Readership of* manga, *however, is not limited to the young. It is not unusual to see business executives with their heads buried in the latest issues of comics specially written for them. In the excerpt below from* The Wilson Quarterly, *Frederick Schodt, a student of Japanese popular culture, discusses the development of comics in Japan. As you read this article, ask yourself why the Japanese have such a passion for* manga.

In his travel book *The Great Railway Bazaar* (1975), Paul Theroux recalls his encounter with a comic book left behind by a young woman seated next to him on a train in northern Japan: "The comic strips showed decapitations, cannibalism, people bristling with arrows like Saint Sebastian . . . and, in general, mayhem. . . . I dropped the comic. The girl returned to her seat and . . . serenely returned to this distressing [magazine]."

Japanese *manga,* or comic books, come as a rude shock to most Westerners. With their emphasis on violence, sex, and scatology, *manga* do not seem to fit the typical Western notion of Japan as a subtle, even repressed, society. Yet *manga* are read and enjoyed by Japanese of every social class.

All told, comics accounted for 27 percent of all books and magazines published in Japan in 1980; the more than one billion *manga* in circulation every year amount to roughly 10 for every man, woman, and child in Japan.

The most popular Japanese comics appear in monthly and weekly magazines. Fat, 350-page boys' comic books—which have circulations as high as three million—combine dramatic stories of sports, adventure, and science fiction with humor. Girls' magazines place their emphasis on tales of love, featuring stylized heroes and heroines. Themes in adult male magazines range from the religious to the risque, mostly the latter; the stories teem with warriors, gamblers, and gigolos. Until recently, Japanese woman had to read comics written for teen-age girls or peruse those designed for their boyfriends or husbands. But in 1980, publishers came to their rescue with two monthlies, *Be in Love* and *Big Comic for Ladies.*

Why do the Japanese have such an unusual appetite for comics?

It is possible that their written language predisposes Japanese to more visual forms of communication. In its most basic form, the individual Japanese ideogram, adopted from the Chinese, is a symbol denoting either a tangible object or an abstract concept, emotion, or action. Cartoonist Tezuka Osamu has said of his comics: "I don't consider them pictures—I think of them as a type of hieroglyphics. . . . In reality I'm not drawing. I'm writing a story with a unique type of symbol."

The comic tradition in Japan dates back almost 900 years. During the 12th century, a Buddhist priest named Toba . . . penned the *Chojugiga* scrolls, literally "humorous pictures of birds and animals." In a style bearing strong resemblance to today's Walt Disney figures, the scrolls showed monkeys, rabbits, and frogs bathing in rivers, practicing archery, wrestling, and worshiping. Refinements in woodblock printing during the 17th century spread cartoons from the aristocracy and the clergy to the common people. [The phrase *manga* was coined in 1814 by the Japanese woodblock print artist Hokusai, using the Chinese ideograms *man* (involuntary or in spite of oneself) and *ga* (picture). Hokusai was evidently trying to describe something like "whimsical sketches." But it is noteworthy that the first ideogram also has the meaning "morally corrupt."] European-style cartoons, often modeled on those of the British magazine *Punch,* became popular during the latter half of the

19th century; during the 1920s, Japanese artists marveled at the "Sunday funnies" in America and quickly adopted their style.

The real comic boom, however, did not take place until after the Second World War. Young Japanese in particular were starved not just for food but also for entertainment. Dozens of small *manga* publications sprang up to satisfy the growing demand, a demand spurred by the appearance in Japan of such American cartoon classics as Chic Young's *Blondie*, serialized and translated in 1946.

To be sure, small children in Japan have always read comics for the same reason that children everywhere do—they are both accessible and fun. But the passage from childhood to adult life has not weaned postwar Japanese from their dependency on comics. Two modern developments help to explain why.

First, Japan has become a very crowded, urban nation, with a population density that ranks 20th in the world. Unlike many other amusements, comics require little physical space, and they can be enjoyed in silence and solitude. Pioneers in headphone amplifiers for electric guitars, tiny tape players, and other miniaturized gadgetry, the Japanese place a premium on not bothering others.

Second, Japan remains a society ruled by mutual obligations and codes of behavior. Individual desires must be subordinated to the good of the group, yet the pressures for individual achievement have, if anything, increased. To the student cramming for examinations, the businessman stuck in the corporate hierarchy, and the housewife trapped at home, *manga* provide an escape valve for dreams and frustrations. And as such, they play a vital part in Japanese popular culture, revealing legacies from the past, ideals of love, attitudes toward work and play, and above all, a thirst for fantasy. . . .

Besides reading them for pleasure, Japanese now rely on cartoons and comics as an effective way to communicate: They can be found on street signs, shopping maps, instruction manuals, electricity and gas bills, and even in phone booths. One Tokyo publisher recently came out with a history of the world in comic-book form. The growing intrusion of *manga* into daily life is one reason that modern Japanese youth, already surrounded by television sets and video tape recorders, are described by pundits in Japan as the *shikaku sedai*, the "visual generation."

READING REVIEW

1. What possible reason does Schodt offer for why the Japanese particularly have become so addicted to comics?
2. What is the origin of the word *manga?* What interesting point, given the nature of many modern comics, does Schodt note about the possible meaning of the word?
3. How has the nature of Japanese society contributed to the popularity of comics?

115 A NEW LEADER FOR PAKISTAN

The election of Benazir Bhutto as Prime Minister of Pakistan in 1988 was interesting for two reasons. First, her election came after years of "Islamization" in Pakistan, which had restricted women's legal and political rights. Second, she took over from the people who had ousted and later executed her father, former Prime Minister Zulfikar Ali Bhutto. In the excerpt below from The New York Times, *an American reporter discusses the problems facing Benazir Bhutto as the first female leader of a Muslim state. As you read the excerpt, consider why some people consider Benazir Bhutto the "heir apparent" to the leadership of Pakistan.*

They danced in the streets of Lahore, Karachi, and Rawalpindi last week when Benazir Bhutto became Prime Minister of Pakistan.

"Power is no big deal," Ms. Bhutto told the nation Friday night, a few hours after assuming office. "What is more important is that people always have respect for you in their eyes."

The Prime Minister . . . seems to embody all the fresh new spirit that Pakistanis hope will infuse their nation after 11 years of military rule and an "Islamization" campaign that diminished women's rights and made a rough, male-dominated frontier nation even more austere and cheerless.

"Out of all that obscurantism comes something so totally opposite!" exclaimed Javed Jabbar, who last week became the first member of the legislature's upper house to shed his independent label and announce that he had decided to back Ms. Bhutto's Pakistan People's Party in the Senate.

The new Pakistan has met and overcome its initial challenge with surprising ease, conducting a fair and peaceful election. But other, perhaps higher, hurdles lie ahead.

Ms. Bhutto, the daughter of former Prime Minister Zulfikar Ali Bhutto, who was overthrown in 1977 and executed two years later, has never held a paying job before and has given few concrete details of where and how she intends to lead the country. Over the years since her father's execution, she has been campaigning vigorously to restore democracy and avenge her father's overthrow and death.

While she is admired for her fierce loyalty to his memory, she is said to tolerate no criticism of him. Many Pakistanis wonder what if any effect her zealous devotion to his memory, including her tendency to gloss over his misdeeds, will have on her policies. By most accounts, Mr. Bhutto rigged elections and suppressed all opposition in the previous era of civilian rule.

Now, the Bhutto daughter faces several important deadlines. She has . . . to form a government that will command the confidence of the National Assembly and . . . to convince the country's overseas lenders that her government will pursue a sound economic policy.

A Pakistani teacher preparing for class

The aid consortium of foreign governments and international lending groups . . . will want to know how Ms. Bhutto's economic team will raise the money for schools, houses, jobs, minimum wage and comprehensive medical coverage she has promised the voters. As the country's debts mount, feudal landlords and business barons pay almost no taxes. Some of them are backers of her Pakistan People's Party.

The money to pay for social programs cannot come from the military, which is variously thought to consume between 40 and 60 percent of the country's budget. Ms. Bhutto has said that to cut military spending would be tantamount to inviting martial law. The military, cushioned by a range of privileges denied most Pakistanis, including schools, good hospitals and subsidized luxury housing, will have to be brought back down to earth gently and slowly.

Internationally, a democratic Pakistan may have new standing, but this does not mean that it can automatically live more easily with the colossus to the East, India. . . . For most Pakistanis, life with India is measured in wars.

Domestically, Pakistani institutions have to be built or revitalized to tackle urgent social needs. At least two-thirds—some say more than three-quarters—of Pakistanis are illiterate. The population of about 100 million is growing by more than 3 percent a year, one of the world's highest rates.

In developing human resources, Ms. Bhutto's gender may have the greatest psychological impact because Pakistan's women need a heightened sense of self-respect and greater involvement in national life, Mr. Jabbar, an important adviser to Ms. Bhutto, said. Under President Mohammad Zia ul-Haq, who was killed in a plane crash last August [1988], women had their legal rights reduced and were generally encouraged to withdraw from public life.

Ms. Bhutto has never portrayed herself as a feminist in a nation that would be conservatively—but not radically—Islamic even without the policies of the late President. In shops, offices, houses and in crowds gathered to see the new Prime Minister, women invariably beam when asked whether it is important that their country will be run by one of them. Do they think a woman can rule a Muslim nation?

"Why not?" is the almost universal reply.

Some of Pakistan's most conservative Muslim theologians take a different view. A few days before the election, they issued a categorical ruling saying that a woman could not head an Islamic state.

But for most voters in a poor country where the power of the landowner or the patronage of the party is all-important, Ms. Bhutto's sex has not been an issue. She is seen in simpler terms: as the head of the Bhutto clan and the astute leader of the Bhutto party. Because there was no male heir willing and able to shoulder the Bhutto mantle, the people flocked to her.

READING REVIEW

1. Why do you think that cutting the Pakistani military's share of the budget would invite the imposition of martial law?
2. Why might Benazir Bhutto's gender have a psychological impact on the development of human resources in Pakistan?
3. Some people have referred to Benazir Bhutto as the "daughter of destiny." What do you think they mean by this?

116 THE FILIPINOS CELEBRATE THE FALL OF PRESIDENT MARCOS

When a number of high-ranking army officers and the minister of defense turned against him in 1986, Ferdinand Marcos resigned as President and fled the Philippines. In a huge demonstration of joy, thousands of Filipinos flocked to the presidential residence, Malacañang Palace. The opulence in which the Marcos family had lived shocked even the most cynical of these palace invaders. In the excerpt below from Granta: The Snap Revolution, *British reporter James Fenton describes his feelings on entering Malacañang Palace. As you read the excerpt, note the response of the Filipinos to what they found at the presidential residence.*

I turned back and walked down the centre of the road to Malacañang [Palace], my feet crunching broken glass and stones. I asked a policeman whether he thought it was safe to proceed. Yes, he said, there were a few Marcos men hiding in the side-streets, but the fighting had all stopped. A child came running past me and called out, "Hey, Joe, what's the problem?" but didn't wait for an answer.

As I came within view of the palace I saw that people were climbing over the railings, and just as I caught up with them a gate flew open. Everyone was pouring in and making straight for the old Budget Office. It suddenly occurred to me that very few of them knew where the palace itself was. Documents were flying out of the office and the crowd was making whoopee. I began to run.

One of the columnists had written a couple of days before that he had once asked his grandmother about the Revolution of 1896. What had it been like? She had replied: "A lot of running." So in his family they had always referred to those days as the Time of Running. It seemed only appropriate that . . . I should be running through Imelda's old vegetable patch. The turf looked sorrier than ever. We ran . . . past the sculpture garden, past where people were jumping up and down on the armoured cars, and up onto the platform from where we had watched Marcos on the balcony. Everyone stamped on the planks and I was amazed the whole structure didn't collapse.

We came to a side entrance and as we crowded in I felt a hand reach into my back pocket. I pulled the hand out and slapped it. The thief scurried away.

Bing [my photographer] was just behind me, looking seraphically happy, with his cameras bobbing around his neck. We pushed our way through to a kind of hall, where an armed civilian told us we could go no further. The journalists crowded round him, pleading to be allowed a look. The man had been sent by the rebel troops. He had given his word of honour, he said. He couldn't let anybody past. But it was all, I'm afraid, too exciting. One of the Filipino photographers just walked past the guard, then another followed, then Bing went past; and finally I was the only one left.

I thought: oh well, he hasn't shot them, he won't shoot me. I scuttled past him in that way people do when they expect to be kicked up the backside. "Hey, man, stop," said the guard, but as he followed me round the corner we both saw he had been standing in the wrong place: the people in the crowd had come round another way and were now going through boxes and packing-cases to see what they could find. There were no takers for the Evian water. But everything else was disappearing. I caught up with Bing, who was looking through the remains of a box of monogrammed towels. We realized they had Imelda's initials. There were a couple left. They were irresistible.

I couldn't believe I would be able to find the actual Marcos apartments, and I knew there was no point in asking. We went up some servants' stairs, at the foot of which I remember seeing an opened crate with two large green jade plates. They were so large as to be vulgar. On the first floor a door opened, and we found ourselves in the great hall where the press conferences had been held. This was the one bit of the palace the crowd would recognize, as it had so often watched Marcos being televised from here. People ran and sat on his throne and began giving mock press-conferences, issuing orders in his deep voice, falling about with laughter or just gaping at the splendour of the room. It was all fully lit. Nobody had bothered, as they left, to turn out the lights.

I remembered that the first time I had been here, the day after the election, Imelda had slipped in and sat at the side. She must have come from that direction. I went to investigate.

And now, for a short while, I was away from the crowd with just one other person, a shy and absolutely thunderstruck Filipino. We had found our way, we realized, into the Marcoses' private rooms. There was a library, and my companion gazed in wonder at the leather-bound volumes while I admired the collection of art books all carefully catalogued and with their numbers on the spines. This was the reference library for Imelda's world-wide collection of treasures. She must have thumbed through them thinking: *I'd like one of them,* or *I've got a couple of them in New York,* or *That's in our London house.* And then there was the Blue Drawing Room with its twin portraits of the Marcoses, where I simply remember standing with my companion and saying, "It's beautiful, isn't it." It wasn't that it *was* beautiful. It looked as if it had been purchased at Harrods. It was just that, after all the crowds and the riots, we had landed up in this peaceful, luxurious den. My companion had never seen anything like it. He didn't take anything. He hardly dared touch the furnishings and trinkets. We both simply could not believe that we were there and the Marcoses weren't. . . .

Another of the rooms had a grand piano. I sat down.

"Can you play?" said my companion.

"A little," I exaggerated. I can play Bach's Prelude in C, and this is what I proceeded to do, but my companion had obviously hoped for something more racy. Beside the piano . . . lay a letter. It was a petition from members of a village, asking for property rights on the land they lived on. It was dated well before the Snap Election. Someone (Marcos himself? The letter was addressed to him) must have opened it, seen it was a petition, popped it back in the envelope and sat down to play a tune. The keys were stiff. I wondered if the piano was brand new.

A soldier came in, carrying a rifle. "Please co-operate," he said. The soldier looked just as overawed by the place as we were. We co-operated.

When I returned down the service stairs, I noticed that the green jade plates had gone, but there was still some Evian water to be had. I was very thirsty, as it happened. But the revolution had asked me to co-operate. So I did.

Outside, the awe had communicated itself to several members of the crowd. They stood by the fountain looking down at the coloured lights beneath the water, not saying anything. I went to the parapet and looked across the river. I thought: somebody's still fighting; there are still some loyal troops. Then I thought: that's crazy—they can't have started fighting now. I realized that I was back in Saigon yet again. *There* indeed there had been fighting on the other side of the river. But here it was fireworks. The whole city was celebrating.

READING REVIEW

1. Why did Fenton think it appropriate that he found himself running through the grounds of Malacañang Palace?
2. Even though he did not find the blue drawing room in the Marcos apartments particularly pleasing to the eye, Fenton remarked to a fellow invader that it was beautiful. Why?
3. What impact do you think the opulence of the Marcos's life style had on the Filipinos who invaded Malacañang? Explain your answer.

---

117 JOMO KENYATTA STIRS NATIONALIST FEELINGS AMONG THE KIKUYU

In the early 1950s, the British government was ready to grant limited political freedoms to the native peoples of East Africa. The European settlers in Kenya, however, were totally against any kind of political reform. Jomo Kenyatta, the Western-educated leader of the independence movement in Kenya, the Kenya Africa Union (KAU), began to preach that the only way for Africans to achieve any kind of freedom was through bloodshed. Out of Kenyatta's pronouncements grew one of the most feared terrorist groups of the twentieth century—Mau Mau. In the excerpt below from Mau Mau From Within, *Karari Njama, a Mau Mau leader, tells how a speech by Kenyatta persuaded him to join the movement. As you read the excerpt, note how Kenyatta used the KAU flag to show that Kenyans would have to fight for their freedom.*

It was 26 July 1952 and I sat in the Nyeri Showgrounds packed in with a crowd of over 30,000 people. The Kenya Africa Union was holding a rally and it was presided over by Jomo Kenyatta. He talked first of LAND. In the Kikuyu country, nearly half of the people are landless and have an earnest desire to acquire land so that they can have something to live on. Kenyatta pointed out that there was a lot of land lying idly in the country and only the wild game enjoy that, while Africans are starving of hunger. The White Highland, he went on, together with the forest reserves which were under Government control, were taken from the Africans unjustly. This forced me to turn my eyes toward the Aberdare Forest. I could clearly see Karari's Hill, almost in the middle of Aberdare Forest. The hill that bears my grandfather's name and whom I am named after. Surely that is my land by inheritance and only the wild game which grandfather used to trap enjoy that very fertile land. This reminds me of my youth . . . in a Boer's farm in the White Highland, but I felt that I must attend to what Jomo Kenyatta would say next.

The Africans had not agreed that this land was to be used by white men alone. "Peter Mbiyu is still in the United Kingdom," he went on, "where we sent him for land hunger. We expect a Royal Commission quickly to enquire into the land problem." He asked the crowd to show by hands that they wanted more land. Each person raised both his hands. And when he asked those who did not want land to show their hands, nobody raised.

Chief Nderi, when he took the platform, assisted Kenyatta's argument by saying that Aberdare was given boundaries which removed land from

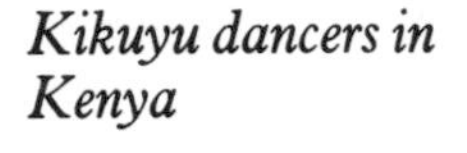
Kikuyu dancers in Kenya

the Nyeri people. He too said that Africans had the right to this unused land. This, spoken by a Government official, proved to all present that Africans had a truly just grievance on the land question.

The other point that Jomo Kenyatta stressed during the meeting was African FREEDOM. He raised the KAU flag to symbolize African Government. He said Kenya must be freed from colonial exploitation. Africans must be given freedom of speech, freedom of movement, freedom of worship and freedom of press. Explaining this to the people, he said that with the exception of freedom of worship, the other freedoms are severely limited with respect to the Africans. Freedom of movement: many Africans have been prosecuted for trespass on European land or for entering a town outside his own district. I personally faced a resident magistrate . . . in December 1949 charged under trespass on a European farm. Without a fine, he sentenced me to three months imprisonment. He refused to my paying money for the sentence.

I was struck by its [the flag's] red colour in the middle of black and green, which signified blood. An hour passed without any description of the KAU flag. Most of the time I was pondering how and when we shall officially hoist that National flag to signify the Kenya African freedom. I recalled Kenyatta's words in 1947 at a KAU rally on the same ground. "The freedom tree can only grow when you pour blood on it, but not water. I shall firmly hold the lion's jaws so that it will not bite you. Will you bear its claws?" He was replied with a great applause of admittance.

When Kenyatta returned on the platform for the third time, after a few other speakers, he explained the flag. He said, "Black is to show that this is for black people. Red is to show that the blood of an African is the same colour as the blood of a European, and green is to show that when we were given this country by God it was green, fertile and good but now you see the green is below the red and is suppressed." (Tremendous applause!) I tried to figure out his real meaning. What was meant by green being "suppressed" and below the red? Special Branch agents were at the meeting recording all the speeches so Kenyatta couldn't speak his mind directly. What he said must mean that our fertile lands (green) could only be regained by the blood (red) of the African (black). That was it! The black was separated from the green by red; the African could only get to his land through blood.

"You also see on the flag a shield, a spear and an arrow," he went on. "This means that we should remember our forefathers who used these weapons to guard this land for us. The 'U' is placed over the shield and indicates that the shield will guard the Union against all evils . . ."

READING REVIEW

1. Why was Karari especially aggrieved that he owned no land?
2. Who do you think Kenyatta was referring to when he spoke of holding open the jaws of the lion?
3. How, according to Karari, did the KAU flag symbolize the need for armed struggle?

118 NELSON MANDELA EXPLAINS WHY THERE IS A SOUTH AFRICAN RESISTANCE MOVEMENT

In its struggle against apartheid, the African National Congress (ANC) largely used the methods of passive resistance. After the massacre of 67 peaceful African demonstrators at Sharpeville in 1960, however, the ANC went underground and changed its tactics, forming a military wing called Umkonto we Sizwe, *or "Spear of the Nation." In 1963, Nelson Mandela and eight others were arrested and charged with founding a terrorist organization—Umkonto. The following year Mandela and seven of the eight were found guilty and sentenced to life imprisonment. In the excerpt below, taken from trial transcripts, Mandela explains why a movement like Umkonto was needed. As you read the excerpt, consider whether the South Africans' grievances justified the use of violence.*

As I understand the State case, . . . the suggestion is that Umkonto was the inspiration of the Communist Party which sought by playing upon imaginary grievances to enrol the African people into an army which ostensibly was to fight for African freedom, but in reality was fighting for a communist state. Nothing could be further from the truth. In fact the suggestion is preposterous. Umkonto was formed by Africans to further their struggle for freedom in their own land. Communists and others supported the movement, and we only wish that more sections of the community would join us.

Our fight is against real, and not imaginary, hardships or, to use the language of the State Prosecutor, "so-called hardships." Basically, we fight against two features which are the hallmarks of African life in South Africa and which are entrenched by legislation which we seek to have repealed. These features are poverty and lack of human dignity, and we do not need communists or so-called "agitators" to teach us about these things.

South Africa is the richest country in Africa, and could be one of the richest in the world. But it is a land of extremes and remarkable contrasts. The Whites enjoy what may well be the highest standard of living in the world, whilst Africans live in poverty and misery. Forty per cent of the Africans live in hopelessly overcrowded and, in some cases, drought-stricken Reserves, where soil erosion and the overworking of the soil makes it impossible for them to live properly off the land. Thirty per cent are labourers, labour tenants, and squatters on White farms and work and live under conditions similar to those of the serfs of the Middle Ages. The other 30 per cent live in towns where they have developed economic and social habits which bring them closer in many respects to White standards. Yet most Africans, even in this group, are impoverished by low incomes and high cost of living. . . .

Poverty goes hand in hand with malnutrition and disease. The incidence of malnutrition and deficiency diseases is very high amongst Africans. Tuberculosis, pellagra, kwashiorkor, gastroenteritis, and scurvy bring death and destruction of health. The incidence of infant mortality is one of the highest in the world . . . . These diseases not only destroy the vital organs of the body, but they result in retarded mental conditions and lack of initiative, and reduce powers of concentration. The secondary results of such conditions affect the whole community and the standard of work performed by African labourers.

The complaint of Africans, however, is not only that they are poor and the Whites are rich, but that the laws which are made by the Whites are designed to preserve this situation. There are two ways to break out of poverty. The first is by formal education, and the second is by the worker acquiring a greater skill at his work and thus higher wages. As far as Africans are concerned, both these avenues of advancement are deliberately curtailed by legislation.

The present Government has always sought to hamper Africans in their search for education. One of their early acts . . . was to stop subsidies for African school feeding. Many African children who attended schools depended on this supplement to their diet. This was a cruel act.

There is compulsory education for all White children at virtually no cost to their parents, be they rich or poor. Similar facilities are not provided for the African children, though there are some who receive such assistance. African children, however, generally have to pay more for their schooling than Whites. According to figures quoted by the South African Institute of Race Relations in its 1963 journal, approximately 40 per cent of African children in the age group between seven to fourteen do not attend school. For those who do attend school, the standards are vastly different from those afforded to White children. In 1960–61 the *per capita* Government spending on African students at State-aided schools was estimated at R12.46. In the same years, the *per capita* spending on White children . . . was R144.57. Although there are no figures available to me, it can be stated, without doubt, that the White children on whom R144.57 per head was being spent all came from wealthier homes than African children on whom R12.46 per head was being spent.

The quality of education is also different. According to the Bantu Educational Journal, only 5,660 African children in the whole of South Africa [graduated] in 1962. . . . This is presumably consistent with the policy of Bantu education about which the present Prime Minister said, during the debate on the Bantu Education Bill in 1953:

> When I have control of native education I will reform it so that Natives will be taught from childhood to realize that equality with Europeans is not for them. . . . When my Department controls Native education it will know for what class of higher education a Native is fitted, and whether he will have a chance in life to use his knowledge.

The other main obstacle to the economic advancement of the African is the industrial colour-bar under which all the better jobs of industry are reserved for Whites only. Moreover, Africans who do obtain employment in the unskilled and semi-skilled occupations which are open to them are not allowed to form trade unions which have recognition under the Industrial Conciliation Act. This means that strikes of African workers are illegal, and that they are denied the right of collective bargaining which is permitted to the better-paid White workers. The discrimination in the policy of successive South African Governments towards African workers is demonstrated by the so-called "civilized labour policy" under which sheltered, unskilled Government jobs are found for those White workers who cannot make the grade in industry, at wages which far exceeded the earnings of the average African employee in industry. . . .

The lack of human dignity experienced by Africans is the direct result of the policy of White supremacy. White supremacy implies Black inferiority. Legislation designed to preserve White supremacy entrenches this notion. Menial tasks in South Africa are invariably performed by Africans. When anything has to be carried or cleaned the White man will look around for an African to do it for him, whether the African is employed by him or not. Because of this sort of attitude, Whites tend to regard Africans as a separate breed. They do not look upon them as people with families of their own; they do not realize that they have emotions—that they fall in love like White people do; that they want to be with their wives and children like White people want to be with theirs; that they want to earn enough money to support their families properly, to feed and clothe them and send them to school. And what "house-boy" or "garden-boy" or labourer can ever hope to do this?

Pass laws, which to the Africans are among the most hated bits of legislation in South Africa, render any African liable to police surveillance at any time. I doubt whether there is a single African male in South Africa who has not at some stage had a brush with the police over his pass. Hundreds and thousands of Africans are thrown into jail each year under pass laws. Even worse than this is the fact that pass laws keep husband and wife apart and lead to the breakdown of family life. . . .

Africans want to be paid a living wage. Africans want to perform work which they are capable of doing, and not work which the Government declares them capable of. Africans want to be allowed to live where they obtain work, and not be endorsed out of an area because they were not born there. Africans want to be allowed to own land in places where they work, and not to be obliged to live in rented houses which they can never call their own. Africans want to be part of the general population, and not confined to living in their own ghettoes. African men want to have their wives and children to live with them where they work, and not be forced into an unnatural existence in men's hostels. African women want to be with their menfolk and not be left permanently widowed on the Reserves. Africans want to be allowed out after eleven o'clock at night and not to be confined to their rooms like little children. Africans want to be allowed to travel in their own country and to seek work where they want to and not where the Labour Bureau tells them to. Africans want a just share in the whole of South Africa; they want security and a stake in society.

Above all, we want equal political rights, because without them our disabilities will be permanent. I know this sounds revolutionary to the Whites in this country, because the majority of voters will be Africans. This makes the White man fear democracy.

But this fear cannot be allowed to stand in the way of the only solution which will guarantee racial harmony and freedom for all. It is not true that the enfranchisement of all will result in racial domination. Political division, based on colour, is entirely artificial and, when it disappears, so will the domination of one colour group by another. The ANC has spent half a century fighting against racialism. When it triumphs it will not change that policy.

This then is what the ANC is fighting. Their struggle is a truly national one. It is a struggle of the African people, inspired by their own suffering and their own experience. It is a struggle for the right to live.

During my lifetime I have dedicated myself to this struggle of the African people. I have fought against White domination, and I have fought against Black domination. I have cherished the ideal of a democratic and free society in which all persons live together in harmony and with equal opportunities. It is an ideal which I hope to live for and to achieve. But if needs be, it is an ideal for which I am prepared to die.

READING REVIEW

1. What two features of South African life did Mandela say Umkonto was fighting against?
2. According to Mandela, why were white South Africans opposed to equal political rights for Africans?
3. Do you think the grievances listed by Mandela justified the use of violence by the ANC? Why or why not?

---

119 THE MEANING OF THE *INTIFADA*

After the Six-Day War in 1967, the Israelis occupied lands held by the Palestinians on the West Bank of the Jordan River and in the Gaza Strip. In time, Israelis began to move into these occupied areas, establishing settlements there. As more and more settlements encroached on their lands, the Palestinians demonstrated against Israeli rule. In late 1987 the demonstrations turned to violence in an uprising that the Palestinians called the intifada, *or "the shaking." Israeli journalist Yoram Binur posed as a Palestinian for six months to see what life was like for Palestinians in the occupied areas. In the excerpt below from the* UtneReader, *he discusses how some Palestinians contribute to the* intifada. *As you read the excerpt, consider the impact that the* intifada *has had on the attitudes of the Israelis and the Palestinians toward one another.*

Before one can speak of the *intifada,* as the Palestinians call the current uprising, one must first understand how the Palestinians have coped with life under the Israeli occupation up to this point. The key concept in this respect is *sumud,* which means "sticking with it," "staying put," "holding fast" to one's objectives and to the land—in a word, survival. Sumud is an attitude, a philosophy, and a way of life. It maintains that one must carry on in a normal and undisturbed fashion, as much as possible. Compared with organized civil disobedience, or passive resistance as preached by Gandhi, sumud is a more basic form of resistance growing out of the idea that merely to exist, to survive, and to remain on one's land is an act of defiance—especially when deportation is the one thing Palestinians fear most.

Although sumud is essentially passive by nature, it has a more active aspect, consisting of gestures that underscore the difference between surviving under difficult conditions and accepting them. During the course of my project, I was several times presented with examples of this active sumud. On one occasion, I met a Palestinian youth . . . who told me about his version of sumud. "Despite the fact that I am a university graduate," he said, "I can't find work in my profession, so I earn my living as a construction worker."

"Where do you work?" I asked.

"In Beit El, up there." He pointed at the hill that overlooked the refugee camp. On the hillside, one could see scattered houses with the European-style, slanted red-tile roofs that are characteristic of the Jewish settlements in the West Bank. "That means you not only work for the Jewish, but you work for the worst of them, for the settlers," I said, in an admonishing tone of voice.

[He] exchanged glances with his friends—as if to ask them whether to include me in their little secret—and replied, "True, we work for the settlers. The money we earn allows us to live here, to be *samidin* (practitioners of sumud), but that isn't all. For us, in this camp, sumud isn't just bringing home money and buying a sack of rice and a few bags of sugar. When I work at the settlement I take advantage of every opportunity to fight them."

"What can you do as a simple laborer?"

"Quite a bit. First of all, after I lay tiles in the bathroom or kitchen of an Israeli settler, when the tiles are all in place and the cement has already dried, I take a hammer and break a few. When we finish installing sewage pipes, and the Jewish subcontractor has checked to see that everything is all right, then I stuff a sackful of cement into the pipe. As soon as water runs through that pipe the cement gets as hard as a rock, and the sewage system becomes blocked."

Two older men who were sitting at a table near ours joined in the conversation. [These men] represented a generation of Palestinians that is haunted by the stinging defeat of 1948, at which time the Arabs either fled—leaving behind their villages and land—or were forcibly deported. But the younger generation, which is more active in resisting the occupation, owes its nationalistic education and inspiration to these elders. The elders are the ones who nurtured and sustained the Palestinians' identification with the villages of their origin. When asked where they are from, even youngsters who have never known an existence other than in the miserable shanties of a refugee camp can proudly name the place of their family's origin—which is often a village that ceased to exist long before they were born.

The intifada, which means "the shaking" (in the sense of shaking oneself free or awake), began with demonstrations in the Jebalya refugee camp on December 8, 1987, spread quickly to other camps, and continues to this day. There have been hundreds of deaths and casualties, mostly among Palestinians.

The intifada, in my opinion, can be understood as the anguished cry of a minority trying to call attention to the discrimination that is being practiced against it, as much as a demand for national liberation. But Israeli officials prefer to speak of "violent disturbances of order," or just plain riots. . . .

For 20 years the Palestinians have lived among us. During the day we have been the employers who profited by their labor and exploited them for all they are worth; in the afternoon we have been the police; in the evening we have been the soldiers at the roadblock on the way home; and

Israeli soldiers confronting a Palestinian

at night we have been the security forces who entered their homes and arrested them. The young Palestinians work in Tel Aviv, Jerusalem, and other Israeli cities. They identify with the values of Israeli society at least as much as they do with their traditional backgrounds. They get a whiff of the democratic privileges that Israeli citizens enjoy, but they cannot share them. The young man who spends his work week among a people living under democratic rule returns to his home, which is only an hour away but which has (in effect, if not officially) been under curfew for 20 years. Any Arab who walks in the streets at a late hour can expect to be detained and questioned about his actions, even during periods of relative calm. He sees and recognizes the value of freedom but is accorded the kind of treatment that characterizes the most backward dictatorial regimes. How can he be anything but frustrated?

In the end, the impression I was left with formed a depressing picture of fear and mistrust on both sides. The Palestinians, employed as a cheap labor force, are excluded from Israeli society, whereas Israeli Jews are satisfied to rule without the least curiosity about how the other side lives. My conclusion is that a continuation of Israel's military presence in the West Bank and the Gaza Strip threatens to change Israel into a place that many people, including myself, will find unlivable. I am tired of witnessing the disastrous results of the occupation every day. And I am frightened that many more people, on both sides, may be doomed to suffer bloodshed and destruction.

READING REVIEW

1. How does *sumud* differ from passive resistance?
2. How does Yoram Binur view the *intifada?*
3. How do you think the *intifada* has affected Palestinian-Israeli relations?

---

120 BEIRUT DIARY

In 1975 fighting erupted between Christian and Muslim factions in Lebanon. Sporadic periods of war have left the capital city of Beirut, once called the "Paris of the Middle East," in ruins. Early in 1989 a pronouncement by the leader of the Christian forces, General Michel Aoun, that he would drive the Syrian Army—supporters of the Muslim forces—from Lebanon, put the people of Beirut squarely in the line of fire once again. In the excerpt below from The New York Times Magazine, *Ihsan A. Hijazi, a Lebanese reporter, describes life in Beirut during this latest bout of hostilities. As you read the excerpt, note how Hijazi, although living in a war zone, tries to live as much of a normal life as possible.*

April 17, 1989. Sporadic shelling this morning. I drive home from my office at midday with a 25-liter canister of gasoline for my electric generator. Just moments after I pass the state-run Lebanese University, a mortar shell strikes the campus. The blast causes my car to wobble, but I make it home to my apartment building . . . in West Beirut. In the afternoon, a lull in the fighting allows me to turn the generator on and use my electric typewriter. I write my daily story for *The Times*.

The bombardment starts up again in the evening. I rush to the balcony and turn the generator off, to prevent a fire. I consider driving my dispatch over to Reuters, where I have been filing for years, but then shells and rockets begin to rain down on our street. My building stands near a major intersection where the Syrian Army has set up a checkpoint. Next door is the residence of the Muslim Prime Minister, Dr. Selim al-Hoss; on the other side is the Muslim-operated television station. All have been a target for repeated shelling from Christian East Beirut ever since the current crisis began on March 14.

Gen. Michel Aoun, who commands the army's Christian forces and heads the Christian Cabinet of Lebanon's divided Government, has set up a blockade of ports controlled by Muslim militias. Aoun regards the Muslim militias as puppets of the Syrians, and has sworn to drive the Syrians from Lebanon.

The Syrians do not plan to leave. On both sides of the Green Line—the nine-mile border that divides Beirut into the Muslim West and Christian East—guns have been firing daily.

A shell crashes outside, followed by the sound of falling glass and debris. Women and children in the building scream. A big cloud of black smoke covers the street. My wife, Mildred, and I rush out of our apartment on the fourth floor and sit down in the stairwell, using a candle to see our way around. The city has been without electricity and water for days. Our building no longer has any glass. . . .

"A shell crashes outside, followed by the sound of falling glass and debris."

We decide to go down to the basement, actually a parking garage, and spend the night there. It is swarming with families from neighboring buildings who are escaping the bombardment. There is no place to sit, let alone bed down. Earlier in the day, I took my older car . . . down there after its windows had been shattered by shrapnel. I have a newer [car] as well. It is a necessity to have more than one car in Beirut, because you never know when one will be put out of commission either by falling shells or bullets.

Mildred and I clean glass off the two front seats of the car, climb in and try to sleep. It is too noisy. Too nervous to sleep, everyone keeps radios turned on for bulletins about the fighting, hoping to hear news of a cease-fire. But no such luck.

I awaken at 4:35 A.M. to a deafening silence. . . .

April 19. . . . Today, people are queuing up in front of bakeries, and at public water fountains with empty plastic water bottles and canisters. The American University Hospital, overflowing with casualties, has been hit by shells several times. The Christians were aiming their guns at the Syrian soldiers who have been guarding the hospital since

1987. Before that, the hospital was an arena for rival Shiite and Druse militiamen.

Ali Jaber, my new assistant, comes to my office early in the morning to tell me he is taking the day off. He wants to drive his mother and sister to the safety of . . . southern Lebanon. "Many shells fell near my house," he says. . . .

I don't leave because running away is not a solution. And after all, I am a journalist with a duty to keep the events on record. It would be easy to say that after years of civil war and the Israeli invasion in 1982, I have gotten used to violence. But violence is not something one can take in stride. I keep asking myself if my luck will hold out—or whether a shell will hit me this time around. . . .

April 23. The day of the garbage. Mountains of trash have piled up on the streets. Garbage collectors are nowhere to be seen. They would not risk their lives to sweep the city. Rats as big as cats are having a field day. Garbage receptacles in buildings are full.

I have our porter look into the situation. He finds a garbage collector who agrees to take away our trash— . . . for a price. . . .

April 24. . . . Around midnight it begins. First, explosions in the distance. Then the thud of crashing bombs, nearer and nearer. We are already in bed. An explosion rocks our street.

"Are you awake?" I ask Mildred. "The shelling is getting worse," she replies. I suggest we get up and put our clothes on in case we need to go down to the basement. We hear shouting outside. The neighbors are leaving to go to the shelter.

It is pitch dark. I turn on my pen-size flashlight and look at my watch. It is 1:35 A.M. Fully dressed, we lie down on our beds, hoping the exchanges will die down.

Gradually they do. We catnap, then my alarm clock goes off. It is 4:55 A.M. Time to get up and go to work. Mildred is asleep.

I shave and take a cold shower. I change my clothes and put on a gray business suit and a red tie. To be well attired is important for morale.

Mildred has left an empty gasoline canister at the door for me to take to the office and have filled. A pump next to my office has kept us well supplied with fuel.

With my briefcase in one hand and the canister in the other, I walk downstairs to my car, warm it up and drive to my office through the empty streets. . . .

April 26. All quiet. When there's no bombing, boredom takes hold. After finishing work at the office, I rush home. The thought of being separated from Mildred during an outbreak of shelling, when telephone lines sometimes go down, is no less frightening than the thought of being hit by a rocket.

But, once home, there is not much to do. Boredom is even worse for Mildred. She hardly goes out. When I leave home, I close both the wooden door and the iron gate behind me. I reopen them when I get back to the apartment. . . .

Our main pastime is watching videos. The television programming is not always interesting (although we do enjoy the comedies, such as "The Cosby Show" and "Perfect Strangers"), so we rent films from the supermarket. Videos, like gasoline for generators, are an important item in the shopping bag of most Beirutis.

April 27. A day of great expectations: the Council of Foreign Ministers of the Arab League is meeting in Tunis to work out arrangements for a cease-fire in Lebanon. Despondent Beirutis are debating whether the conference will put an end to their agony. In the street, in homes and at offices, radios are on all the time as people listen anxiously for news. . . .

The news from Tunis does not come until late afternoon, after I have returned home. Local radio stations keep interrupting their programs with bulletins about the resolutions of the Arab ministers, who have decided that a comprehensive cease-fire, applying to all of Lebanon, should begin at noon tomorrow. A team of Arab observers will be rushed in to monitor the truce.

Civilians are worried what will happen between now and the cease-fire deadline. Sure enough, Beirut soon begins to shake to the sound of explosions as artillery duels break out on the Green Line. . . .

April 29. . . . The morning newspaper reminds us that as many as 1,000 cease-fires have come and gone during 14 years of civil strife. The Arab League truce is the fifth since the present cycle of bloodletting erupted on March 14.

Nonetheless, you can tell there is a glimmer of hope—although not many really believe the peace and quiet will last. . . .

April 30. It is Easter Sunday on the Greek Orthodox calendar. The two governments have decided that Monday will be a national holiday to observe this religious occasion, and May Day will also be a holiday. Holidays are one of the few things left that still bring Christians and Muslims together. Next week, it will be the turn of the Muslims to celebrate: government offices will be closed for two days in observance of Eid el-Fitr, which marks the end of Ramadan and a month of fasting. . . .

Bishop Elias Audeh, the Greek Orthodox prelate of Beirut, is angry when he delivers his sermon at his church in the Christian quarter. . . . In an obvious allusion to Lebanon's warlords, he says, "They have renounced God in favor of weapons of mass destruction." He adds, "If Christ had been a war god, we would have renounced Him. But he is a messenger of peace."

During these desperate times, the Lebanese have become more religious. Even churches in mainly Muslim West Beirut are jampacked with the faithful this Sunday. And two days ago, a mosque up the street from my apartment could not accommodate all believers. Many prayed on the sidewalk outside. The imam, or preacher, like Bishop Audeh, condemned the indiscriminate violence of the previous weeks. But the shelling just goes on.

READING REVIEW

1. Why is Hijazi's apartment building in the firing line of the Christian forces?
2. Why is the feeling of hope about the cease-fire tempered by the fear that the peace might not last?
3. How does Hijazi try to live as normal as possible? Why do you think it is important for him to do this?

---

121 DAILY LIFE IN A MEXICAN SHANTYTOWN

Over the last 25 years, thousands of Mexicans have left the rural areas for Mexico City in search of work. Since housing was limited or expensive, these urban immigrants simply squatted on whatever empty land they could find, building shacks of scrap metal and other cast-off materials. Typically the life of these shantytown inhabitants is pictured as one of poverty, squalor, and random violence. In the excerpt below from Networks and Marginality: Life in a Mexican Shantytown *by Larissa Adler Lomnitz, an anthropologist describes daily life in the shantytown of Cerrada del Condor on the southern outskirts of Mexico City. As you read the excerpt, note the similarities and differences between life in a shantytown and life in an ordinary city neighborhood.*

The initial impression is of an assemblage of low, single-story shacks or brick cabins made of inexpensive materials and scattered at random. It has a transient look, more like a camp than a permanent settlement. Roofs are weighed down with stones, wires hang from power lines, tins and metal scraps are found in heaps around the dwellings, bricks and old plumbing fixtures are apparently strewn about in disorder. There is a characteristic shantytown smell. . . .

The place looks extremely dry and dusty most of the year. During the rainy season, however, the alleys become rivers of mud. Some bushes and small trees grow on the slopes, between the houses, but they do not seem to yield any noticeable shade. The general impression is neither urban nor rural; the shacks are too small and too close together for a typically rural environment. . . .

The dwellings are unpainted structures made mostly of bricks or adobe. They have little mortar and no outside finish, so that the owner may easily take them apart and reuse the bricks elsewhere. Most homes are one-room dwellings with a wooden door and no windows. The door is normally left open during the day, and there is a plastic or fabric hanging across the opening for privacy. Most settlers grow flowers or ornamental plants in tin cans placed around the house or hung on the walls. Outside each door there is usually a metal washbasin where water

Mexico City today

is stored for personal washing, bathing children, washing dishes, and doing the laundry. . . . The washbasins may also be a source of additional income for housewives who take in washing. A washboard made of fiber or some similar material completes the installation. Clotheslines with dripping laundry are seen everywhere in the shantytown.

During the daytime, radios are blaring from nearly every door. Women and young girls are busy washing, cooking, and minding the small children playing in the gutter in front of the homes. The style of dress is largely urban. Though many construction workers still wear straw hats and *huarache* sandals, otherwise the men dress like the Mexico City working class: dungarees, shirt, and shoes. Elderly migrant women tend to wear dark-colored dresses with skirts below the knees and a shawl . . . for covering the head, as is customary in the countryside. Younger women mostly wear secondhand urban dress such as blouses with skirts or cheap print dresses. Young girls wear blouses with short skirts or pants, as well as inexpensive dresses, all of which may be found in the stores or at the nearby market. Young boys are dressed in hand-me-downs from their brothers, mostly ill-fitting clothes, with their shirt-tails hanging out. Synthetic fabrics and plastics are dominant; women as well as children characteristically wear shoes made entirely of molded plastic. . . .

A typical day in [the shantytown] starts before sunrise, when most men and women get up. Around 6 A.M., most men as well as some women go to work. Many walk to work, others take the bus. As the sun rises over the mountains the bustle in the shantytown begins. Lining up in front of the public water faucet are long queues of women, children, and old men, waiting to fill their buckets. Most of these buckets are made of empty used cans. . . . Some of the old men balance two of these cans at the ends of a wooden yoke, which they use to carry water to the homes of settlers for a few centavos. The public water faucet is the informal meeting place of the shantytown, much like the village well was in the countryside. There is a great deal of exchange of news and gossip while waiting in line with the empty buckets.

Most of the women start working on their laundry early in the morning. While they soak and scrub in front of their homes, the transistor radios are blasting soap operas or popular music. Most shantytown women are soap opera fans and rarely miss an episode. Meanwhile, young girls help their mothers in sweeping, running errands, and watching over their small brothers. Little boys, as a rule, are more pampered than little girls, though they too have to help with errands, particularly carrying water. There are two school shifts; some children go to school in the mornings, whereas others go in the afternoons. Those children who are not away at school or running errands for their mothers are usually seen playing around the dwellings in groups according to age. . . . There are also a few gangs of adolescent boys who are no longer going to school and who do not yet have jobs. They may be seen sitting around near the entrance to the shantytown or leaning against a wall, talking.

During the morning hours there are small groups of jobless men talking outside the shops where beer is sold. By midmorning the shantytown is bustling with activity. Street vendors walk by offering their wares to the women who work or sit out of doors. Elderly men and women set out stands in front of their homes with small amounts of merchandise. The items for sale on the street include bread, clothing, chairs, ice cream, fruit, and so on. . . . About noon, the children who go to school on the afternoon shift start washing up or taking a bath in the tanks in front of their homes. They eat their lunch of tortillas, beans, or noodle soup. After they go and the children from the morning shift return, the women can relax for an hour or so. In the afternoon they may finish their housework, listen to the radio, or watch a soap opera on television. There is also a lot of gossiping and visiting among relatives and neighbors on afternoons.

Television is an important cultural influence in the shantytown. Children watch television after school; if they do not have a set at home they visit with neighbors who do. More important, ownership of a television set tends to ensure the presence of men [at home] after work.

Between 7 and 8 P.M. there is a light evening snack, mostly coffee and tortillas, and then to bed. The lucky owners of a television set may sit up or watch the screen from their beds until late at night.

READING REVIEW

1. Why do the shantytown brick cabins have little mortar and no outside finish?
2. What aspect of rural life has been maintained in the urban shantytown?
3. How does shantytown life compare to life in an ordinary city neighborhood? Illustrate your answer with examples from the excerpt.

---

122 GUERRILLA PRIEST

A controversial religious movement to develop in recent years is liberation theology—the idea that God demands social justice for and deliverance of the poor and oppressed. Most of the founders of this movement were young Latin American Catholic priests. Their analysis of Latin America's political and economic problems was Marxist in nature, and the usual solution they offered was socialism. Sometimes, these priests forsook the pulpit and took up arms in the struggle for liberation. In the excerpt below from Volume II of Latin American Civilization, *edited by Benjamin Keen, Camilo Torres, a Colombian priest who was killed in 1966, explained how he can be a revolutionary yet not be a Communist. As you read the excerpt, consider whether Torres was correct in joining the armed struggle for liberation.*

Because of the traditional relations between Christians and Marxists, and the Church and the Communist Party, it is quite likely that erroneous suspicions and suppositions will arise regarding the relations of Christians and Marxists within the United Front, and of a priest and the Communist Party.

This is why I want to clarify to the Colombian people my relations with the Communist Party and its position within the United Front.

I have said that I am a revolutionary as a Colombian, as a sociologist, as a Christian, and as a priest. I believe that there are elements within the

Communist Party which are genuinely revolutionary. Consequently, I cannot be anti-Communist either as a Colombian, as a sociologist, as a Christian, as a priest.

I am not anti-Communist as a Colombian because anti-Communism in my country is bent on persecuting the dissatisfied, whether they be Communists or not, who in the main are poor people.

I am not anti-Communist as a sociologist because the Communist proposals to combat poverty, hunger, illiteracy, and lack of housing and public services are effective and scientific.

I am not anti-Communist as a Christian, because I believe that anti-Communism condemns the whole of Communism, without acknowledging that there is some justice in its cause, as well as injustice. By condemning the whole we condemn the just and the unjust, and this is anti-Christian.

I am not anti-Communist as a priest because, whether the Communists realize it or not, there are within their ranks some authentic Christians. If they are working in good faith, they might well be the recipients of sanctifying grace. Should this be true, and should they love their neighbor, they would be saved. My role as a priest, even though I am not exercising its prerogatives externally, is to lead all men to God. The most effective way to do this is to get men to serve the people in keeping with their conscience.

"I do want all men to act in accordance with their conscience, to look in earnest for the truth, and to love their neighbor effectively."

I do not intend to proselytize among the Communists and to try to get them to accept the dogma and teachings of the Catholic Church. I do want all men to act in accordance with their conscience, to look in earnest for the truth, and to love their neighbor effectively.

The Communists must be fully aware of the fact that I will not join their ranks, that I am not nor will I ever be a Communist, either as a Colombian, as a sociologist, as a Christian, or as a priest.

Yet I am disposed to fight with them for common objectives: against the oligarchy and the domination of the United States, and for the takeover of power by the popular class.

I do not want public opinion to identify me with the Communists. This is why in all my public appearances I have wanted to be surrounded not only by the Communists but by all revolution aries, be they independent or followers of other movements.

It matters little that the press is bent on depicting me as a Communist. I prefer to follow my conscience, rather than give in to the pressures of the oligarchy. I prefer to follow the directives of the Pontiffs of the Church rather than those of the pontiffs of our ruling class. . . .

READING REVIEW

1. Why was Torres unable to be anti-Communist as a Christian?
2. Why was Torres willing to fight alongside the Communists?
3. Should priests become as deeply involved in revolutionary movements as Torres did? Why or why not?

123 OBJECTIVES OF THE CONTADORA PROCESS

In January 1983 the presidents of Mexico, Venezuela, Colombia, and Panama met at Contadora Island, Panama, to try to work out a resolution to the crisis in Central America. Later that year they issued a document called Contadora Document of Objectives, *which called for an arms freeze, a reduction of foreign military personnel, and an end of insurgency in the region. This initiative to bring peace to Central America—often called the Contadora Process, or simply Contadora—turned out to be little more than a working paper, for a number of countries objected to one or more of its objectives. In the excerpt below, the major objectives of Contadora are listed. As you read the excerpt, consider how Contadora was a major change in Latin American attitudes toward outside influence in regional issues.*

The signatory states, considering:

The situation prevailing in Central America . . . is characterized by an atmosphere of tension that threatens security and peaceful coexistence in the region . . .

Declare their intention of achieving the following objectives:

To promote detente and put an end to situations of conflict in the area, restraining from taking any action that might jeopardize political confidence or obstruct the achievement of peace, security and stability in the region;

To ensure strict compliance with the . . . principles of international law, whose violators will be held accountable;

To respect and ensure the exercise of human, political, civil, economic, social, religious and cultural rights;

To adopt measures conducive to the establishment and, where appropriate, improvement of democratic, representative and pluralistic systems that will guarantee effective popular participation in the decision-making process and ensure that the various currents of opinion have free access to fair and regular elections based on the full observance of citizens' rights;

To promote national reconciliation efforts wherever deep divisions have taken place within society, with a view to fostering participation in democratic political processes in accordance with the law;

To create political conditions intended to ensure the international security, integrity and sovereignty of the States of the region;

To stop the arms race in all its forms and begin negotiations for the control and reduction of current stocks of weapons and on the numbers of armed troops;

To prevent the installation on their territory of foreign military bases or any other type of foreign military interference;

To conclude agreements to reduce the presence of foreign military advisers and other foreign elements involved in military and security activities, with a view to their elimination;

To establish internal control machinery to prevent the traffic in arms from the territory of any country in the region to the territory of another;

To eliminate the traffic in arms, whether within the region or from outside it, intended for persons, organizations or groups seeking to destabilize the Governments of Central American countries;

To prevent the use of their own territory by persons, organizations or groups seeking to destabilize the Governments of Central American countries and to refuse to provide them with or permit them to receive military or logistical support;

To refrain from inciting or supporting acts of terrorism, subversion or sabotage in the countries in the area;

To establish and co-ordinate direct communication systems with a view to preventing or, where appropriate, settling incidents between States of the region;

To continue humanitarian aid aimed at helping Central American refugees who have been displaced from their countries of origin, and to create suitable conditions for the voluntary repatriation of such refugees, in consultation with or with the co-operation of the United Nations High Commissioner for Refugees (UNHCR) and other international agencies deemed appropriate;

To undertake economic and social development programs with the aim of promoting well being and an equitable distribution of wealth;

To revitalize and restore economic integration machinery in order to attain sustained development on the basis of solidarity and mutual advance;

To negotiate the provision of external monetary resources which will provide additional means of financing the resumption of intra-regional trade, meet the serious balance-of-payments problems, attract funds for working capital, support programs to extend and restructure production systems and promote medium- and long-term investment projects;

To negotiate better and broader access to international markets in order to increase the volume of trade between the countries of Central America and the rest of the world, particularly the industrialized countries, by means of a revision of trade practices, the elimination of tariff and other barriers, and the achievement of price stability at a profitable and fair level for the products exported by the countries of the region. . . .

READING REVIEW

1. Which two Central American countries troubled by political turmoil prompted the Contadora Process?
2. Analysts often divide the objectives of Contadora into four categories—political, military, social, and economic. Give examples of each category.
3. Some people have suggested that Contadora signaled a major change in the way Latin Americans dealt with their region's internal affairs. What, in your opinion, was the nature of this change?

Colombian soldiers inspecting an airplane seized from drug traffickers

124 THE TRAGEDY OF COLOMBIA

Assassinations have become an everyday occurrence in Colombia's major cities. Much of the violence is the work of the drug cartels that run the cocaine trade to Europe and the United States. In recent years violence has taken on a political character, with party officials and election candidates being the major targets of the death squads. In the excerpt below from The World Press Review, *a Spanish journalist provides a vivid illustration of how violence has become an accepted part of life in Colombia. As you read the excerpt, note how violence has entered the culture of the country.*

Two bodyguards watch a car on a Bogotá street. "I am safe as long as someone else does not pay them more than I do," observes the car's owner.

Jaime Jaramillo, who became head of the leftist Union Patriotica (UP) party after the assassination . . . of the former head, Jaime Pardo, does not take off his bulletproof vest even on the floor of the congress. Two of Jaramillo's seven bodyguards have been kidnapped.

Some 2,000 Colombians—police officers, guerrillas, politicians, and civilians—met violent deaths in 1987. Murders, kidnappings, disappearances, terrorist attacks, armed confrontations, and death threats are everyday fare in the Andean country next door to Central America. But now a new type of violence has erupted: the "dirty war." The drug traffic, combined with fear from recent election gains by the UP, has given rise to *listas negras*, death lists issued by paramilitary groups. Some of the lists are published in the national press; one of them contained the names of 34 well-known union leaders, politicians, retired officers, and human rights workers.

Some of the names have been scratched, such as that of Hector Abad, director of the Human Rights Committee in Antioquia and a candidate for mayor of Medellín. Abad and Leonardo Bentacur were shot down as they drove to the funeral of union leader Luis Felipe Veléz, who had been killed hours earlier. Eight days after he took over from Abad, Luis Fernandez Veléz, vice president of the University of Antioquia, was found dead in his car.

The University of Antioquia makes the crime pages more frequently than the education page. More than 20 professors and students have been murdered, and half a dozen have disappeared.

In the midst of this bloodbath, the armed forces have announced that the country has 130 citizen armies, mostly farmers and ranchers, armed with legal weapons. In Bogotá, Medellín, and Cali, long lines of applicants for gun permits wait in front of government offices. Gen. Miguel Maza Márquez, head of the criminal investigation police, recently said that in Medellín, Colombia's second largest city, several schools "recruit young men and train them to shoot long-range and short-range weapons. There is a national demand for trained assassins."

Medellín, an industrial city, has a population of 2.7 million—of whom 500,000 live in absolute poverty. The slums that surround the city are filled with the unemployed. Colombia's major drug dealers also live in Medellín, and the paramilitary groups operate from there. . . .

If Medellín is Colombia's most violent city, Guaviare holds the record as the most violent region. Its murders have become a web of intrigue that no official investigation has been able to penetrate. In San José, the capital of Guaviare, the bullet and the machete have become the leading causes of death, and the morgue is never empty. . . .

The violence in San José has taken on a political character. [In 1987] the city's mayor and several candidates in the municipal elections were killed. "We were well positioned to win in the area," says Jaramillo, "but they killed our candidates and we cannot risk more people." In the past two years, 500 UP workers have been murdered.

Colombia is in a war without front lines, says a Colombian historian now in exile in Spain. "They are killing people of every political persuasion. Every side resolves its differences by killing its opponents."

The bookstores of Bogotá have added a new section: "Violence." One of the best books on this theme, *Colombia, Violencia y Democracia*, was commissioned by the government. Its 10 authors, all professors at the National University, are now on a death list.

READING REVIEW

1. What are *listas negras*?
2. What do you think is meant by the statement,"Colombia is in a war without front lines?
3. How does the journalist indicate that violence has become a part of Colombian culture?

---

125 THE ECONOMIC MANIFESTO OF THE QUEBEC PARTY

The Quebec Party, which favored the complete separation of Quebec from Canada, was founded in 1970. In its election manifestos, the Quebec party made a point of showing how federalism—and outside interests like United States companies—had worked against the development of the province's economy. In the excerpt below from The Revolutionary Process in Quebec *by Pierre Vallieres, the party provides an explanation of Quebec's economic problems and how these problems might be alleviated after independence. As you read the excerpt, consider the economic and political impact of Quebec's separation from the rest of Canada.*

An Economy to be Understood

Quebec's economy is not really underdeveloped. It has a prominent industrial character and provides the gamut of services normally found in developed countries.

The motor of this economy, Montreal, is one of the largest economic centres in eastern North America.

In addition, the economy of Quebec is largely open to the outside. Imports and exports are essential to its function.

Finally, the average income of Quebecers, while lower than the Canadian average, remains nevertheless comparable to that of the industrial world.

These few facts should indicate that the transformation of the Quebec economy, as necessary as it is, cannot be inspired by economic policies followed by this or that underdeveloped country. . . .

The Great Ailments

It also must be stated that this economy works very badly.

It is an economy which has aged in many of its vital sectors. . . . Closings of paper, chemical, shoe, clothing and textile factories and the collapse of a part of the agricultural sector are the most visible results of this industrial senility.

A bilingual traffic sign in Quebec City, the heart of French-speaking Canada

Secondly, it is a badly balanced economy. It has absorbed only partially the great waves of worldwide industrialization of the last 80 years. Light industry of the first industrial revolution (clothing, textiles, furniture, shoes) still occupies an abnormally important place in the modern context.

Thirdly, it is an economy completely divorced from the society which supports it. . . . Nearly all major economic decisions have been made by financial interests and entrepreneurs outside our milieu . . . first by the English-Canadian group . . . then more and more by American interests. . . .

A colonial mentality was thus maintained in Quebec long after the exterior characteristics of a colonial economy disappeared. . . .

Foreign Control Limitations

It is necessary to establish several categories of foreign capital investment in the Quebec economy. According to the nature and activity of the business, it can be permitted or forbidden to be controlled from the outside, and in certain cases even exclude all outside interests.

Exclusively Quebec sectors: The first category deals with sectors where foreign interests would be outlawed in just about all its forms, and where the transfer of even a minority block of shares would not be acceptable.

Examples: The mass media, the distribution of printed matter, books, primary steel works.

Majority Quebec sectors: The second category deals with those sectors where a certain portion, even an important one, could be foreign controlled, as long as this participation is below 49 per cent.

Examples: Banks, trust and insurance companies, railroads and certain manufacturing industries. . . .

Sectors open to foreign control: This concerns a third category of enterprises, where foreign interests could have a majority control.

Examples: Coca-Cola and industries using completely new technology.

Quebec-Canada

Our program proposed two elements of association between Quebec and Canada [after independence]: first a customs union, then a monetary union.

The customs union recognizes simply that Quebec exports an important part of its production to the other Canadian provinces and that these provinces have essential markets in Quebec.

Nothing would be more ridiculous than to begin independence with a tariff war between the two countries. . . . This is why we say with assurance that the moment Quebec sovereignty appears inevitable, Canada will accept without difficulty the customs union project. . . .

Should the proposed monetary union fail and we have to conduct our commercial relations only with Canada, we propose that the initial accords go no further than tariff agreements augmented by agreements on transport.

The co-ordination of fiscal polices could wait.

In the event of a monetary union, the question takes on another aspect and the requirements of co-ordination become more precise.

This is particularly difficult to establish between countries that have long had their own monetary institutions. . . .

But since monetary union already exists in Canada, our case is far easier. All that is required is that, when Quebec becomes independent, the two new countries—each with its own monetary institutions—agree to co-ordinate their policies closely. . . .

READING REVIEW

1. According to the Quebec party, what were the "great ailments" of Quebec's economy?
2. How did the Quebec party plan to end foreign domination of Quebec's economy?
3. What do you think would be the economic impact on the Canadian economy if Quebec withdrew from the Federation? Give reasons for your answer.

126 A CHILD OF THE TROUBLES

A generation of children have grown up in Northern Ireland knowing no other life but "the Troubles." With the death toll at over 2,500 people, what impact has this had on these children? American journalist Roger Rosenblatt sought to answer this question by talking to young people who had been personally touched. In the excerpt below from the Manchester Guardian Weekly, *he talks to a teenage girl, Elizabeth, whose brother, mother, and grandfather had all been killed in the violence. As you read the excerpt, note Elizabeth's attitude to "the Troubles."*

Elizabeth['s] . . . voice is quiet, her smile hesitant. Every feature is gentle—the way the long hair waves, the way the lidded eyes give solace. She may have the face of her mother.

"Did they ever find out who did the shooting?"

"The bullets in her body were from the IRA. They've got two fellas in jail for it now. My father works with their fathers in the brewery. He's quite friendly with them, actually. He just has pity for the ones who done it."

The man jailed for the killing of her grandfather was a member of the militant Ulster Volunteer Force.

"And Patrick [her brother]? How was he killed?"

"It was a Catholic fella. They have him locked up too." All three, then, died in different parts of the violence. "When we were younger, we couldn't understand it. We didn't know where to turn or who to blame. We asked the adults, and the adults, they all had different views on it. I kept askin', Why is all this happenin' to *us?*". . .

"Did it shake your belief in God?"

"Not in God. In man."

She goes on about her life: about cooking and cleaning for her father, about the occasional movie she gets to (*Friday the 13th*—"a good scare") and the occasional book (*Across the Barricades*). She suddenly seems invested with an ancient image. She is Ireland, this girl; not Northern Ireland, but the whole strange place, that western chip of Europe stuck out in the Atlantic with no natural resources but its poetic mind and a devouring loneliness. In peacetime that loneliness is intense but beautiful. In time of war it is merely intense. Here is Elizabeth at the window watching rain. Or Elizabeth shopping for groceries. Or Elizabeth walking home under that tumultuous blue-black sky. I could see it. Children often relish being alone, because alone is where they know themselves and where they dream. But thanks to the war, these Belfast children are alone in a different away. Elizabeth is not dreaming of what she will be. She looks about her and knows quite well what she will be, and what her life and that of her children will be in that dread city. And . . . she wants out.

"Do you think that you could marry a Protestant boy?"

"If I find one nice enough. [A graceful laugh.] But if I ever did get married, I'd end up emigratin'. I would not want to live here, bringin' up my own children in the Troubles. 'Cause I was hurt. And I wouldn't want that to happen to them."

It is easy to picture Elizabeth as a parent, because she seems a parent already. . . . She has been rushed into adulthood. Now she must take care of her father as if she were his parent—he who does not like to talk about the Troubles, or about the past, and who seems to have settled, quite justifiably, for a life of determined peace and quiet. He may never change. A grown-up parent sees life in stages, knows fairly well when a child will outgrow or overcome this and that. But how does a child-parent know the same about grown-ups? In a sense, more patience and understanding are asked of these children than of any real parent.

You wonder, in fact, if they begin to love their parents a little less for the multitude of responsibilities imposed on them. Or, for that matter, if they love them less for the danger they are all in. I remembered reading in Philippe Aries's *Centuries of Childhood* that in primitive worlds the high infant mortality rate inured parents against caring for their children too much because they knew they would probably lose them. Does the same obtain in places where there is a high parent mortality rate? Perhaps the children here begin to withhold some of their love from their parents as a pre-emptive strike against the assassins. It would be reasonable. It would be reasonable too if they loved them less simply for being grown-ups, for being partly responsible for the weeping in the streets. Yet they seemed to love their parents more, not less. They love them with greater caution, since whatever these children touch may explode or disappear. Still, when they spoke of their parents, it was with the most delicate mixture of faith, encouragement, pride, fear and regret. . . .

"Do you think that one side in the Troubles is more right than the other?"

"No," says Elizabeth, "neither is wrong. But they need somethin' to bring them together. I really don't know where fightin' gets anybody. It's only goin' to bring more dead, more sadness to the families." . . .

"Don't *you* want revenge?" I ask.

She seems stunned by the question, and regards me with a look both pitying and severe. "Against whom?" she says.

READING REVIEW

1. According to Rosenblatt, how are Belfast children alone in a different way from other children?
2. Why does the author state that Belfast children might love their parents a little less?
3. How would you describe Elizabeth's attitude to life? Explain your answer.

127 *GLASNOST* AND JOURNALISM

Mikhail Gorbachev's policy of glasnost *has introduced a new form of journalism in the Soviet Union—investigative reporting. Soviet journalists have found the transition to this form of work difficult after years of simply spouting the Party line. And Soviet bureaucrats have not helped—when questioned they first become wary, then defensive, and then aggressive. Vitali Vitaliev, however, has been successful in this new venture, writing exposés—on crime, the Soviet mafia, Soviet neo-fascism, and the lack of social justice. In the excerpt below from the* Manchester Guardian Weekly, *Vitaliev writes of a wasteful practice that has been going on for years. As you read the excerpt, ask yourself what impact investigative journalism will have on Soviet society.*

Russian-English dictionaries do not contain the word *pokazukha*. There is no direct English equivalent: the closest is probably "window-dressing." Literally, *pokazukha* means "boasting about non-existent achievements". The concept is not easy for the western reader to understand: if achievements do not exist, what is the point of boasting about them? But the fact is that *pokazukha* was one of the major causes of stagnation and social injustice.

The traditions of *pokazukha* in Russia go back to the 18th century when Prince Grigory Potiomkin (1739–1791) constructed fake cardboard villages on the banks of the Volga to impress Catherine the Great. *Pokazukha* is hard to combat.

Even Gorbachev was subjected to it in the first month of his rule when he decided to pay a visit to the ordinary flat of an ordinary Soviet citizen. He was taken to a plush apartment with excellent furniture and lots of books and was genuinely impressed by the apparent prosperity of his hosts. But, having tea, he looked at the bottom of his cup and saw the stamp of the CPSU [Communist Party of the Soviet Union] Central Committee canteen. He was so angry he left the flat immediately and never tried to repeat an impromptu visit like that again.

A friend of mine was living in that very block in Proletarsky district. The day before the visit he saw new furniture being delivered to the flat by lorry. The day after Gorbachev's visit the same lorry took the furniture away.

When I made up my mind to deal with *pokazukha* at economic exhibitions, the subject was still a no-go area. For many years all such criticism was silenced. Of course I could have tried to write about the USSR Exhibition of Economic Achievements, the archetype of *pokazukha*, but I decided that, to start with, it was better to go somewhere in the provinces. So I went to Frunze, the capital of Kirgizia, a central Asian Soviet republic with one of the lowest living standards in the country.

The exhibition of economic achievements occupied 50 acres on the outskirts of Frunze. I was alone there—no other visitors. Which probably explains why, when I entered the pavilions, their staff appeared dumbfounded and watched me suspiciously, as if I were a kind of madman.

"Hey, what are you doing in here?" The napping woman curator in the Agriculture Pavilion woke up and approached me threateningly.

"Just browsing around. Can't I do that?" I wondered.

"No, you can't. It's a closed exhibition."

A closed exhibition is like a four angled triangle.

All the spacious halls of the Agriculture Pavilion were stuffed with food. Piles and Piles of smoked, boiled, dried sausages (28 different sorts); sweets, cakes and puddings in beautiful boxes. There were dairy products I'd never seen before—kunmiss (horse's milk) among them. There were prunes the size of an apple and pumpkins the size of globes. And above this horn of plenty there were diagrams and posters exhorting ever greater production of food.

Troubled by this lonely visitor, the director of the pavilion appeared. She explained that the exhibition was intended solely for the participants of the plenum of the Kirgizia Party Central Committee, which was to open in a couple of days.

"But some of the food may have perished by then," I said.

"Never mind. We'll replace them," the director replied cheerfully.

"Are those products on sale in Frunze food shops?" I asked.

The director stared at me sternly, the way parents look at children when they are being naughty.

"Walk around the shops and see for yourself."

And I saw. In the shops: wrinkled liver sausage . . . , canned sprats in tomato sauce, sticky, vomitingly-sweet candies. That's all.

"Have you got Grapes in Chocolate or Apricots in Chocolate," I asked sales girls, remembering the exhibits in the pavilion. They shot piercing looks at me and gave no reply.

At the exhibition (in the Standards and Quality Pavilion): cheap and beautiful footwear, bright and fashionable clothes for children, lacy underwear, T-shirts with funny drawings.

In the shops (Frunze central departmental store): rubber high boots in Gulliver sizes, light beach shoes (in the middle of winter); brown boots, clumsy and heavy like convicts' chains. . . . Queues for women's underwear and men's socks. Near the entrance, a huge crowd storming the street stall selling jerseys of Armenian make.

"Are jerseys hard to get in Frunze?" I asked a man vainly trying to penetrate the crowd.

"Everything is hard to get here," he replied, throwing himself into the mob.

I'm sure members of the Kirgizia Communist Party Central Committee were pleased with what they saw at the exhibition and went back to their offices thinking everything was OK in the republic. But wouldn't it be better for them to walk once around the city shops?

I managed to find out that the annual cost of the exhibition to the state was 1,031,000 roubles [about $1.6 million]. Illusions are costly.

The drawing which accompanied my *Krokodil* [a satirical magazine] story, "Distorting Mirror", depicted the famous sculpture of the worker and the peasant woman which decorates the entrance gates of the All-Union Exhibition—with one difference: instead of the sheaf of wheat, they were holding a piece of sausage over their heads. Several years ago it would have been considered sacrilege. The publication of the story and the cartoon gives hope that in the near future we will stop throwing dust into each other's eyes.

READING REVIEW

1. What is *pokazukha*?
2. What was the reaction of the bureaucrats in Kirgizia to Vitaliev's questions on the republic's exhibition of economic achievements?
3. How do you think this new form of journalism will affect Soviet society? Explain your answer.

---

128 THE COMMUNIST ROLLER COASTER

After Mikhail Gorbachev introduced the policies of glasnost *(opening) and* perestroika *(restructuring) in the Soviet Union, calls for similar reforms arose from all over Eastern Europe. The calls were the loudest in Poland, where the struggle for democratization had been going on for more than 20 years. These calls were answered in 1989, and the changes came thick and fast. Within a matter of weeks the outlawed union Solidarity was made legal, the first open election since World War II was held, and Solidarity was invited to form a government. In the excerpt below, the possibilities and dangers of these changes are discussed in an editorial from* The New York Times. *As you read the excerpt, consider the affect of the "roller coaster" of change on the Polish people.*

Nowhere has the ride been jumpier than in Poland. Communist reforms, prodded by popular pressure, have moved even faster there than in the Soviet Union. Just *weeks* ago, Poland's Solidarity union was illegal. Now, President Wojciech Jaruzelski is ready to ask Solidarity to lead the next government. Astonishing change—and the ride ahead will be riskier still.

Reform has so ignited expectations that moderate leaders urgently conclude it's better for Solidarity to lead than for Poland to thwart

President Bush and Solidarity leader Lech Walesa in Gdansk, Poland

impatient workers and consumers. President Bush has pledged to mobilize Western aid. Meanwhile, the United States holds its breath as the roller coaster sinks and climbs.

In April, legalization of the union and free election of a fraction of Parliament seemed a breathtakingly bold leap. Yet the timetable envisioned then was soon overtaken by events, notably the sweeping repudiation of the Communists in the June voting and the clumsy rigidity of their response. . . .

The challenge facing any Polish government today is to radically transform a command economy, smothered in bureaucracy. That means liberating the productive potential of farmers, attracting investors, nurturing new enterprises, and closing uneconomical old ones.

The prescription doesn't differ much from the reform agendas of the Soviet Union or Hungary. What sets Poland apart is the advanced state of its economic crisis and of its popular struggle for change. Poles began that struggle in 1956 when they toppled a Stalinist leadership and halted collectivization of agriculture. In 1970, 1976 and 1980 they rebelled against food price increases that lowered living standards without hope of long-term gain. By the 1980's, stagnation had led to repeated strikes and the formation of Solidarity as a permanent opposition vehicle.

To his great credit, General Jaruzelski, who once tried to crush Solidarity with martial law, came to understand that radical reform could no longer be delayed, and that without Solidarity's participation reform had scant chance of success. But the careful opening to which he initially agreed has been overwhelmed. In June's election Poles repudiated the Communists, gave Solidarity a de facto mandate for a government role and signaled smaller parties that they would have to show more independence if they hoped to survive.

In response, the Communist regime offered only a reshuffle of familiar figures and another 1980-style "trust us" price shock. Grass-roots pressure cannot be contained by such tired rigidities. With the independent parties in full parliamentary revolt against Communist nominees and the Solidarity rank and file mobilizing for further strikes, the most prudent course, once more, was to be breathtakingly bold.

Solidarity indicates it recognizes what the limits are: it is willing to respect Warsaw Pact commitments and leave military and security matters in Communist hands. General Jaruzelski, as President, retains the power to command the army, appoint presidential ministers and order elections.

Unmanageable change in Poland is the last thing reform Communists anywhere need now. Soviet nationalities, and workers too, are alarmingly restless about the still-unrealized promise of perestroika. In Poland, Solidarity's seasoned leaders worry about runaway expectations.

A Solidarity-led government is a desperate gamble to manage the accelerating change. All who want a freer Eastern Europe . . . will hope it succeeds.

READING REVIEW

1. Why, according to the editorial, is the situation in Poland different from those in the Soviet Union and Hungary?
2. In your opinion, what does the writer of the editorial think of General Jaruzelski? Explain your answer.
3. How do you think this rapid political change will affect the Polish people? Give reasons for your answer.

---

129 A MESSAGE FROM THE APOLLO 11 ASTRONAUTS

On July 20, 1969, one of the great events in the history of space flight and exploration took place—the first manned landing on the moon. After landing their lunar module, astronauts Neil Armstrong and Buzz Aldrin spent about a day collecting samples and running experiments on the moon's surface. They then rejoined their compatriot Mike Collins in the command module for the journey back to earth. On the night of July 23 they made a live television broadcast back to earth, the content of which is included in the excerpt below. As you read the excerpt, consider the impact of the moon landing on space exploration.

Armstrong: Good evening. This is the Commander of Apollo 11. A hundred years ago, Jules Verne wrote a book about a voyage to the moon. His spaceship, Columbia, took off from Florida and landed in the Pacific Ocean, after completing a trip to the moon. It seems appropriate to us to share with you some of the reflections of the crew as the modern day Columbia completes its rendezvous with the planet earth and the same Pacific Ocean tomorrow. First, Mike Collins.

Collins: Roger. This trip of ours to the moon may have looked to you simple or easy. I'd like to say that it has not been a game. The Saturn V rocket which put us into orbit is an incredibly complicated piece of machinery. Every piece of which worked flawlessly. This computer up above my head has a 38,000-word vocabulary, each word of which has been carefully chosen to be of the utmost value to us, the crew. This switch which I have in my hand now has over 300 counterparts in the Command Module alone. In addition to that, there are myriad circuit breakers, levers, rods, and other associated controls. The SPS engine, our large rocket engine on the aft end of our Service Module, must have performed flawlessly or we would have been stranded in lunar orbit. The parachutes up above my head must work perfectly tomorrow, or we will plummet into the ocean.

We have always had confidence that all this equipment will work, and work properly, and we continue to have confidence that it will do so for the remainder of the flight. All this is possible only through the blood, sweat and tears of a number of people. First, the American workmen who put these pieces of machinery together in the factory. Second, the painstaking work done by the various test teams during the assembly and retest after assembly. And finally, the people at the Manned Spacecraft Center, both in management, in mission planning, in flight control, and last but not least, in crew training. This operation is somewhat like the periscope of a submarine. All you see is the three of us, but beneath the surface, are thousands and thousands of others, and to all those, I would like to say thank you very much.

Aldrin: Good evening. I'd like to discuss with you a few of the more symbolic aspects of the flight of our mission, Apollo 11. But we've been discussing the events that have taken place in the past two or three days here on board our spacecraft. We've come to the conclusion that this has been far more than three men on a voyage to the moon. More, still, than the efforts of a government and industry team. More even, than the efforts of one nation.

We feel that this stands as a symbol of the insatiable curiosity of all mankind to explore the unknown. Neil's statement the other day upon first setting foot on the surface of the moon, "This is a small step for a man, but a great leap forward for mankind," I believe sums up these feelings very nicely. We accepted the challenge of going to the moon. The acceptance of this challenge was inevitable. The relative ease with which we carried out the mission, I believe, is a tribute to the timeliness of that acceptance.

Astronaut Edwin E. Aldrin, Jr. on the moon

Today, I feel we're fully capable of accepting expanded roles in the exploration of space. In retrospect, we have all been particularly pleased with the call signs that we laboriously chose for our spacecraft, Columbia and Eagle. We've been particularly pleased with the emblem of our flight depicting the U.S. eagle bringing the universal symbol of peace from the earth, from the planet earth to the moon, that symbol being the olive branch. It was our overall crew choice to deposit a replica of this symbol on the moon. Personally, in reflecting the events of the past several days, a verse from Psalms comes to mind to me. "When I consider Thy heavens, the work of Thy fingers, the moon and the stars which Thou hast ordained, what is man that Thou art mindful of him."

Armstrong: The responsibility for this flight lies first with history and with the giants of science who have preceded this effort. Next with the American people who have through their will indicated their desire. Next, to four administrations and their Congresses for implementing that will; and then to the agency and industry teams that built our spacecraft, the Saturn, the Columbia, the Eagle, and the little EMU, the space suit and backpack that was our small spacecraft out on the lunar surface. We would like to give a special thanks to all those Americans who built the spacecraft, who did the construction, design, the tests, and put their hearts and all their abilities into those crafts. To those people, tonight, we give a special thank you, and to all the other people that are listening and watching tonight, God bless you. Good night from Apollo 11.

READING REVIEW

1. What point do you think Mike Collins was trying to make?
2. Why do you think Buzz Aldrin said it was inevitable that the challenge of going to the moon would be accepted?
3. What contributions do you think the moon landing made to space exploration?

---

130 BOOKS, GADGETS, AND FREEDOM

Developments in computers and the electronic media have revolutionized the ways information is stored, retrieved, and transmitted. Many people worry that the growing dependence on these "electronic gadgets" will make another form of communication—the printed word—obsolete. In the excerpt below, Peruvian novelist Mario Vargas Llosa discusses the dangers of these gadgets winning out over books. As you read the excerpt, consider the impact of audio-visual culture on freedom.

Books mean ideas, words, fantasy, the practice of intelligence. Nothing has pushed forward cultural life as much as the invention of printing, nor has anything contributed more to its democratization. From Gutenberg's times until today, the book has been the best propeller and depositor of knowledge, as well as an irreplaceable source of pleasure.

However, to many its future is uncertain. I recall with anguish a lecture I heard at Cambridge a few years ago. It was entitled "Literacy Is Doomed," and its thesis was that the alphabetic culture, the one based on writing and books, is perishing. According to the lecturer, audio-visual culture will soon replace it. The written word, and whatever it represents, are already an anachronism since the more avant-garde and urgent knowledge required for the experience of our time is transmitted and stored not in books but in machines and has signals and not letters as its tools.

The lecturer had spent two weeks in Mexico where he had traveled everywhere, and even in the underground he had no difficulty, though he spoke no Spanish, because the entire system of instructions in the Mexican underground consists of nothing but arrows, lights, and figures. This way of communication is more universal, he explained, for it overcomes, for instance, language barriers, a problem congenital to the alphabetic system.

The lecturer maintained that all Third World countries, instead of persisting in those costly campaigns aimed at teaching their illiterate masses how to read and write, should introduce them to what will be the primary source of knowledge: the handling of machines.

The formula that the proud speaker used with a defying wink still rings in my ears: "not books but gadgets." And, as a consolation to all those who might be saddened by the prospect of an illiterate world, he reminded us that the alphabetic period in human history had in any case been short-lived.

The lecturer did not think the alphabetic culture would totally vanish nor did he wish it to do so. He forecast that the culture of the book would survive in certain university and social enclaves for the entertainment and benefit of the marginal group interested in producing and consuming it.

The exponent of this thesis—which I have outlined very roughly—was not Marshall McLuhan, the Canadian prophet who said the book would "die" by 1980. . . . The speaker was Sir Edmund Leach, eminent British social anthropologist, then provost of King's College. Coming from a distinguished mandarin of the alphabetic culture of our time, such statements should not be taken lightly.

It is true that for many people the written word is becoming more and more dispensable. Books are less important even to the literate people of today (considering the time they devote to them and the effect books have on their lives) than they were to the literate people of the past.

We must be appalled at this, because although I doubt the prophecy of Professor Leach will come true, if it does it will be a disaster for humanity. Together with the books, and their writers and readers, something else will vanish: the culture of freedom.

My pessimism is based on two certainties. First, audio-visual culture is infinitely more easily controlled, manipulated, and degraded by power than is the written word. Because of the solitude in which it is born, the speed at which it can be reproduced and circulated, and its lasting mark on people's conscience, the written word has put up a stubborn resistance against being enslaved. With its demise, the submission of minds to power—to the powers—could be total.

Second, the audio-visual product tends to limit imagination, to dull sensibility, and to create passive minds. I am not a retrograde, allergic to audio-visual culture. On the contrary. After literature I love nothing more than the cinema, and I deeply enjoy a good TV program. But even in a the few countries such as England where TV has reached a high level of artistic creativity, the average TV program, that which sets the pattern, attempts to embrace the widest possible audience by appealing to the lowest common denominator.

The nature of culture—either literate or audio-visual, free or enslaved—does not stem from historical determination, from the blind evolution of science. The decisive factor will always be man's choice. If books and gadgets are caught in a deadly fight and the latter defeat the former, the responsibility will lie with those who chose to allow it to happen. And that may be their last choice.

But I do not think this Orwellian nightmare will really occur. Fortunately for us writers and readers, our fate is linked to that of freedom, that illness or vice caught by humanity rather late in history that affects a good part of mankind in an incurable way.

READING REVIEW

1. Why is the form of communication found in the Mexican underground system more universal than alphabetic communication?
2. According to Vargas Llosa, who would be to blame if gadgets did indeed win out over books?
3. Do you think the new audiovisual culture represents a threat to freedom? Why or why not?

---

131 THE OPENING OF THE BERLIN WALL

In 1961 a frantic East German government tried to stem the exodus of its citizens into democratic West Germany. In the middle of the night of August 13, 1961, East Germany sealed its borders with the West, proclaiming that none of its citizens could travel to West Germany without official permission. Two days later, on August 15, construction crews began building the infamous Berlin Wall, which came to signify the hardened attitudes of the cold war. For years, few people believed that the East German government would ever dismantle the hated symbol of communism. Then, with the beginnings of glasnost *and* perestroika *in the Soviet Union, people throughout Eastern Europe began clamoring for democratic reforms and freedom of movement. Under pressure from Soviet leader Mikhail Gorbachev, the East Germans began to relax their rules on emigration. And on November 9, 1989, East German officials told a disbelieving world that they were ready to open the Wall. In the excerpt below from* Time, *George J. Church describes the opening of the Berlin Wall. As you read the excerpt, consider what the opening of the Wall might mean for Communist governments throughout Eastern Europe.*

For 28 years it had stood as the symbol of the division of Europe and the world, of Communist suppression, of the xenophobia of a regime that had to lock its people in lest they be tempted by another, freer life—the Berlin Wall, that hideous, 28-mile-long scar through the heart of a once proud European capital, not to mention the soul of a people. And then—poof!—it was gone. Not physically, at least yet, but gone as an effective barrier between East and West, opened in one unthinkable, stunning stroke to people it had kept apart for more than a generation. It was one of those rare times when the tectonic plates of history shift beneath men's feet, and nothing after is quite the same.

At the stroke of midnight on Nov. 9, a date that not only Germans would remember, thousands who had gathered on both sides of the Wall let out a roar and started going through it, as well as up and over.

What happened in Berlin last week was a combination of the fall of the Bastille and a New Year's Eve blowout, of revolution and celebration. At the stroke of midnight on Nov. 9, a date that not only Germans would remember, thousands who had gathered on both sides of the Wall let out a roar and started going through it, as well as up and over. West Berliners pulled East Berliners to the top of the barrier along which in years past many an East German had been shot while trying to escape; at times the Wall almost disappeared beneath waves of humanity. They tooted trumpets and danced on the top. They brought out hammers and chisels and whacked away at the hated symbol of imprisonment, knocking loose chunks of concrete and waving them triumphantly before television cameras. They spilled out into the streets of West Berlin for a champagne-spraying, horn-honking bash that continued well past dawn, into the following day and then another dawn. As the daily *BZ* [newspaper] would headline: BERLIN IS BERLIN AGAIN. . . .

When the great breach finally came, it started undramatically. At a press conference last Thursday, Schabowski [East Berlin Communist party boss] announced almost offhandedly that starting at midnight, East Germans would be free to leave at any point along the country's borders, including the crossing points through the Wall in Berlin, without special permission, for a few hours, a day or forever. Word spread rapidly through both parts of the divided city, to the 2 million people in the West and the 1.3 million in the East. At Checkpoint Charlie, in West Berlin's American sector, a crowd gathered well before midnight. Many had piled out of nearby bars, carrying bottles of champagne and beer to celebrate. As the hour drew near, they taunted East German border guards with cries of *"Tor Auf!"* (Open the gate!)

On the stroke of midnight, East Berliners began coming through, some waving their blue ID cards in the air. West Berliners embraced them, offered them champagne and even handed them deutsche mark notes to finance a celebration (the East German mark, a nonconvertible currency, is almost worthless outside the country). "I just can't believe it!" exclaimed Angelika Wache, 34, the first visitor to cross at Checkpoint Charlie. "I don't feel like I'm in prison anymore!" shouted one young man. Torsten Ryl, 24, was one of many who came over just to see what the West was like. "Finally, we can really visit other states instead of just seeing them on television or hearing about them," he said. "I don't intend to stay, but we must have the possibility to come over here and go back again." The crowd erupted in whistles and cheers as a West Berliner handed Ryl a 20-mark bill and told him, "Go have a beer first."

Many of the visitors pushed on to the Kurfürstendamm, West Berlin's boulevard of fancy stores, smart cafés and elegant hotels, to see prosperity at first hand. At 3 a.m., the street was a cacophony of honking horns and happily shouting people; at 5 some were still sitting in hotel lobbies, waiting for dawn. One group was finishing off a bottle of champagne in the lobby of the Hotel Am Zoo, chatting noisily. "We're going back, of course," said a woman at the table. "But we must wait to see the stores open. We must see that." . . .

West Germany, the country most immediately and strongly affected, was both overjoyed and stunned. In Bonn members of the Bundestag [the West German parliament], some with tears in their eyes, spontaneously rose and sang the national anthem. It was a rare demonstration in a country in which open displays of nationalistic sentiment have been frowned on since the Third Reich died in 1945....

Running through the joy in West Germany, however, was a not-so-subtle undertone of anxiety. Suppose the crumbling of the Wall increases rather than reduces the flood of permanent refugees? West Germany's resources are being strained in absorbing, so far this year, the 225,000 immigrants from East Germany, as well as 300,000 other ethnic Germans who have flocked in from the Soviet Union and Poland. According to earlier estimates, up to 1.8 million East Germans, or around 10% of the population, might flee to the West if the borders were opened—as they were last week all along East Germany's periphery. (Within 48 hours of the opening of the Wall, nearly 2 million East Germans had crossed over to visit the West; at one frontier post, a 30-mile-long line of cars was backed up.) West Germans fear they simply could not handle so enormous a population shift....

The reaction is another indication of how the sudden mellowing of the East German state and the crumbling of the Wall have taken the West by surprise. The West German government has done little or no planning to absorb the refugees: it has left the task of resettlement to states, cities and private charity. "There is no real contingency plan for reunification" either, admits a Kohl confidant. Only in recent days has a small group been assigned to examine the reunification question, and it has not even been given office space.

Much will depend, of course, on whether, and how soon, Krenz [the East German leader] delivers on his rhetoric of freedom. The conviction that they will be able to decide their future could indeed keep at home most East Germans who are now tempted to flee; it is difficult to see anything else that might....

In the end it does not matter whether Eastern Europe's Communists are reforming out of conviction or if, as one East German protest banner put it, THE PEOPLE LEAD—THE PARTY LIMPS BEHIND. What does matter is that the grim, fearsome Wall, for almost three decades a marker for relentless oppression, has overnight become something far different, a symbol of the failure of regimentation to suppress the human yearning for freedom. Ambassador Herder [East German ambassador to the United States] declared that the Wall will soon "disappear" physically, but it might almost better be left up as a reminder that the flame of freedom is inextinguishable—and that this time it burned brightly.

READING REVIEW

1. Why do West Germans have mixed emotions about the refugees who are streaming into their country?
2. Imagine that you were an East Berliner on the night of

November 9, 1989. How would you have felt when they opened the Wall?

3. How do you think the opening of the Berlin Wall affected the Communist regimes throughout Eastern Europe?

---

132 ROCK MUSIC AND POLITICS

During the 1980s many rock artists began to use their music to drive home a social message to their listeners. Perhaps the most notable example of this was the Live Aid Concert of 1985. Broadcast live from Philadelphia and London to an audience of around 1.5 billion people, the concert raised more than $70 million for famine relief in Africa. The excerpt below from The Economist *explores the development and meaning of this marriage of rock and politics. As you read the excerpt, ask yourself how the writer views the role of rock musicians in politics.*

"The revolution will not be televised." So sang Gil Scott-Heron, one of the few musicians to have made a career out of unashamedly political pop music, on his 1984 album of the same name. "Sorry Gil—it's gonna be televised and rerun." Thus Little Steven, one-time guitarist with Bruce Springsteen, in a 1989 song called, appropriately, "Revolution".

As far as rock goes, the revolution was televised on July 13, 1985. That was the day when, according to Bob Geldof, 2 billion people watched and listened to Live Aid. Even allowing for hyperbole, it is impossible to imagine anything other than rock music drawing such numbers and carrying a message so far. It was a lesson quickly learnt. Amnesty International sponsored two rock tours, and was in turn preached about by artists such as U2; membership has soared. When the Anti-Apartheid Movement had its 70th birthday tribute to Nelson Mandela broadcast live in Britain, and relayed to the rest of the world, it gave Little Steven and Gil Scott-Heron, as well as such veterans of politics and pop as Harry Belafonte and Stevie Wonder, a chance to get their messages to a worldwide audience.

This new media power comes as the climax of Robin Denselow's excellent new history of political pop [*When the Music's Over: The Story of Political Pop*]. It charts the achievements, tragedies and squabbles of the wide range of musicians who have tried to mix the popular and the political.

The book starts with the folk revival of the 1950s, dominated by figures such as Ewan MacColl in Britain and Pete Seeger in America, musical journalists always ready to put the issues of the day into song. People have always sung about their working lives; so folk music and socialism seemed made for each other.

The Live Aid Concert of 1985

Rock music was different. The consumers were teenagers—as were many of the performers. Rock therefore focused on authority in general (read: parents) rather than on ideology. Politics was merely part of the system. The Who summed it up in "Won't Get Fooled Again":

Meet the new boss

Same as the old boss. When the big stars of the 1960s and 1970s—increasingly isolated from the real world of their fans—gave any consideration to politics, they rarely managed to get further than "Peace and love" or "Smash the system". Political rock was something of an oddity. Minor stars played to devoted audiences in small venues, and the world did not change.

Since Live Aid, rock superstars have realised the value of putting politics into their music. The rock generation has grown up—and grown-ups care about politics. People over 20 (though perhaps not those over 30) feel good about buying CDs with a *soupcon* of caring and social relevance, and rock stars are happy to provide it. Feeding the starving, freeing political prisoners, breaking down apartheid, saving the rain forests: all that goes down well. Revolutionary socialism, however, does not.

Those objectionable concerns reflect another change: rock music is moving into the third world. Live Aid, which put affluent rock music at the service of third-world poverty, stood at a slightly uncomfortable halfway house on the road to globalism. Since then the music has followed the issues. "World music" records are selling more and more; artists from Mali (Salif Keita) or Panama (Ruben Blades) are becoming stars. Amnesty International's Human Rights Now tour . . . went to places most "world tours" ignore, such as India, Zimbabwe, Ivory Coast and Argentina; and it was a tour where a Senegalese singer, Youssou N'Dour, could share the billing with Bruce Springsteen.

These influences are making rock richer as a musical form. They will probably also keep it political. When different cultures make contact, political sparks will always fly. Musicians of the third world, besides, are not prisoners of the teenage record-buying market; they are free to write about aspects of life besides sex (thinly disguised as love); and that means politics. In all, it would have made Bob Marley, the greatest figure in the history of political pop and the third world's first home-grown superstar, a happy man.

READING REVIEW

1. Before the 1980s what did rock music focus on? Why?
2. How has involvement in politics changed rock music? Give reasons for your answer.
3. How do you think the writer of the excerpt feels about the involvement of rock musicians in politics? Explain your answer.

Coronado Press Inc.: From "Funeral Operation of Pericles" by Thucydides from *The Speeches of Thucydides* by H.F. Harding. Copyright © 1973 by H.F. Harding.

Judy Daish Associates Limited on behalf of Tom Pickard: From *Jarrow March* by Tom Pickard. Copyright © 1982 by Tom Pickard. First published by Allison & Busby.

J.M. Dent & Sons Ltd.: From "The Heiligenstadt Will" from *Beethoven's Letters,* translated by J.S. Shedlock, B.A., selected and edited by A. Eaglefield-Hull. Published in 1926 by J.M. Dent & Sons Ltd.

Doubleday, a division of Bantam, Doubleday, Dell Publishing Group, Inc.: From *My Enemy, My Self* by Yoram Binur. Copyright © 1989 by Yoram Binur. From "Introduction" (Retitled: "The Burning of the Books") by Louis P. Lochner from *The Goebbels Diaries: 1942–1943* by Goebbels. Copyright 1948 by Doubleday, a division of Bantam, Doubleday, Dell Publishing Group, Inc. From "Excerpts from the Parti Quebecois Economic Manifesto" (Retitled: "The Economic Manifesto of the Quebec Party") from *Pierre Vallieres: The Revolutionary Process In Quebec* by Nicholas M. Regush. Copyright © 1973 by Nicholas M. Regush. From "Belfast" from *Children of War* by Roger Rosenblatt. Copyright © 1983 by Roger Rosenblatt.

Lindsay Drummond: From "India Follows Gandhi" (Retitled: "Gandhi Emerges as India's New Leader") from *Glimpses of World History* by Jawaharlal Nehru. Copyright 1942 by John Day Company.

The Economist Newspaper Ltd.: "Vox Pop" (Retitled: "Rock Music and Politics") from *The Economist,* April 29, 1989, Vol. 311, Number 7600. Copyright © 1989 by The Economist Newspaper Ltd.

Giulio Einaudi Editore S.p.A.: From Chapter 57 of *The Travels of Marco Polo* (Retitled: "Kublai Khan's Great Park at Shangdu"). Published in the United States by The Orion Press.

The Free Press, a division of Macmillan Publishing Co., Inc.: "A Woman's Hundred Years" from *Chinese Civilization and Society: A Sourcebook,* edited by Patricia Buckley Ebrey. Copyright © 1981 by The Free Press.

Garamond, Ltd.: From *The Anglo-Saxon Chronicles* (Retitled: "A Saxon View of William the Conqueror"), translated and conflated by Anne Savage. Copyright © 1982 by Phoebe Phillips. Originally a Phoebe Phillips/Heinemann book.

Government of India Press: From *Excavations at Harappa* by Madho Sarup Vats. Published by Government of India Press, 1940.

Grove Press and Unwin Hyman Ltd.: From *The Book of Songs,* translated from the Chinese by Arthur Waley. First published in 1937.

Harper & Row, Publishers, Inc.: From *Danton's Death* (Retitled: "Robespierre and Saint-Just Defend the Arrest of Danton") by George Buechner, translated and adapted by James Maxwell. Copyright © 1961 by Chandler Publishing Company. From "A Day in the Castle" (Retitled: "The Table of a Thirteenth-Century English Lord") from *Life in a Medieval Castle* by Joseph and Frances Gies. Copyright © 1969 by Joseph and Frances Gies. From "Martyrs of Palestine" from *A History of Rome Through the Fifth Century,* Volume II: The Empire, edited by A.H.M. Jones. Copyright © 1968 by A.H.M. Jones.

Harper & Row, Publishers, Inc. and Methuen & Co. Ltd.: From "The Peasant Bodo" from *Medieval People* by Eileen Power. Copyright 1924 by Methuen & Co.

Sherwood Harris and his agents, Raines & Raines: From *The First to Fly: Aviation's Pioneer Days* (Retitled: "The First Flight Across the English Channel") by Sherwood Harris. Copyright © 1970 by Sherwood Harris.

Harvard University Press: From *The Making of the New Deal: The Insiders Speak,* edited by Katie Louchheim (Retitled: "Eleanor Roosevelt's Contribution to the New Deal"). Copyright © 1983 by the President and Fellows of Harvard College. From "Belgrade and Rhodes" (Retitled: "Suleyman the Magnificent Captures Belgrade") from *Suleiman the Magnificent, 1520–1566* by Roger Bigelow Merriman. Copyright 1944 by the President and Fellows of Harvard College. From "History, Book XVII" from *Diodorus of Sicily,* translated by C. Bradford Welles. Copyright © 1963 by the President and Fellows of Harvard College.

D.C. Heath & Company: From "The Heroic Tsar" (Retitled: "The Great Czar") from *Peter the Great Changes Russia,* Second Edition, edited by Marc Raeff. Copyright © 1963, 1972 by D.C. Heath & Company.

Heinemann International: From "The Rivonia Trial" (Retitled: "Nelson Mandela Explains Why There is a South African Resistance Movement") from *No Easy Walk to Freedom* by Nelson Mandela. Copyright © 1965 by Nelson Mandela.

The Heritage Press: From "A Day In The King's Life" (Retitled: "A Day in the Life of Louis XIV") from *The Memoirs of Louis De Rouvroy Duc De Saint-Simon Covering the Years 1691–1723,* selected, translated and edited by Desmond Flower. Copyright © 1959 by The George Macy Companies, Inc. Copyright renewed © 1987 by The Heritage Press.

David Higham Associates Ltd.: From "5th November (Tuesday) A Most Horrible Conspiracy Discovered" (Retitled: "The Gunpowder Plot") from *A Jacobean Journal* by G.B. Harrison. Published by Routledge and Kegan Paul, 1941.

The Hogarth Press Ltd.: "Music in a Spanish Town" (Retitled: "Two Poems of the Spanish Civil War") by Laurie Lee.

Henry Holt and Company, Inc.: From "Advice to Schoolboys" from *Wings of the Falcon, Life and Thought of Ancient Egypt,* translated and edited by Joseph Kaster. Copyright © 1968 by Joseph Kaster.

Holt, Rinehart and Winston, Inc.: From "Ivan the Terrible's Punishment of Novgorod in 1570" from *Medieval Russia: A Source Book, 900–1700,* translated and edited by Basil Dmytryshyn. Copyright © 1967 by Holt, Rinehart and Winston, Inc.

Horizon Press: From "Blind Man and Lame Man" from *The Intimate Folklore of Africa* by Alta Jablow. Copyright © 1961 by Alta Jablow.

Houghton Mifflin Company: From "Inca Sun Worship" (Retitled: "The Incas: Worshippers of the Sun"), and from "Man of Destiny" (Retitled: "The Great Liberator") from *Latin American Civilization: The Colonial Origins,* Vol. I, Third Edition, edited by Benjamin Keen. Copyright © 1974 by Houghton Mifflin Company. From "Camilo Torres, Priest and Revolutionary" (Retitled: "Guerrilla Priest") from *Latin American Civilization: The National Era,* Vol. II, Third Edition, edited by Benjamin Keen. Copyright © 1974 by Houghton Mifflin Company.

Charles Knight & Co. Ltd., an imprint of A & C Black (Publishers) Ltd.: From "Incidents of the Siege" from *Annals of the Indian Rebellion 1857–58,* compiled by N.A. Chick, edited by David Hutchinson. Copyright © 1974 by Charles Knight & Co. Ltd. First published in Calcutta in 1859.

Kodansha International LTD: From "Reading the Comics" (Retitled: "The Japanese Passion for Comics") by Frederik L. Schodt from *Manga! Manga! The World of Japanese Comics.* Copyright © 1983 by Kodansha International LTD.

Little, Brown and Company: From *Life on Earth: A Natural History* by David Attenborough. Copyright © 1979 by David Attenborough Productions Ltd.

Mario Vargas Llosa: From "Books, Gadgets and Freedom" by Mario Vargas Llosa from *The Wilson Quarterly,* Spring 1987.

Larissa Adler Lomnitz: From "Some Impressions of Shantytown Life" from *Networks and Marginality: Life in a Mexican Shantytown* by Larissa Adler Lomnitz, translated by Cinna Lomnitz. Copyright © 1977 by Larissa Adler Lomnitz. Published by Academic Press.

Los Angeles Times Syndicate International: From "The Bloody Anarchy in Colombia" (Retitled: "The Tragedy of Colombia") by Sol Fuertes from *El País,* Madrid.

Macmillan Publishing Company: From *Woodrow Wilson and the Lost Peace* (Retitled: "The Germans are Informed of the Terms of the Treaty of Versailles") by Thomas A. Bailey. Copyright 1944 and renewed © 1972 by Thomas A. Bailey. From "Women of Power: Leaders, Doctors, and Witches" (Retitled: "Women Leaders in North American Indian Societies") from *Daughters of the Earth: The Lives and Legends of American Indian Women* by Carolyn Niethammer. Copyright © 1977 by Carolyn Niethammer.

Ewan MacNaughton Associates as agents for The Daily Telegraph PLC: From "Dunkirk: May 28–June 4, 1940" (Retitled: "The Evacuation of Dunkirk") by Douglas Williams from *The Daily Telegraph,* London, June 1, 1940. Copyright © 1940 by The Daily Telegraph PLC.

McGraw-Hill Publishing Company: From *Prehistoric Men,* Eighth Edition, by Robert J. Braidwood. Copyright © 1964, 1967, 1975 by Scott, Foresman and Company.

Monthly Review Foundation: From "Karari's Hill" (Retitled: "Jomo Kenyatta Stirs Nationalist Feelings Among the Kikuyu") from *Mau Mau from Within* by Donald J. Barnett and Karari Njama. Copyright © 1966 by Donald L. Barnett.

William Morrow & Company: From "Mao, Chuteh, and Chouen-Lai" (Retitled: "A Portrait of Mao Zedong") from *My China Years: A Memoir* by Helen Foster Snow. Copyright © 1984 by Helen Foster Snow.

Thomas Nelson & Sons Ltd.: From *Akbar* (Retitled: "A Day in the Life of a Mogul Emperor") by Laurence Binyon. First published May, 1932.

The New York Times Company: From "At China's Ministry of Truth, History is Quickly Rewritten" (Retitled: "Rewriting History in China") by Richard Bernstein from *The New York Times,* June 12, 1989. Copyright © 1989 by The New York Times Company. From "Pakistan is Sure of Its Leader, Less Sure of Her Plans" (Retitled: "A New Leader for Pakistan") by Barbara Crossette from *The New York Times,* December 4, 1988. Copyright © 1988 by The New York Times Company. From "Beirut Diary" by Ihsan A. Hijazi from *The New York Times* Magazine, May 28, 1989. Copyright © 1989 by The New York Times Company. From "The Communist Roller Coaster" from *The New York Times,* August 18, 1989. Copyright © 1989 by The New York Times Company.

W.W. Norton & Company, Inc. and David Higham Associates Limited: From "Animals and Sportsmen" (Retitled: "Sports in England") from *The English: A Social History, 1066–1945* by Christopher Hibbert. Copyright © 1987 by Christopher Hibbert.

Obunsha Co. Ltd.: From "From the Village to the Factory" (Retitled: "The Living Conditions of Japanese Industrial Workers During the Meiji Period") by Yanagida Kunio from *Japanese Manners and Customs in the Meiji Era.* Published by Obunsha Co. Ltd. in 1957.

Oceana Publications Inc.: From *The Splendor That Was Africa* (Retitled: "Mansa Musa's Pilgrimage") by Ricky Rosenthal. Copyright © 1967 by Rita Rosenthal.

Ohio State University Press: From *On the Commonwealth: Marcus Tullius Cicero,* translated by George Holland Sabine and Stanley Barney Smith. Copyright 1929 by the Ohio State University Press.

L. Jay Oliva: From "The Purge Trials" (Retitled: "The Trial of Nikolai Bukharin") from *Russia and the West from Peter to Khrushchev,* edited by L. Jay Oliva. Copyright © 1975 by L. Jay Oliva.

Oxford University Press (Oxford): From "Codex Theodosius" by Theodosius and from "The Diet of Worms, 1521" (Retitled: "Luther's Refusal at the Diet of Worms") from *Documents of the Christian Church*, Second Edition, selected and edited by Henry Bettenson. Copyright © 1963 by Oxford University Press.

Pathfinder Press: "Appeal on Czechoslovakia" (Retitled: "Soviet Dissidents Decry the Invasion of Czechoslovakia") by Pyotr Grigorenko and Ivan Yakhimovich from *Samizdat: Voices of the Soviet Opposition*, edited by Saunders. Copyright © 1974 by the Anchor Foundation.

Penguin Books Ltd.: From "Lao Tzu: Tao Te Ching" from *Chinese Classics: Tao Te Ching,* translated by D.C. Lau. Copyright © 1963, 1982 by D.C. Lau. From pp. 453–457 of *The Politics* by Aristotle, translated by T.A. Sinclair, revised by Trevor J. Saunders (Penguin Classics, Revised Edition, 1981). Translation copyright © 1962 by the Estate of T.A. Sinclair; revised translation copyright © 1981 by Trevor J. Saunders. From pp. 180–183 of *The Last Days of Socrates* by Plato, translated by Hugh Tredennick (Penguin Classics, Revised Edition, 1969). Copyright © 1954, 1959, 1969 by Hugh Tredennick.

Pennsylvania State University Press: From "Orthodoxy, Autocracy, Nationality" (Retitled: "Czar Nicholas I's Approach to Government—Orthodoxy, Autocracy, Nationality") from *Life and Thought in Old Russia,* edited by Marthe Blinoff (University Park, PA, 1961), pp. 192–193. Copyright © 1961 by Pennsylvania State University Press.

Peters Fraser & Dunlop Group Ltd.: From "Back to Malacañang" (Retitled: "The Filipinos Celebrate the Fall of President Marcos") by James Fenton from *Granta,* 18. Published in 1986 by Granta Publications Ltd.

Prentice-Hall, Inc., Englewood Cliffs, NJ: From "France on the Eve of Revolution" (Retitled: "The People State Their Grievances") from *The French Revolution,* edited by Philip Dawson. Copyright © 1967 by Prentince-Hall, Inc. From "The Ems Dispatch" (Retitled: "Bismarck 'Edits' the Ems Dispatch") from *Bismarck: Great Lives Observed,* edited by Frederic B.M. Hollyday. Copyright © 1970 by Prentice-Hall, Inc. From "By an 'Idéologue'" (Retitled: "A View of Napoleon's Character") from *Napoleon: Great Lives Observed,* edited by Maurice Hutt. Copyright © 1972 by Prentice-Hall, Inc. From "The Question of Taxation: The Stamp Act Congress" (Retitled: "The Colonists' View of Taxation") from *Problems in American History,* Fourth Edition, Volume 1/through reconstruction, edited by Richard W. Leopold, Arthur S. Link, and Stanley Coben. Copyright © 1952, 1957, 1966, 1972 by Prentice-Hall, Inc.

Princeton University Press: From *Ancient Near Eastern Texts Relating to the Old Testament* (Retitled: "Sargon II's Conquests"), Third Edition, edited by James B. Pritchard. Copyright © 1950, 1955, 1969 by Princeton University Press.

Random House, Inc.: From "Lycurgus" (Retitled: "The Making of Spartan Soldiers") from *Lives from Plutarch: The Modern American Edition of Twelve Lives,* edited by John W. McFarland et al. Copyright © 1966 by John W. McFarland, Pleasant F. Graves, Jr. and Audrey Graves.

St. John's University Press: From "The Wisdom of Confucius" from *Asian Institute Translations, No. 2, The Hsiao Ching,* edited by Paul K.T. Sih, translated by Mary Lelia Makra. Copyright © 1961 by St. John's University.

Salem House Publishers, Ltd.: From Chapter 5 of *Voices of the French Revolution,* by Richard Cobb, General Editor, and Colin Jones, Editor. Copyright © 1988 by Phoebe Phillips Editions.

Charles Scribner's Sons, an imprint of Macmillan Publishing Company: From *Digging up the Past* (Retitled: "The Task of the Archaeologist") by Sir Leonard Woolley. Copyright 1930 by Charles Scribner's Sons; copyright renewed © 1958 by C. Leonard Woolley.

Simon & Schuster, Inc.: From "The Darkest Days" (Retitled: "The Discovery of Anne Frank's Hiding Place") from *Anne Frank Remembered: The Story of the Woman Who Helped to Hide the Frank Family* by Miep Gies with Alison Leslie Gold. Copyright © 1987 by Miep Gies and Alison Leslie Gold.

Denis Mack Smith: From "A Foreign Volunteer at the Battle of the Volturno, April 2, 1860" (Retitled: "A Volunteer's View of Garibaldi at the Battle of the Volturno") from *Garibaldi: Great Lives Observed,* edited by Denis Mack Smith. Copyright © 1969 by Prentice-Hall, Inc.

Chester G. Starr: From *Rise and Fall of the Ancient World* by Chester G. Starr. Copyright © 1960 by Rand McNally & Company.

Summit Books, a division of Simon & Schuster, Inc.: From "Contadora: Document of Objectives (September 1983)" (Retitled: "The Objectives of the Contadora Press"), and from "Dana Munro: U.S. Policy Toward Nicaragua" (Retitled: "A Change in United States Policy Toward Nicaragua") from *The Central American Crisis Reader,* edited by Robert S. Leiken and Barry Rubin. Copyright © 1987 by Robert Leiken and Barry Rubin.

Time, Inc.: "France: Battle of the Sorbonne" from *Time* Magazine, May 17, 1968. Copyright © 1968 by Time, Inc. From "After nearly three decades as the cold war's premier symbol, the Wall crumbles" by George J. Church from *Time* Magazine, November 20, 1989. Copyright © 1989 by Time, Inc.

Charles E. Tuttle Co., Inc.: From *Everyday Life in Traditional Japan* (Retitled: "Actors and Entertainers in Feudal Japan") by C. J. Dunn. Copyright © 1969 by C.J. Dunn.

University of California Press: From "Saladin and the Third Crusade" (Retitled: "Saladin's Courage and Steadfastness") from *Arab Historians of the Crusades —Selected and Translated from the Arabic Sources* by Francesco Gabrieli, translated and edited by E.J.

Costello. Translation copyright © 1969 by Routledge & Kegan Paul Ltd.

University of Chicago Press: From *The History: Herodotus,* translated by David Grene. Copyright © 1987 by The University of Chicago. From "Eunomy" by Solon from *History of Western Civilization,* Topic II, pp. 5–9, by the University of Chicago College History Staff.

University of North Carolina Press: From "6 August 1945" (Retitled: "The Morning of the 500-ton Bomb") from *Hiroshima Diary: The Journal of a Japanese Physician, August 6–September 30, 1945* by Michihiko Hachiya, M.D., translated and edited by Warner Wells, M.D. Copyright © 1955 by The University of North Carolina Press.

Viking Press, a division of Viking Penguin, Inc.: From "From Bern to Berlin" (Retitled: "Two Testimonials for Albert Einstein") from *Albert Einstein: Creator and Rebel* by Banesh Hoffmann with the collaboration of Helen Dukas. Copyright © 1972 by Helen Dukas and Banesh Hoffmann.

Vitali Vitaliev: From "Seeing is Believing" by Vitali Vitaliev (Retitled: "Glasnost and Journalism") from *Manchester Guardian Weekly,* June 18, 1989. Copyright © 1989 by Vitali Vitaliev.

Wadsworth Publishing Company: From "Descriptions of Towns" (Retitled: "Muslim Towns and Trade in North Africa") from *The Medieval Town* by John Mundy and Peter Riesenberg. Copyright © 1958 and renewed © 1986 by John H. Mundy and Peter Riesenberg.

A.P. Watt Limited on behalf of The Executors of the Estate of Robert Graves: From *Gaius Suetonius Tranquillus: The Twelve Caesars,* translated by Robert Graves, revised by Michael Grant. Translation copyright © 1957 by Robert Graves; revised translation copyright © 1979 by Michael Grant. From *Greek Myths,* Illustrated Edition, by Robert Graves. Copyright © 1958, 1981 by Robert Graves.

PHOTO CREDITS

The Beginnings of Civilization: Page 2, Beryl Goldberg; 5, FPG International; 8, Monkmeyer Press Photo Service; 12, The Granger Collection; 16, The Bettmann Archive; 19, Hans Huber/The Stock Shop; 21, D. Banerjee/Dinodia Picture Agency; 24, Historical Pictures Service; 27, Culver Pictures, Inc.

Civilizations of the Mediterranean World: Page 33, Historical Pictures Service; 38, 41, FPG International; 45, Nita Winter/The Image Works; 49, Josip Ciganovic/FPG International; 52, The Granger Collection.

The World in Transition: Page 57, Historical Pictures Service; 61, TASS/SOVFOTO; 64, Historical Pictures Service; 66, Ken Lambert/FPG International; 68, TASS/SOVFOTO; 75, The Pierpont Morgan Library; 83, The Granger Collection; 85, Topham/The Image Works; 89, HRW Photo; 91, Cameramann International; 97, Jason Lauré; 100, HRW Photo by John White.

The Emergence of Modern Nations: Page 104, Historical Pictures Service/FPG International; 109, Parisport/Sygma; 112, Historical Pictures Service; 119, Superstock International; 122, Reuter Photo/FPG International; 125, Historical Pictures Service; 131, Culver Pictures, Inc.; 134, Historical Pictures Service; 144, Cameramann International; 149, Culver Pictures, Inc.; 153, The Granger Collection.

The Development of Industrial Society: Page 154, Topham/The Image Works; 161, Photoworld/FPG International; 162, Topham/The Image Works; 164, Superstock International; 168, Library of Congress; 171, FPG International; 178, The Granger Collection; 181, Library of Congress; 190, Steve Shapiro/Life Picture Service/Time, Inc.; 193, Photoworld/FPG International.

World War in the Twentieth Century: Page 199, Paul Thompson/Photoworld/FPG International; 202, National Archives; 207, UPI/Bettmann Newsphotos; 212, HRW Photo; 217, Margaret Bourke-White/LIFE Picture Service/Time, Inc.; 222, The Granger Collection; 228, 229, The Dutch Tourist Office; 232, Keystone Pictures/Photoworld/FPG International; 233, Shunkichi Kikuchi/Magnum.

The World Since 1945: Page 236, FPG International; 245, Gerard Aime/The Image Works; 249, J. Langevin/Sygma; 255, Fujihira/Monkmeyer Press Photo Service; 260, Pastner/FPG International; 267, M. Milner/Sygma; 273, Rudi Herzog/FPG International; 279, Rick Maiman/Sygma; 282(L), Beryl Goldberg; 282(R), FPG International; 289, Leighton Mark/UPI/Bettmann Newsphotos; 292, NASA/The Image Works; 299, Rob Taggart/UPI/Bettmann Newsphotos.

0
B 1
C 2
D 3
E 4
F 5
G 6
H 7
I 8
J 9